D0016160

WHITE CIRCUS

WHITE CIRCUS

A SKIING LIFE WITH THE CRAZY CANUCKS

KEN READ

WITH MATTHEW FISHER

KEY PORTER BOOKS

To my parents,
who always kept it
in perspective

Copyright © 1987 by Ken Read and Matthew Fisher

All rights reserved. No part of this work covered by the copyrights
hereon may be reproduced or used in any form or by any means —
graphic, electronic or mechanical, including photocopying, record-
ing, taping or information storage and retrieval systems — without
the prior written permission of the publisher.

Care has been taken to trace ownership of copyright material con-
tained in this book. The publishers will gladly receive any information that will enable them to rectify errors or omissions affecting
references or credit lines in subsequent editions.

Canadian Cataloguing in Publication Data
Read, Ken
   White circus

ISBN 1-55013-038-2

1. Read, Ken.   2. Skiers – Canada – Biography.
3. Skis and skiing.   I. Fisher, Matthew.
II. Title.

GV854.2.R43A3 1987   796.93'092'4   C87-094123-2

Key Porter Books Limited
70 The Esplanade
Toronto, Ontario
Canada   M5E 1R2

Design: Word & Image Design Studio Inc.
Typesetting: Q Composition Inc.
Printed and bound in Canada

87 88 89 90 6 5 4 3 2 1

CONTENTS————

Preface   vii

I   PRELUDE

1   The Perfect Race   3

II   THE MAKING OF A WORLD CUP RACER

2   The Early Years   11
3   A Season in Europe   22
4   The Crazy Canucks   33
5   World Cup Breakthrough   46

III   THE WORLD CUP

6   Serge Lang   59
7   "Der Kaiser" — Franz Klammer   67
8   Money   76
9   The Media   85

IV   A SKIING LIFE

10   Our Life   97
11   The Servicemen   109
12   Fear of Falling   118

V   THE SEASON OF 1980

13   Kitzbühel   129
14   Wengen   145
15   From Chamonix to Lake Placid   156
16   Lake Placid   163

VI THE LAST OF THE CRAZY CANUCKS

17 The Podborski Story   183
18 Government and Sport   196
19 Past, Present, and Future   205
20 What It All Meant   212

Appendix   216

PREFACE

No one was more surprised than I when Anna Porter approached me to write a book. After my retirement in 1983 I had considered the idea, yet in spite of strong encouragement from my father, memories and personalities were too recent . . . too fresh.

I welcomed Anna's offer. She said it was a tongue-in-cheek article by John Portwood in *Calgary Magazine* that had triggered her interest. Since Nancy Greene's memoirs in 1968, no one had written a book about ski racing in Canada. I agreed it was time to tell our story—it is both my story and the story of the Crazy Canucks.

No writer could be better equipped to assist me than Matthew Fisher. Matthew covered the World Cup from 1977 to 1984. For eight years he traversed the globe as the vital link with Canada's amateur athletes competing overseas. Matthew knew intimately the events and personalities that shaped the "Canadian decade."

I'm grateful to those who helped sharpen my memory of events: my closest friends from skiing, Konrad Bartelski, Robin McLeish, Tim Gilhooly, and Mike Irwin; my parents who perhaps knew the triumphs and disasters better than I; and my wife Lynda, who patiently provided counsel.

Finally, there is an army of volunteers who can't be forgotten. They made it all possible. Without the dedication of the parents and helpers who froze their feet and thanklessly contributed hundreds of hours to gatekeeping, timing, course preparation . . . the Crazy Canucks would never have been able to show Canadians what we can truly aspire to.

I
PRELUDE

THE
PERFECT
RACE

CHAPTER ONE

January 12, 1980

I T IS FIVE MINUTES to seven in the morning at the Park Hotel, Kitzbühel, when the alarm clock rings.

I wake up, roll over and turn the alarm off. Then, as always on a race day, without even looking out the window to see what the weather is like, I return to the warmth of my eiderdown, to run in my mind's eye down the world's most famous and most feared downhill course.

Training and racing: it is part of the routine, the mind-set, which has to be established at the start of every winter day. To win demands an instinctive mastery of the course. To acquire this mastery takes hours of mental rehearsal. While my room-mate, Tim Gilhooly, who cartwheeled into a fence and fractured his leg two days ago, lies awkwardly in the bed, I imagine myself in the starting hut, three kilometres and a world away, atop Kitzbühel's storied Hahnenkamm.

What I am trying to achieve in my stream of consciousness is a perfect run. I want to see and feel everything as I will see and feel it five and a half hours from now, when my body as well as my mind is at the top of the mountain. I need to touch on and solve all the difficult pieces of Kitzbühel's puzzle, to find the ideal line, the path that will let me gain the few hundredths of a second that will put me ahead of the pack.

I picture myself standing in the starting gate, poles at the edge, timer at my side, ready to thread my way down the hill, past two long conga lines of cowbell-toting, ski-mad Austrians, to the huge, bowl-like finish area in the valley below.

With two swift pushes and two skates I am off. I drop quickly into an aerodynamic tuck and my body is thrown down the steep incline. Even though I am hunched over, with my arms close to my sides and my face pointed forward, I command myself to relax, to be loose. Five seconds into the race I start the first turn, a slight line adjustment to the right, which sets me up for an S-turn on a rough, icy sidehill that was so chewed up in training that they had to apply a blowtorch to it every night to smooth it down. This traverse is followed quickly by a broad left-hand turn. I have to set up wide to get precisely the right trajectory. Otherwise I will not be prepared to push off an abrupt ledge, into the Mausfalle, or "Mousetrap." "Mousetrap."

Despite its reputation, the Mausfalle is more intimidating than difficult. A racer flies no more than thirty metres into the air from the ledge, landing about half way down the icy 200-metre slope. But I have to do it in such a way as to be ready for the acceleration and G-force pull which occur in the sharp compression at the bottom of the trap and, more importantly, for the change of terrain that follows as I exit below on to a very flat slope leading into the broad, left-hand opening to the Carousel.

Two years ago, in 1978, my skis banged together here, slamming me face-first into the snow. Forward momentum carried me into a fence. The Austrian star, Franz Klammer, who had crashed at the same spot a few minutes before, came and fished me out.

Such negative memories have no place in a pre-race reverie, however. I have yet to decide whether to run a tight or wide line. I have been running wide in training, but it came to our attention that a tight line might really be a mite faster, because it is smoother and shorter. I go through it this way in my dream, but I still have not decided what will work best for me in the race. I postpone the decision until moments before I leave the starting gate for real.

The Carousel consists of a gigantic S-turn. The first turn, which takes me out of the Mausfalle, is nothing more than a set-up for the second. In 150 metres, I have accelerated from sixty to one hundred kilometres per hour. Now I look for the gate at the tail-end of the second turn. To find it, I must do a 180-degree turn, beginning in a wide arc, fifty metres from the gate. It is crucial that I achieve the right timing and trajectory. If I am too high or too low I will have to release my edge for an instant, which will cost me time, and probably victory. I stand on my right-hand ski and push as hard as I possibly can, driving my outside arm down.

Should I execute the Mausfalle and the Carousel correctly, I will be well placed to skirt the tricky roll at the top of the Steilhang, or "steep wall." If I do not hit the entrance to the Steilhang as I want to, I could end up in the crowd. In my dream I get it right, continuing to ski down a very short, steep slope of solid ice on to a track which cannot be seen from the top of the wall. Coming into the second turn at high speed is a leap of blind faith. Because my eyes cannot tell me where I am going, I have to believe I have begun the curve at the right spot. To set up, I have to drop over the little roll and then start hitting my edges as hard as I can, simply driving down on them, staring directly ahead as the fence approaches on the left side. Then, with the fence clearly in view, my brain recalls what it has learned from half a dozen close inspections during the preceding week. I literally cannot see where I am going, but I must cut back to the right immediately by standing on my left ski. The trick is to do this as directly and smoothly as possible. I have to carve the turn so that I can carry most of my speed on to the long, telling flats that follow.

Until now the ride has been extremely rough. The mountain is coming at me so fast that I can't think. But I know I am doing well. My mind races ahead of my skis. It is not anticipating: it is reacting to what it has learned by rote. To the uninitiated I must appear to be travelling at a mad speed. Everything is a blur but, paradoxically, I maintain a sharp focus. The mountain is ingrained in my mind: the best line, the perfect feel, flawless turns.

So far, the race has lasted thirty-five seconds. Now, for the first time, I have a chance to actually see and contemplate what I am doing, instead of responding to the mountain from memory. I go back into my tuck for the next twenty seconds, letting my skis glide. Before dropping down into the Alte Schneise, I am rushed on to a very narrow catwalk, the Bruckenschuss, which is no more than ten metres wide.

International Ski Federation rules require that downhill slopes be at least thirty metres wide, but Kitzbühel, and Wengen, Switzerland, where we will race next week, were designed years before the rules were made, and have been granted "classic" exemptions. Such catwalks are not, in my opinion, dangerous. They add character and charm to a course, and give racers a very strong sense of their speed.

A slight turn on the catwalk called the Gschösswiese, and my right elbow is within inches of a picket fence which marks the outer extremity of the course. There have been occasions when people have made small mistakes and fallen into the fence, but this is unusual. When I go through, my only concern is to let my skis slide and glide. I try to keep off my edges, to squeeze as much speed out of this section as I can.

The track ends with a blind, ninety kilometre-per-hour drop on to the Alte Schneise. This very rough, 200-metre sidehill traverse is a clearing. In summer, cows graze here. In January, with the cows in the barn, it is where the Hahnenkamm is usually won or lost.

In 1975, when I first raced here, I lost a ski in the Alte Schneise and ended up on my head. Again, today, I feel as if I have no control over what I am doing or where I am going. I am in a sort of free-fall. My skis bounce crazily in front of me. But I make a controlled descent in the sense that, as my skis plummet I follow them down, pulled by gravity.

Now, no matter how bumpy it gets, I must maintain my tuck. If I can do this for the entire length of the traverse, I can make good my escape with a speed of about 120 kilometres per hour.

Next I come to a sweeping right turn into the Seidlalm. This is a flat meadow in which there is a series of blind turns. After the intensity of the Alte Schneise this is an extreme, but welcome, change of pace. The Seidlalm is so elementary that many racers ignore it in training. But they do so at their peril. If its simplicity renders me inattentive, I will begin to meander, lose time or even worse, catch an edge and fall. I follow the tracks left in the snow by those who have gone before me. My shoulders are low, my hands well out in front. The skis are running. The wax must be right.

When I leave the Seidlalm, I find myself, for the first time, skiing on a broad pitch. The Lärchenschuss is perhaps fifty metres across and consists of one, rather simple, right turn. But the breadth of the course is deceptive. It obscures the fact I am accelerating again so I must be especially vigilant. *Never underestimate the challenge.*

From the Lärchenschuss I race into the Oberhausberg. A house is in front of me, but the beaten track tacks to the left for a moment; then I am boomeranged into a sharp right turn. It is straightforward, easy: bump, push, land, turn, release, turn again, keep pushing around, and now hold the tuck, feel the speed, decelerate for a moment. The lull before the storm.

Just below and to my left, I finally see the finish area. All that remains of the race are thirty-five seconds of the most savage and spectacular downhill racing anywhere.

This run is so steep, it's like dropping out of the sky. To finish safely, it is imperative that the second turn out of the Oberhausberg and over the Hausberg Kante, is made at exactly the right angle. In the first jump I am airborne for no more than five metres, but I land gingerly, absorbing as much of the shock as I can with my knees, while turning my body and then my legs back to my left through a slight compression. I release my knees to pre-jump a small bump, turn again slightly through another compression, and then complete a seventy-five degree twist before I hit the next bump. If I don't get this right, I will shoot across the sidehill traverse, losing precious momentum and time.

As I career into view of the 30,000 spectators at the bottom of the hill, I send a white plume of snow high into the sky behind me. The key now is to find the optimal line and to hold it by staying in my tuck. But, because of the speed and other forces involved, it is impossible. I have just accelerated again from seventy to 120 kilometres per hour. I move back and forth, a black dot dancing across the mountain, hands and head pushed forward towards the holes in my ski tips. To regain my balance, I stand up for a millisecond. Like overheated pistons, I feel my thighs and calves seizing up. On a Canadian highway the police would be after me. I have reached a top speed of 130 kilometres per hour.

There is one last bump ahead, and one more compression that jerks my knees towards my head. The mountain, having spent almost all of its energy, is trying one last time to defeat me. I have become a guided missile, streamlined as much as possible, for the last surge. I attempt to remain attentive to what passes beneath my feet, while searching desperately for an extra hundredth of a second. But it is too late. I am already across the finish line. The dream is over.

The best day of my ski racing life is about to begin.

II

THE MAKING
OF A WORLD
CUP RACER

THE
EARLY
YEARS

CHAPTER TWO

J UST AS I CANNOT REMEMBER learning how to walk, I have
absolutely no recollection of learning how to ski. But I have
very few memories of my early life that do not include skiing.

Like virtually every other member of the Canadian ski team,
it was my good fortune to be born into a family with a strong
skiing background. In our case at least, I think it is fair to say
that a family that skis together stays together. Our parents
both skied. Whether we were good or bad, young or old, big
or little, they encouraged us to join them.

In the post-war years my mother, Dee, who had grown up
in Quebec, was a skier of some distinction. In 1948 she won
the Canadian downhill and combined championships, and finished third in the slalom. For a time she was probably the
third-best woman skier in the country, behind the Wurtele
twins, Rhona and Rhoda.

My father, John, had been a fair hockey player in Montreal
in his youth, but with the birth of their first child, my sister,
Janet, he forsook the sport, and became an avid recreational
skier.

I was born in 1955 in Ann Arbor, Michigan, where my father
was doing graduate work in pediatrics. The folks at the ABC
television network made much of this fact whenever I raced
at Kitzbühel or in the Olympics. Why, I was almost American!
However, I remember nothing of my American years. By the
time I was three the family, which also included my older
brother, Ron, had moved to Vancouver. My father accepted a
position as assistant professor of public health and pediatrics
at the University of British Columbia. Every winter weekend
we went skiing at Mount Seymour or Mount Baker.

A three year-old doesn't really ski. He spends most of his time on a ski hill on his bum. But I guess I knew enough to know I was having fun, even if I was not paying much attention to technique. I have no memories of how it happened, but I assume that with the help of my parents, and of Ron and Janet, who had already become adept skiers, I acquired the mechanical skills necessary to stay upright. By the time I was four or five years old I was no longer sliding along on the seat of my pants.

My father has a favourite story about me during this period. We used to go skiing sometimes at Stevens Pass, in Washington. To protect me from being mowed down by faster skiers in the moguls, he would snowplough behind me. As we came into the lower part of the course, where it was flatter and smoother, he knew others would spot me in time so he went on ahead. When he reached the bottom of the hill, stopped and turned around, I was nowhere to be seen. Then, suddenly, straight ahead of him on the crest of the hill, I appeared, and with a joyous whoop began schussing towards him at full speed. He told me that, from that moment on, he knew I was going to be a downhiller. Who knows? Maybe his story is apocryphal, but I want to believe it.

My mother was the great skier, but it was my father who took us to learn to ski. Though he was a pediatrician, this wasn't work. He delighted in watching children mature. He took us from the snowplough-between-his-legs stage, to guiding us down a hill while we held on to his ski pole.

It is a joy I now share occasionally with my nieces and nephews. It is something very special to watch youngsters tackle a sport in a spirit of pure exuberance. I think particularly of my young nephew, Andrew, who has cystic fibrosis. He has some physical limitations which frustrate him, but on skis, he's the king.

When we were good enough, we were handed over to my mother, a prodigiously talented skier who liked the challenge of tough hills. She provided much more sophisticated instruction and a competitive edge that really appealed to me. She taught me about limits and, by her example, about the will-power that is required to win ski races. She told me about her own victories. I wanted to do the same as her.

In my middle and late teens, and then later, when I was with the Canadian National Ski Team, my father once again became the predominant parent, as far as my ski racing was concerned. He tempered my dreams with steady doses of reality, explaining in plain terms the hard work and the steps I had to follow to get where I wanted to be. He was also the great sounding board who would talk to me, patiently, when I was frustrated. He helped me to maintain a diplomatic veneer, occasionally, when I was in an absolute fury over some decision or other. He absorbed my rage. Of course, he not only did this for me, but for my brothers and my sister, too. He always helped us to return to our own little fights with renewed vigour and understanding.

My first race was a slalom near Vancouver, in the spring of 1962. A few of the best racers from the area had returned from competition and were on hand for this loose, informal event. Karen Dokka, who had skied for Canada at the Squaw Valley Olympics, two years before, was one of them. After the race I remember going up to her and saying, "We're tied!" In fact, we were. We had both missed gates and been disqualified.

That summer my father transferred to Queen's University in Kingston, Ontario, to become head of the Department of Preventative Medicine in the medical faculty. It was a giant step up the ladder for him, but the move from the mountainous splendour of British Columbia to the flatlands which abut Lake Ontario meant that we no longer had access to the kind of skiing we had grown accustomed to. The local hill, Cataraqui, was operated by the Kingston Ski Club, but it was tiny and only had rope tows. Everyone encouraged us to drive north to Ottawa, to check out the hills across the river, at Camp Fortune. The Gatineaus were nothing like the mountains of BC or Washington, but there were several active ski clubs and a large, enthusiastic ski community.

I remember very clearly our first day at Camp Fortune. It was bitterly cold, perhaps minus twenty or thirty degrees, Celsius. I took the poma lift up Skyline, which was the expert side of the resort. The pomas were very stiff. I hopped on, small, freezing, and very much alone. For me, then, Skyline was a huge hill and I was terrified. The next thing I knew I had done a 180-degree spin and was screaming for my parents. The tow stopped; I got off and skied to the bottom. My parents decided it might be best if I tried a chairlift which ran parallel to the poma lift. I got on and rode up the hill without incident, but when I tried to get off, my pole caught on the safety bar.

As my father skied blithely away, I was left dangling about ten feet in the air.

It was a not a propitious initiation to skiing in the east. But, from that time on, we found that the five hours we spent commuting to and from the Gatineau Hills each weekend were to be worth it. In no time at all I was living, eating, and breathing skiing. I could not wait to escape Kingston on Fridays for Smiths Falls, Carleton Place, Ottawa and, after about two and a half hours on the road, our chalet at Camp Fortune.

They may not have had the mountains of Europe or the North American West, but Camp Fortune and the Ottawa Ski Club had a structured racing organization which involved hundreds of kids. Unlike the Nancy Greene League, which tends to lump all the children together, the kids at Fortune were divided so that no child ever felt at a disadvantage because of his weight and size. Best of all, I got to know a bunch of kids who loved to bomb down the hill. We built bumps and executed spread-eagles in masses of ten or fifteen kids. We chased one another everywhere. To test our mettle, we'd schuss Slalom, which was an intimidating pitch to a ten year-old, on the far side of the resort. We'd begin half way down. As the day progressed and our confidence increased, we'd bite off ever larger chunks of piste. Out of such innocent foolishness are formed the skiers who become racers, and the racers who become champions.

At Christmas, for national team members and midget skiers alike, there was a special camp to re-emphasize basics — how to snowplough and set an edge properly. It was a mite boring, but it was effective. Most of the coaches were parents, but some were very good skiers and excellent teachers. For a time this small club in the Gatineaus may have run the best ski racing system in Canada. It turned out racers such as Currie Chapman, who now coaches the Canadian women's team, and the Clifford sisters, world champion, Betsy, and former national team member, Susan.

Such was the fun we had blasting down the slopes at Fortune that, quite often, the coaches had real difficulty tracking us down so that we could be put through a formal program with gates and technical training. The Fortune program was varied. We were not obliged to concentrate solely on Alpine skiing, but were involved in a regime which also included ski-jumping, slalom, downhill and cross-country. Cross-country was always

the weak sister because it involved the most work, but jumping was immensely popular. My original jumping coach was
Fred Morris, who later became Canadian program director for
ski-jumping. World Cup winner, Horst Bulau, was a graduate
of Morris's side of the Fortune system.

At my level jumping was pure joy, not hard work. A rope
tow ran beside the jumps, so we didn't even have to lug our
skis and bodies up the mountain to do it all over again. Ski-
jumping also made a practical contribution to my development as an Alpine racer. It taught me how to manoeuvre my
body in such a way that I could deal safely with the complex
forces of gravity and aerodynamics which came into play every
time I was launched off a downhill bump. As a youngster
pushing myself to the limits of my ability on the jumps, I
acquired an acute sense of what those limits were. The critical
factor in jumping is speed at take-off. Whether it is on a puny
midget jump, or a ninety-metre monster, whether ski-flying
or downhill racing, the athlete must not exceed the critical
point beyond which the body loses control of the angle or
attitude that holds it in flight. Camp Fortune's jumping program, in teaching me this and many other lessons, benefited
me greatly as a downhill racer.

I had one particularly good friend in Ottawa. Richard Graves
was a little bigger than I was. His size worked against him in
the Alpine program, in which co-ordination was important,
but it gave him an advantage in the Nordic events, except on
the midget jump, which was already too small for him. When
we were eleven years old, he showed up one day with a special
pair of jumping skis and proceeded to successfully jump Lock-
aberg, the sixty-metre jump. That's where I drew the line. I
did not have any specialized equipment, and I was still having
a great time in the Alpine program. Until then, there had been
a small, undeclared war within me: would I become a ski
jumper or an Alpine racer? Alpine had won.

Nine years later, Richard and I met again at Garmisch-
Partenkirchen, West Germany. I was there representing Can-
ada at a World Cup downhill competition. He was there as a
member of the Canadian jumping team for one of the Vier
Schanze Tournée competitions, part of the jumping World
Cup. Each of us must have made the right choice.

Richard's brother, Phil, and his sister, Sue were also, briefly,
members of the national Alpine ski team. Mr. Graves and Mr.

Livingston (Fred and Doug were always "Mister" to this ten-year-old) were my first real coaches. They encouraged me, and taught me a lot about the rudiments of the sport, but most of all they made skiing fun. The gratitude of a ten-year-old is fleeting. Their reward for so many weekends with frozen hands and feet was to see my beaming face and then my back as I took off down the hill.

As anyone who knew me back then will attest, I talked of almost nothing but skiing and the singular thrill it gave me. I lived for the winter weekends and the holidays, when I could slip on the boards in Quebec or the northeastern US, and lose myself in the pleasure of skiing. Through these years my parents were extraordinarily supportive, but never pushy. They created opportunities for us, and instilled within us the idea that if we explored the world and developed to our maximum potential, we would be happier and more useful citizens.

I was lucky to have devoted parents who were always on call, to ski with me or to provide me with a lift to some faraway hill. But I had more. As the third-oldest child, I had a brother and sister to look up to and, by then, a younger brother, Jimmy, to encourage. Ron and Janet started later in the sport than Jim and I. They paved the way for me and they provided thousands of hours of informal instruction when we went free skiing.

Janet was good at all sports, but a master of none. Ron was not inclined towards sports — he is a mathematician and the genius of the family, now working as the systems manager for the Calgary Olympic organizing committee. But he was also a fair racer, good enough for a time to be a member of the Alberta team. Having a slightly older brother was a great motivating factor. Through these years he was my yardstick until, when I was fourteen and he was seventeen, I beat him in my first downhill race.

We stayed in Kingston and skied at Camp Fortune for five years. By the time I was ten years old, I was winning everything, and beating the racers in the category above me, but my skiing was still very inconsistent. I was making too many mistakes. During our last winter in central Canada, when I was twelve, I made a very foolish error while mucking around on a hill at Fortune. I broke my right leg in two places, ending my season a few days before Christmas.

We always took the week off school before the holidays to get a jump on our skiing. We had rented a chalet in Old Chelsea, near Camp Fortune. It was pouring rain, one day, as I trained gates on Marshall Hill with my mother, Ron and Janet. This meant climbing the hill after every run. I was a typical twelve-year-old: I didn't want to climb the hill! I became petulant. Instead of staying with the family, I created my own little ski jump and went at it. On one run I caught my tip as I was launched off the precipice, and I smacked into the ground. My leg snapped. My mother was concerned for me, but not very impressed by my stunt. Until then, I had felt that I could do no wrong on skis. This episode was a quick, cruel lesson in human frailty. I was vincible.

There are many skiers in western Canada who look down their noses at their skiing counterparts in Ontario and Quebec whose mountains, they feel, are really no more than piddling hills. They are mistaken.

As I learned at Camp Fortune, the size of the hill is not the most important element in the development of a ski racer. What is important? Skiing must be enjoyed for what it is. An ethusiastic program in which the participants enjoy lots of camaraderie and *bonhomie*, can go a long way towards making up for any shortcomings in vertical drop.

Skiing in the east can actually be advantageous to a young racer. The conditions are more difficult than in the west. There is rock-like artificial snow, colder temperatures, and shorter, more crowded pistes which lend themselves to slalom, or technical skiing, rather than flat-out, hell-bent-for-leather downhill racing. To become a good downhill racer, a solid technical base is essential. In the west it is easy to become spoiled by lush powder, and runs which seem to stretch forever, before the necessary basics are acquired.

A look down a list of recent Canadian racers confirms that the east has produced more than its share. Kathy Kreiner, Betsy Clifford, Steve Podborski, Laurie Graham, Liisa Savijarvi, Todd Brooker, Dave Irwin and the Stemmles, Brian and Karen, all learned to ski in Ontario or Quebec. By dint of hard work and good coaching, they acquired sufficient technique in their public school years to win the attention and support that enabled them to escape the eastern hills, and get on to the bigger slopes out west. There, they could ski long runs, and become accustomed to their greater variety and scope. This essential, western phase in their maturation as ski racers usually occurred between their twelfth and fourteenth birthdays. Like small-town hockey players with dreams of the big time, they left everything they knew and loved to find out how good they could be.

I was lucky. I didn't have to make such a difficult choice. When I was twelve, my father became the head of the department of Community Health Sciences at the University of Calgary. It was a great challenge for him and a real break for me. I was heading for the Rocky Mountains at the ideal moment in my career.

I HAD ONLY SEEN CALGARY and its nearby mountains from the back seat of the car, when we made the annual trek from Vancouver to Montreal, in the early 1960s, to visit my grandparents. But my mother had skied in the Canadian Championships at Mount Norquay, near Banff, in 1948. She was full of stories which I loved to hear about the great skiing and scenery.

She told me about the days before ski lifts were common, when competitors had to climb all the way up the mountain to ski down into the huge bowl at Norquay. She gave me a vision of powder snow that lasted forever on thin, winding tracks surrounded by lodgepole pine trees. She also told fabulous tales of trekking to Skoki Lodge, Temple Lodge, and Lake Louise, where the château stood proudly over the lake, facing a massive, beautiful wall of glacial ice. She sketched a very romantic picture. My imagination was totally engaged. I could hardly wait for my chance to do what she had done.

The move west was at a time of transition in my life. I was coming off a broken leg, and was at that exciting and critical stage of life when boys become young men. At the time, my first year in Alberta seemed very difficult but, in retrospect, it went very smoothly. Old and trusted friends had been abandoned, and R.G. Sinclair Public School in Kingston Township was left behind. I was now part of a new, proudly western crowd, in a new, proudly western racing program, racing on much bigger, more demanding hills.

I began the ski season in C class open racing, but by year's end I had moved up to the A class. I was progressing rapidly.

After a year spent looking for the best situation, my parents decided to take out a family membership at the Lake Louise Ski Club. This brought me into contact with Mike Wiegele. Mike was an Austrian carpenter and ski racer who, upon realizing that he was not going to make it to the top in Europe, decided to emigrate to Canada. He subsequently set up shop as a ski instructor in the Rockies. His love of skiing is undiminished to this day. He now runs a successful heli-skiing outfit in the Cariboos in the BC interior.

Mike's philosophy was not complicated. He felt very strongly that young skiers should ski, ski, ski, and then, when they were sick of skiing, go back and ski some more. He wanted, or rather demanded, that his racers be out on the hill the day Lake Louise opened for skiing. And he expected them to be out there still, five or six months later, when the lifts stopped for the summer.

When the resort was closed he and his brother, Norbert, or the other assistant director of the Lake Louise ski school, a Swiss émigré, André Schwartz, took us on to glaciers in nearby Banff National Park and made us turn the boards some more. No matter how small the patch of snow or ice, he wanted us to ski on it.

Mike also arranged for us to do physical training on a full-time basis, the year round. In this, he was a visionary, well ahead of his time. In Canada, in the late 1960s, skiing was something most coaches and racers turned their attention to in November, and forgot when the snow receded.

At this time we were spending our weekends and most of our summers near Tunnel Mountain, at Banff. We lived in a small cluster of homes with other families — the Kents, the Hillands, the Harvies, the Rooneys — who also had kids in ski racing. The area is now, more-or-less, part of Banff, but back then it was quieter and more remote. There were deer, mountain sheep, and ravenous black bears to contend with in the spring. One time I was outside working on a pair of skis for a race when a bear came foraging in front of the ski storage building. A few snowballs corrected the problem. Of course, I was only one step from the safety of the house!

I helped out for several summers at Camp Horizon, a Kinsman retreat for the mentally and physically handicapped. My father worked as a volunteer at the same camp with children who had diabetes. At this time my entire existence revolved around skiing. I was already a failed baseball player. If I wasn't good at something, I didn't want to play. Maybe it's a character flaw — it drives my wife, Lynda, crazy — but I want to do everything well, immediately. This was my source for the will to win, but it made it very hard for me to take up new sports. Rather than struggle with baseball, I moved on to other summery sporting pursuits — such as skiing! In my spare time I'd run, hike around the mountains, or go cycling, often by myself.

In late August, 1969, Mike dropped by the house to ask Ron and me to climb the Bow Glacier with him on the weekend. He wanted to see if the snow was suitable for a training camp. It was to be a fartlek, a tough ten-mile hike in which we would run on the flats and walk on the incline so that our pulse rates were always up.

So, off we went, hard on Mike's heels. He was always in exceptional shape. To keep up with him required extraordinary effort. But we did it and the Bow Glacier was deemed suitable. The next weekend we and the youngsters all went on a fartlek up the glacier to train gates. It was the kind of program that made me into a national team skier.

Our wiry Austrian coach was widely regarded as a tough, demanding man. But Mike was a European. He realized better than most Canadian coaches that if skiers from this tiny ski country were to have a chance at success, we would have to outwork the Europeans. We couldn't match the natural advantages they found on their doorsteps.

Among the racers from Mike's modest program who made the national team were Mike Irwin, Chris Kent, Bobby Allison, and my younger brother Jim (who specialized in slalom and giant slalom).

Lake Louise was an ideal location at which to learn the game. It had everything a young skier could imagine. There were short runs, long runs, soft snow, hard snow, miles of track and luscious powder at the Purple Bowl. I learned every nook and cranny of the ski area, including virgin back bowls that didn't have any lifts.

During my second year with Mike, when I was fourteen, I made the Alberta team. I was getting some encouraging downhill results, but then I broke my leg again — this time while doing serious giant slalom training. It was to be my last injury for twelve skiing-filled years.

THE FIRST TIME I thought of myself as a ski racing champion was back in the east, when I won the John Snow Trophy in Vorlage. I was ten years old. Betsy Clifford, Sue Graves, and Currie Chapman had their names on the same trophy and I began to dream occasionally — it was not yet an obsession — that I might one day join them in Europe. I understand that trophy is still kicking around Ottawa. Perhaps it is an influence on some youngsters just as it once was on me.

While with Mike Wiegele, my reveries became a little more complex and focused. On the difficult Lake Louise men's Olympic downhill run — so-named because, at one time, the resort hoped it would host the 1972 Olympics, which were actually held at Sapporo — I began to see myself as the dashing Swiss megastar, Bernhard Russi. From film and video clips, I concluded that he was the consummate racer. He was handsome, urbane, and at ease in English, French, or German. And, boy, could that man ski! I imagined myself as him, with my arms and legs relaxed and supple. I copied the Russi tuck, and his superb, compact stance while airborne. I always tried to choose the line I thought the great Bernhard would take.

From these fantasies came the notion that I, too, might one day tame the great European mountains. My chance came sooner than I expected.

A
SEASON IN
EUROPE

I N 1972, MY FATHER took a sabbatical from the University of Calgary. For professional reasons, and to expose us all to another way of life and a much more competitive skiing universe, he and my mother decided we should move to Switzerland for a year. He would work with the World Health Organization at the University of Lausanne. I would ski and go to school.

So, it came to pass that the second of the four preparatory phases leading to a place on the national team, was now over. I was seventeen. I had skied first in eastern, and then in western Canada. The crucial third phase, in Europe, where I decided that ski racing was how I wished to spend the first years of my adult life, was beginning. The fourth stage, when I joined the Canadian Alpine team as a junior member, was only twelve months away.

After a summer at the Griffin camp, high on the Kokanee Glacier in BC, and at another summer camp in Whistler, BC, we flew to Geneva and a completely different, much more professional skiing regimen. I left behind me a land where snow was available for no more than eight or nine months a year. Now I was among a group of excellent young racers who were accustomed to year-round skiing.

Thanks to the efforts of my parents, within a few months there were not many good mountains in Switzerland, France, or Austria, that had not favoured me with a couple of hours of their time. I used the opportunity well. I improved by leaps and bounds, gaining time on my as yet unknown rivals back in Canada.

It seems to me that when Canadian racers are ten or twelve years old, they are as good as Europeans of the same age. But, by the time they are sixteen or seventeen, the Europeans have improved to such an extent that there may be as much as a ten- or fifteen-second gap between them, in most races. The difficulty for Canadians is that, in these vital years, they don't get nearly as many hours of skiing as the Europeans do.

With the exception of a few city slickers, such as Switzerland's Peter Müller, who grew up in a suburb of Zurich, European racers are almost always from Alpine villages. They grow up on farms or in small hotels beside or on top of their hills. Whenever the weather is good, they go skiing.

Switzerland is the leading ski nation in the world today, and has been since the Austrians slipped at the beginning of the decade. Judging by the obvious points of comparison, this should not be so. Based upon population, the number of ski clubs and juvenile racers, Austria should be well ahead of the Swiss and everyone else.

But, in their everyday lives, the Swiss have created a structured, productive racer-delivery system. Theirs is a benevolent dictatorship in which all power lies at the top, but all levels are thoroughly consulted and involved in decision-making. To coach the Swiss World Cup team is to be the top dog in skiing in Switzerland, but much prestige also accrues to the coaches responsible for individual World Cup and Europa Cup disciplines, and to the development coaches who find and nurture the best ten and twelve-year-olds.

Switzerland has a multi-tiered program which is broken by region within the country. They try to find the best young racers, and draw them away from their clubs temporarily, for consultation and evaluation. The intention is to bring these big fish from little ponds into a much larger talent pool, so they can learn exactly how they rate and what they must do if they are to continue improving. Then, just as suddenly, these youngsters are returned to their clubs or regions to make sure they don't dry up or get swollen egos.

The Swiss move their racers through six different levels. These levels are differentiated by youth (six and five), talent (four and three) and results (two and one). Each racer is encouraged to advance as quickly as possible through the numbered levels. In time, most racers meet their limitations, accept the fact and retire from competition. But, if they do not meet the highest standard they are seldom bitter about it, because they know exactly how they progressed and where they failed. Many of these highly-trained skiers re-enter the program as coaches.

At all times Karl Fresner, an Austrian expatriate, and his predecessor, Rolf Hefti, have kept a very close watch on all their coaches and racers. They have designed a program that requires racers to train in all three disciplines (downhill, slalom and giant slalom) with equal fervour. Until recently, few other countries took such multi-disciplinary training seriously.

The Swiss Federation also insists that each racer acquire a trade or profession before being allowed to devote all his or her time to the national team. Peter Müller, for example, the current world downhill champion, is a wealthy man. He is also a licensed tree surgeon.

In Switzerland, all males must do military service in their late teens or twenties, and annual tours of duty until they are into late middle age. Ski racers are not exempted, but most unit commanders are willing to let them adjust their schedules, and allow them to have furloughs for races and important training camps.

In Austria, formal education is virtually impossible within the racer development program. Military service, which is normally compulsory, is waived for national ski team members: presumably they are thought to be providing an essential service to the country as skiers.

In Austria, racers are usually developed within an almighty provincial system, with the best youths getting a chance to try out for the national squad. Provincial federations guard their fiefs jealously. The Tyrolean and Salzberg federations battle each other for overall control and the chance to have as many of their racers on the national team as possible. And so only a few crumbs are left for the youth of the other skiing provinces, Styria, Carinthia, and East Tyrol.

In Switzerland, too, there are regional or factional rivalries. When disputes arise, opponents are sometimes divided along linguistic lines, with those who speak German, French, Italian and Romansh each having a different point of view. But these wrangles are much less obvious, and less destructive, than in Austria because the national federation controls all the levers, and arbitrarily settles disagreements.

The Swiss boss, Fresner, enters each season with a precise appreciation of the condition and capabilities of his racers. He achieves this by watching and working with them during the summer and fall. The Austrian head coach in my era, the legendary Charlie Kahr of Schladming, tolerated a much more haphazard, individualistic approach to racer development. He relied on intense competition within the team to motivate his boys.

In his heyday, Kahr was a brilliant technician and strategist, and a major help to racers such as Franz Klammer. But as he grew older, he became less and less enthusiastic about his work. The results of his inattention to detail are evident in the Austrian team of today. While Fresner and his eager acolytes developed many racing prodigies, Kahr could find none to challenge his old guard. Austria's leading downhill performers today, Peter Wirnsberger, Leonhard Stock, Helmut Hoeflehner, Anton Steiner, and Erwin Resch, have been on the circuit since Steve Podborski and I were virtual World Cup rookies. There is no one on hand to depose them.

It is as if the Austrians expect that by sheer numbers they are bound to reclaim their mantle as skiing's greatest power. Of course, there is something to their logic: with so many thousands of racers to choose from, Austria's team must surely one day rise from the ashes to blaze in glory again.

Obviously, I am partial to the Swiss system, however. It gives racers a better chance to meet their potential within a structured, caring setup. I would love Canada to have such a strong arrangement for identifying talent and nurturing it, but frankly, given the high cost of transport, the way our geographic and political realities pit east against west, and haves against have-nots, plus the pre-eminence of ice hockey which lures away so many of the best athletes, such a development is unlikely, at least on the male side.

But Canada's tiny program does have something the Europeans would like to have. As Heinz Kappeler, a product of the Swiss system, and our downhill coach from 1977 until 1982, has said to me many times, European officials envy the Canadians. We were sufficiently motivated that we never required close supervision. Whether it was dryland or on-snow training, we seized every chance to improve. Our commitment to the sport was often greater because we were deprived of friends and family for so much of the year. We had nothing but each other and our sport. It was and is an intangible advantage that counts for a lot.

We, like our hockey counterparts, brought another quality to competition. As Soviet hockey coaches know, the wild card in any match with the Canadians is their "heart." A system may build an athlete, but it won't necessarily create desire. This was the bottom line . . . we loved to ski fast.

The Canadian racer is generally from a comfortable middle class, professional, urban family. With very few exceptions, such families are the only ones who can afford the sport. The fathers are doctors, lawyers, engineers, teachers, senior public servants, airline pilots or businessmen; the mothers tend to be university-educated, traditional, stay-at-home types, determined that their children have the best of everything, and every opportunity to excel. If their parents aren't willing or able to offer such opportunities — such as dozens of weekends in the mountains — young Canadian racers don't stand much chance of challenging the best European racers, most of whom step from the cradle on to a ski slope. For example, Switzerland's downhill sensation, Michela Figini, grew up within a few yards of a ski lift in the Italian-speaking canton of Ticino. Her long-time Canadian rival, Laurie Graham, was raised in southern Ontario, 3,000 kilometres away from the kind of mountains Figini was skiing on every day. To get Laurie to the same level, her parents had to be able to afford to truck her to the mountains whenever school allowed.

The European advantage continues after they begin competing against the Canadians. When the weather sours, the European goes home to have a home-cooked meal. When it happens to a Canadian, he sits in a hotel and stews. Because he lives close to mountains which the Canadian can only visit, the European enjoys an average of five or six days of training per week, over the course of the season, compared to the Canadian's three.

For a Canadian to be the best in his age group or category is not difficult. In many cases, he will achieve victory by default, which is no victory at all. The skier within a small provincial ski community, such as Alberta, usually competes with skiers of disparate abilities and potential, rather than against the best young racers from across the nation. Consequently, he (or she) finds it much more difficult to improve.

In Switzerland, proximity to good hills and thousands of like-minded youngsters, means easy access to low cost, high-level competition. Ski racers as young as ten years of age are brought into the system. During our year in Europe my younger brother, Jim, won the ten-to-twelve age category in the Swiss Romande regional championships. He was tapped for inclusion in the level six program until the Swiss coaches were told not to bother — because he was Canadian.

Canadians are not exposed to such intense competition until they are, perhaps, sixteen years old. By then, ice hockey and other interests, and the high cost of ski racing have stripped away much of the available talent. Until or unless the government or another wealthy sponsor unexpectedly plunks down the millions of dollars that would be required for a world-class training facility, with glacier skiing and a specialized ski high school, it will be nearly impossible for Canada to compete on anything like even terms against the Alpine nations.

Otherwise, the only alternative is to select a small team of the very best and concentrate all human and financial resources on them. It is a system that goes against the Canadian ethic of equality, but it is the only alternative. A few good late bloomers may be missed in such a system, but most of the exceptional talents will be given a chance to flower.

THAT WINTER IN EUROPE I trained occasionally with the British team and its Austrian coach, Dieter Bartsch, who later became the architect of the Swiss women's team's many successes. I raced in the same downhill race as the Swiss World Champion, Bernhard Russi, and in the same slaloms and giant slaloms as the German-speaking Italian star, Gustav Thoeni. By spring, I had been transformed into a very good, seventeen-year-old racer. To be exposed to European competition, to participate in intense year-round racer development, and to watch how the best racers skied, had also given me the impetus to make ski racing my life.

Skiing suddenly became for me a full-time pursuit, with on-snow training and competition throughout the year. This was my first exposure to sophisticated glacier training and detailed physical programs designed to optimize performance. It was also a time when many lasting friendships were established. The "Three Musketeers" of the British team, Konrad Bartelski, Peter Fuchs, and Willy Bailey, took me under their collective wing and showed me around. They gave me lessons that would bear fruit within two years. Sadly, Peter was killed in a freak car accident in 1979. And Willy died in 1986 while doing what he loved best. He was consumed by an avalanche while skiing in powder snow at his second home in Verbier, Switzerland. These were reminders of how fragile our existence is.

Konrad became my closest friend on the World Cup. Back in 1973 we got off to a rocky beginning. He didn't think too much of the garrulous young Canadian whom Peter had befriended and invited to his home in Scotland. With time, we found that our interests meshed: travel, an evening's adventure chasing the fairer sex (at which Konrad was particularly adept) and ski racing. Konrad, more than anyone, made me feel at home in Europe.

While in Europe I was given permission to join the Canadian B team for a few races on the Europa Cup. The coach of that team told me that my FIS (International Ski Federation) ranking — which determined my seeding and start number — had improved only by virtue of the fact that I had competed in Europe where FIS points were generally lower, and therefore better, than in North America. When I came back to Canada he predicted I would be eaten alive, because I wasn't good enough. His comments were made innocently enough, but they stuck in my craw. I resolved to prove him wrong.

When I returned home, I petitioned the Canadian Ski Association to be invited to a camp for what was then called the Can-Am team. (It's now referred to as the Nor-Am team, and constitutes the second rung in Alpine skiing behind the World Cup). My FIS points warranted such a promotion, but they insisted that I attend a preliminary ski camp, so that my skiing ability could be judged. The camp, which was really nothing more than a week of intense free skiing, was held in Sunshine Village, in Banff National Park, under the direction of the head coach of the Canadian team, Scott Henderson. Due to poor snow conditions we could only ski for seven days, but Scotty was sufficiently impressed to invite me back for a Can-Am team try-out camp in British Columbia.

There were about twenty men competing for eight places on the Can-Am team when we gathered at Kimberley. Among them were a few people whom I would eventually get to know much better, including my future brother-in-law, Derek Robbins. Derek had been on the 1972 Olympic team, but had injured a knee and was trying to regain his old form.

The team was coached by Butch Boutry, a down-to-earth, don't-give-me-any-crap kind of guy, from Nancy Greene country, Rossland, BC. Butch decided that in the course of training we would run a series of slalom, giant slalom and downhill timed trials and, from these tests, on the basis of a World Cup-style point-scoring system, we would qualify for the team.

From the start there were some real surprises. The person who dominated training was a young downhiller from Don Mills, Ontario, by the name of Steve Podborski. An outsider, and only sixteen years old, no one had even considered him a possibility to make the team.

By the end of the camp, when all the points were added up, it was clear that some of the older fellows, like Derek Robbins, had been beaten out. But as we sat together awaiting news of our fate, most of us had no idea whether our names were on Butch's list. I had won a few giant slalom trials, had done reasonably well in the downhill, and had not embarrassed myself in the slalom, but where that left me in the overall standings, which included the results of about thirty runs, I had no idea.

"I'm not going to bother telling you who got how many points," Butch began. "As you know, these results were arrived at using a World Cup points system. And the names of the men on the Can-Am team are: Gary Aiken, Yvon Blackburn, Steve Podborski, Rob Safrata, Tom Irwin (a cousin of Dave Irwin of Thunder Bay, who was already a B team member), Gord Acton, André Senécal, and, last, but not least, Ken Read."

On the four-hour bus ride back across the Continental Divide we got a good little party going. At a pit stop somewhere on the Radium-Banff highway, everyone piled out the door for a break. Everyone, that is, except Steve, who tried to exit the bus by way of a window. But he caught his feet on the lip of the window and ended up cracking his noggin on the asphalt. He was already so benumbed with joy that the accident appeared not to hurt him.

I was in seventh heaven, too. The journey was like a dream. Despite lofty ambitions, I had entertained no real expectation that I would make the Canadian team in my first attempt. I was eighteen years old, and as happy as any young man in the Rockies.

In Calgary my parents accepted the news of my elevation very cautiously, but their coolness did not surprise me. As volunteers within the organization, they knew far better than I the Byzantine political machinations of the Canadian Ski Association. They wanted to see written confirmation that I was on board before getting excited. As in so many things, they were right. Official protests were filed against Steve and me by the Ontario and British Columbia divisions. Their reasoning: he was too young and no one knew who I was.

Butch told us later that he gave the divisions an ultimatum. Either they abide by his selections or find a new coach. Eventually a compromise was worked out. The whole team was to have a review period during which we were to be scored at Can-Am races according to the World Cup points system then in use. (FIS rankings, which determine seeding, and are worked out using a convoluted mathematical formula taking a racer's two best finishes of the year and measuring them against the time of the winner, were not part of the equation.)

Under Butch's compromise setup, anyone falling behind was to be cut. As it turned out, only one person was dropped. Steve and I became fully-fledged national team members.

THROUGH ALL THESE YEARS I continued to attend school. Before leaving for Switzerland, I was lucky enough to sneak through grade eleven, despite a heavy ski racing load that took me away from classes for weeks at a time, in the heart of the school year. While overseas, I took a few grade twelve courses by correspondence. This meant that when I returned to North America the next year, and raced on the Can-Am circuit, I also had to go back to school to complete my grade twelve.

Ski racing and school: the terms are almost mutually exclusive. To take ski racing seriously requires a tremendous amount of time away from home, starting at about the age of fourteen or fifteen. This is why Steve Podborski and Todd Brooker only got roughly grade ten educations.

I was fortunate to have parents who urged me to go as far as possible at school. I also had a high school vice-principal who was willing to do everything in his power to make sure I got through.

Bill Kelly, of Queen Elizabeth High School in Calgary, was my academic adviser and go-between with the teaching staff. He asked teachers to turn a blind eye to my comings and goings until late in the school year, when I would be very far behind.

Then word would come down that I was expected to spend more time in class, and I did.

It wasn't always easy. However, I once came into a social studies class after having been almost six months on the road. The teacher slapped a test paper on to my desk. I shuddered at the thought of the horrible surprises it might contain. It was a geography test: the questions were about the southern Tyrol and Canberra, among other places. I had visited a lot of the places on the test paper, and those I hadn't, I had dreamed about. I got the highest mark in class! Had it been anything else — like mathematics — I would have been dead meat.

Geography was one subject that always came easily to me. I have always been extraordinarily interested in maps. I want to know exactly where I am. For many years, I kept tracings of my road journeys around the world on maps I bought specially for the purpose. My closets are still full of boxes of them, and of huge atlases.

Those who know me now or from my years with the ski team might laugh at the idea, but I was a football player for three years in high school. In grade ten I sat on the bench. In grade eleven I was a two-way lineman on the junior varsity. When I returned for grade twelve, after a year in Europe, I started on the offensive line, but ended up on defence when we were finally knocked out of contention in the playoffs.

Angelo Mosca, Ken Read will never be! I was small, but I worked hard at learning how to block and tackle. And at that level, effort determines a lot. Anyway, it was wonderful preseason training, and gave me a few contacts with schoolmates that I never got in class because I was seldom there. To this day, I have almost no chums from my high school years. That was the price of skiing.

Because I insisted on it, I was able to miss some training camps in June to attend school, but few other young racers were ever granted these exemptions. Schooling was something my head coaches, Scott Henderson and, later, John Ritchie, never seemed to understand. Several racers were given an ultimatum: attend school or ski race. To me, this was unfair. With the right attitude, it was possible to succeed at both. The Canadian school system is flexible enough to allow students with other, short-term priorities (like skiing) to pick their way slowly through an academic program.

With the possible exception of the Swiss, most European teams also preferred that their racers not go to school. Only a few, such as Uli Spiess of Austria, Andreas Wenzel of Liechtenstein, and the West Germans, Michael Veith and Christian Neureuther, even tried to take university courses during their racing years. I don't believe any of them got as far as they had hoped. A notable exception was the West German star of the early 1980s, Irene Epple, who is just now completing a degree in medicine.

Somehow, I always made it through from one grade to the next until, when I was nineteen, the next grade was first year at the University of Calgary. I was to spend many spring sessions there, inching towards a degree. To those who ask me how I managed it, I always reply that it was easy! I enjoyed it. After exercising the body for ten and a half months of the year, to exercise the mind was like a vacation. Shortly after my retirement, I spent a full year at the University of Western Ontario, completing a Bachelor of Arts degree in economics at the merry old age of twenty-eight.

THE
CRAZY
CANUCKS _____ *CHAPTER FOUR*

THE CAN-AM CIRCUIT was a riot of fun and games, a wintry,
cross-continent odyssey with a bunch of good guys and
committed coaches. In form and atmosphere, if not in the
quality of sport exhibited, our travels must have resembled
the epic bus journeys of men like Satchel Paige, who barn-
stormed for years across the US in the days of the Negro
baseball leagues. We began the winter at Whistler, BC; went
over to Pincher Creek, Alberta; south through Montana and
Idaho to Salt Lake City, Park City and Snow Basin, near Ogden,
Utah; northeast to Aspen and the Roch Cup races; then across
the Great Plains to Buck Hill, Minnesota, near Minneapolis
for a parallel slalom; on through the Iron Range to Thunder
Bay for a week of technical races; and then via the blustery
north shore of Lake Superior to Ottawa, Montreal and Thet-
ford Mines, Quebec, for a series of slalom and giant slalom
races. The season finale was at Lake Placid, in upstate New
York.

Skiing and partying in a comfortable, North American environment was a grand experience for an eighteen-year-old, but
at season's end I had had enough of it. My year abroad had
whetted my appetite for major international competition. I
missed the thrill of racing in Europe. I missed the special
atmosphere that exists in a ski resort in which heated nuts,
wurst, and *blauwein* are for sale in the finish area, where race
announcements are made in several languages, and the competition is so keen that only the best racers from half a dozen
nations have a chance of winning.

The Can-Am circuit was a step backwards from the Europa
Cup, which I had been introduced to briefly the year before,

when I lived in Switzerland. It was like playing in the International Hockey League after playing in the American Hockey League. Neither one is quite the big leagues, but the general level of skiing on the Europa Cup is several notches higher. By hook or by crook, I made a personal vow that I would be back in Europe for the next season. The fact that I was only the tenth-best Canadian downhiller at the time, and was even further back in the technical events, never entered my calculations. I became obsessed with returning to Europe.

And fortune smiled upon me. In 1973 the Canadian team on the World Cup was really only three men: Jim Hunter, Dave Murray, and Dave Irwin. The coach, Scotty Henderson, felt it was time to broaden the program, so he invited all the kids from the Can-Am team, plus a few others who had performed well in Canada, to attend a month-long camp with the A team that summer high in the wintry Argentine and Chilean Andes. For the first and last time, conditions there for training were good — we returned many times in later years, but were either rained on, snowed out, or suffered from altitude sickness and had to return home. But that wonderful summer, fifteen of us had a chance to train under every conceivable type of winter snow condition. This, incidently, was the first gathering of a clan that was soon to be known to the ski racing world as the Crazy Canucks. Our month in the Southern Hemisphere was such a good experience that many of us were transformed from rather ordinary skiers into something much better.

Scott Henderson was a former racer who had come close to winning a few times, but never quite succeeded, before a bad leg fracture obliged him to retire in 1970. He expected everyone to work as hard as he did and that was very hard, indeed. Everything he did, we did, whether it was fifty pushups, fifty situps, a four-mile run or twenty hill sprints. From 7:00 a.m. to 6:00 p.m. we were all expected to meet the high standards he set for himself.

Every few days, Scotty would select a certain aspect of skiing for particular emphasis. The running joke was that it was Scotty's "tip-of-the-week." One week the message was: "Sit back slightly on your skis and carve your turns with the tail end of the ski." He'd drill it in with each training run until we got it right. Then we'd move on to something else, such as hand placement to form a better aerodynamic foil: "Hands up, hands up, hands up."

With such hard physical work and emphasis on the basics we thrived under Scotty's patient coaching. His approach was hardly inspirational, but it worked. Within a few weeks, the motley crew had begun to take shape as a world-class team. Almost single-handedly, Scotty was creating the Crazy Canucks.

Hunter, Irwin, and Murray had done reasonably well in Europe in 1974, but Scotty wanted to complement and push them along by adding a new ingredient. He had in mind a younger group, consisting of a specific type of racer — chargers who would work hard, and who were not afraid to point the skis straight down and go for it. He wanted fellows who would tuck through hell if he asked them to. His selections were made mostly on the basis of timed trials.

My goal in South America was to place in the first five in every training run — that would place me in serious contention for a place on the team. I thought I had a chance at catching Irwin and Murray, but I did not presume to think that I could finish ahead of Hunter. I didn't either, except on one occasion, when he fell on his behind.

As it turned out, I came fairly close to meeting my objective, as did Gary Aiken and Steve Podborski. The competition was very close, and everyone knew it. We all became a little anxious towards the end of the month, wondering who would be invited to the next camp in Europe, and who would return to the Can-Am team. A million bedtime mental calculations could not resolve the puzzle of who was ahead and who was behind. The other question was how many newcomers Scotty thought he could afford to bring to Europe, without hindering the results of those already on the team. A complicating factor was that the Canadian Skiing Association (CSA) was chronically short of cash. It had already had trouble funding the small teams that had previously competed in Europe.

One day in late August, 1974, I was sitting in the lobby of the Hotel Portillo with Steve. We were minding our own business, admiring the Chilean Andes while waiting for afternoon tea, when Scotty approached us. He said that he'd like to have a talk with us downstairs. A National Film Board of Canada crew was on hand. Would we mind talking with him in front of the cameras for a few minutes? Steve would go down first. I would follow.

Five minutes later Scotty reappeared in the lobby without Steve. I went downstairs with him and sat down in front of the director, Giles Walker, and his crew. The film, which was about our summer training, was to be entitled, *No Way They Want to Slow Down*.

When the cameras were rolling Scotty smiled and said, "Kenny, we've decided to take you to Europe with us this fall. We'll have six racers on the World Cup. You'll be joining Jim Hunter, Dave Irwin, David Murray, Steve Podborski, and Gary Aiken."

A year before, Butch Boutry had given me the news about the Can-Am team in a hotel in British Columbia, and I had been shocked. This summer I had once again worked my hardest and hoped for the best, but I had no great expectation that I would get to hear that I had done it. Then . . . Bingo! I was shocked again. I had made it! Scotty had made a remarkable, courageous decision. Our youth and the CSA's financial predicament be damned. The Crazy Canucks were at full strength and ready for Europe.

JIM HUNTER WAS CLEARLY the best of the bunch in 1974. He was already in the first seed and, in my mind, I knew that I wasn't likely to beat him. But Irwin and Murray were beatable. So were Aiken and Podborski. I had proven that to myself a few times in South America and I set out to do it again.

"Jungle Jim" Hunter was the workhorse of the team, and the standard against which we judged ourselves. He was a brash, outspoken man who could always be heard at the dinner table and in the video room. He did a very high volume of training and made sure we all knew it. How could we not know? He insisted on doing 100 one-arm push-ups in the hotel lobby.

Jim was always at the top of the hill at the beginning of the day and still skiing when they closed the lifts six or seven hours later. That was easy enough to understand, but away from the hill he was a real enigma for the rest of us. He was a man who was going to conquer the world because the Lord had told him that he would. He told us this in the fall. When spring came and he hadn't scored more than a handful of World Cup points, he boasted that he would win next season. The Lord had told him he would.

There was no denying that Jim was a good skier who, for several winters, danced on the fringe of greatness. He almost became one of the best ski racers in the world. We didn't have to understand him to follow his lead. In fact, his sermonizing, often with Bible in hand, was a powerful motivating factor. He was the hare we all chased. To beat him was a special pleasure.

Jim clawed his way to the top. No one was ahead of him to provide an example. He did it alone. I reckon that his singular devotion to training was designed to make up for lost time. He only started racing when he was fourteen years old. Eight years later, he was ranked in the first fifteen in the world in downhill, and had made a credible showing in giant slalom, winning the first run of a World Cup GS in 1972. These achievements reflected his remarkable dedication. This farmer's son from western Saskatchewan had had to outwork the Europeans by a lot to get close to them. It was a lesson worth remembering.

In our first year together, Jim showed us how much work it took to succeed as a ski racer. In this, he was the architect of much of our eventual success, but he was not part of our two World Cup victories in 1975, or of our strong team showings at other races. Try as he might, his results slowly declined, and he turned bitter.

Jim was dropped from the team after the 1977 season, his dream of being one the world's best shattered by a dreadful season. He was furious about this, and the way the team seemed to have passed him by. I cannot emphasize enough how we used his example to scale the heights. I don't think he fully realizes how important he was to our success.

WHEN I FIRST WENT to Europe with the Canadian team David Murray was twenty-one years old, and a blond-haired flower child — we called him "Maharishi Yogi Mur."

David was a mellow guitar picker from laid-back Vancouver, a proficient windsurfer, a jumbo jet pilot's son who found life groovy and had an eye for very attractive women. He was another late starter who, in his own, much different way, was as determined to make it to the top as "Jungle." But while Jim's approach was to bowl over anything in his path and shout about it, "Mur" kept to himself. He tried to analyze everything. He spent thousands of hours alone, working on his technique and the mechanics of skiing, figuring things out for himself. He even figured out how to repair his own ski boots. He did the same with his guitar. When I first met him, he was learning his first chords from a music book. By the next time I saw him, he'd become a pretty fair player. Eventually, he became an outstanding player, but it was for his own pleasure, not for the entertainment of others. He'd go up to his room, close the door, and strum away.

Such was David's success as a skier that he had already achieved a ninth in downhill at the 1974 World Championships when I joined the team. That winter, he was ranked in the top thirty in the world in the FIS standings. His style was stiff and somehow unnatural, but I think this was a consequence of his late start as a skier. It took him a long time to get going. His seasons usually built to a crescendo in January and would then peter out. He was unlucky. As good as he was, and as hard as he worked, he never won a race, although he came within an eyeblink several times. Once, in a race at Schladming where I was first, he was only six-hundredths of a second behind me.

But "Mur" kept such disappointments in perspective. He was happy to do his best, and that was often very good, indeed.

THE BEST SKIER in our sextet was Dave Irwin, who was twenty. Alone among us he had a background that was similar to that of the European racers. From infancy, he was almost always on skis at Loch Lomond, the hill his father operated near Fort William (now Thunder Bay). Years of experience had given Dave an innate sense of how to ski well. He was also tremendously strong, a real ox of a man. "Thunder Thighs" or "Stump" were nicknames that clearly described his physical attributes. His pants had to be specially tailored to contain his legs. We were all, always, impressed.

Dave's strength and his proficiency as a skier gave him a quiet confidence that none of the rest of us possessed. But I think his self-assurance and prodigious talent sometimes worked against him. Because he knew how good he was, he worked less than the rest of us. He liked to have a good time and would occasionally forget the sport for a while to pursue young ladies. These small flaws made him vulnerable to those with more systematic methods.

At Schladming, in December, 1975, Dave shattered the competition by scoring a huge victory. He had much to be proud of on that day in Styria. He attacked one of the most treacherous courses I've ever seen, and defeated the host country's favourite son, Franz Klammer, and another hotshot Austrian, Klaus Eberhard, by almost two seconds.

But as good as Dave was that day, he was never to win another World Cup race. After the Christmas break, in Wengen, he posted the best interval time, but he came into the final three turns too tightly. He bounced off a net, slid halfway down a hill, recovered and went through the finish. A sure victory became twelfth place. That he finished at all was a tremendous testament to his audacity and strength.

The next day, on the same course, in what was the back end of a downhill double header, he attacked again, and again did not give the hill the respect it merited. As a result, he cartwheeled off at the Minschkannte, on the upper part of the mountain, losing consciousness as his body smashed into a restraining net. It took a hospital stay in Interlaken, in the valley far below, to sort him out. (A videotape of the spectacular crash was used in Swiss life insurance commercials.)

A few weeks later, on his first training run at the Innsbruck Olympics, he ignored warnings from the coaches about a difficult bump near the bottom. He fell again, sending shivers down all our spines because of what it might mean for his head. Fortunately, he walked away from that one, but from that point forward he was never the same skier. He lost the dynamic skiing style that had, for a brief moment, made him the best ski racer in the world, and the only man who could challenge and defeat Klammer.

This is not to say that Dave ever lost his tenacity. Despite a plague of crashes later at places such as Hintertux, Val Gardena, Cortina, and Wengen (again), he stuck with us through six more painful seasons.

GARY AIKEN IS THE LEAST well-known of the six racers who went to Europe in the fall of 1974. He was twenty-one years old — two years older than me, and four years older than Steve. Gary was from Warfield, BC, a small-town boy who grew up between the slightly larger centres of Trail and Rossland, deep in the British Columbia interior.

Gary was a skier with a lovely, deft touch. Betsy Clifford called him "The Snake," because of his smooth, slippery racing style. Like many of the racers who grew up in the interior, Europe came as a shock to him, and he only lasted two years there with us. He was like the American TV character, the Fonz. He was the main man back in his own small pond, but in Europe he was totally out of his element. He called European breakfasts, which were heavy on the buns and wursts, "hockey puck breakfasts." He was a ham-and-eggs kind of guy.

I remember vividly how, at lunch in Megève, during our first season on the World Cup, he was halfway through his lunch before he discovered that he was eating ox tongue. The Europeans consider this a delicacy, but Gary stuck it on the end of his fork and flapped it around with disdain. We quickly lost our appetites.

On the Can-Am circuit, Gary was always far ahead of me, but when we went to Europe our positions were reversed. The life wasn't for him. He was much happier to be at home in Warfield shooting the breeze with his pals. By the spring of 1976, he had his wish. He lives there now, working for Cominco.

IN LATER YEARS, Steve Podborski was known to one and all as "Pod," but back in our first year on the World Cup he was always referred to as "The Kid." I think his first season in Europe put quite a zap on his brain, and he actually regressed a bit as a racer. Only seventeen, rather immature and lacking in confidence, he came to Europe with superb technique, but not much else. Thrust into an environment with a multitude of languages, people, and cuisines to cope with, he spent a lot of that first European winter walking around with wide-open eyes. But unlike Gary Aiken, Steve didn't fight the experience. He tried to learn from it.

There was a debate at the time as to whether Steve was being pushed too quickly through the system. I think he lacked the maturity to handle some of the situations he was thrown into, but ultimately he had the talent and ability to overcome them. And by going to Europe so young he, and racers such as Kathy Kreiner (who won a World Cup at sixteen), Todd Brooker, and Laurie Graham, gained valuable experience which helped to make them champions. If Steve had languished in

Canada for a year or two more, I do not believe he would have accomplished all he did.

THE EARLIER AN ATHLETE is exposed to the quirks of foreign countries and the intensity of international competition, the better are his or her chances to learn from them, and eventually compete on equal terms with everyone else. One reality that will never change is that the heart of ski racing is in central Europe. Most of the racers are Europeans and most of the races will always be held there. If you cannot adapt to, or reach an accomodation with European life, you are doomed. The careers of many talented Canadian and American racers have foundered because they could not adjust. Gary Aiken, who came to Europe a few years later in life than we did, could not.

I had an easier time of it on the continent, and was able to adapt and progress more quickly than Steve and some of the others, because I knew from the outset what I was up against. With my family providing personal and logistical support, I had already been to Val d'Isère and Kitzbühel when I was seventeen. I spoke French. My friend, the British racer, Konrad Bartelski, spoke perfect German. He taught me enough of the language, and of Teutonic ways, that I could get by. Several of the younger Austrians, including the European junior downhill champion, Uli Spiess, had also become friendly with me. In time, my language skills blossomed. Europe became my second home.

"Jungle Jim" was already well known for his showboat antics, and for his annual boast that he was about to win the title. Nonetheless, he had earned a measure of respect because he performed well. The more astute European observers had quietly noted that he and the two Daves had finished in the twenties and thirties regularly during the previous season. With Hunter in the first seed, Murray and Irwin in the second, Aiken and Podborski in the third, and me in the fourth, there were indications aplenty that Canada was improving.

We flew to Europe in November, 1974, from Canadian Forces Base Uplands, near Ottawa. It was a military Boeing 707, the "Sport Canada Special" to Lahr, West Germany. The flight was jammed with military personnel, their families and other government-supported athletes. K-rations were standard fare.

Dressed in ill-fitting blazers and gaudy ties, we were on our best behaviour. No complaints. The price was right.

Upon our arrival in the Black Forest, we still faced a hellish drive to the mountains. We hated every minute of this never-ending day, but we put up with it gladly to save a bit of our budget. If it wasn't for such cost-saving measures, I would probably have been back on the Can-Am circuit, checking into motels and checking out coffee shops in several dozen provinces and states.

We were to have driven an Opal that winter, but because it was unavailable when we arrived, the rental agency gave us a red Mercedes, dubbed "The Red Chariot," which we kept for the duration of our stay. Our other transportation consisted of a one-of-a-kind Volkswagen bus. To make space inside for passengers, we had to jam all our skis and a lot of our other gear on to the roof. Those in the front seat wore t-shirts and shorts because of the heat. Yet it was so cold in the back seat that, even with a team-issue, down parka and heavy winter boots, constant vigilance was needed to avoid frostbite.

Compared to what the team has now, or had in our salad days in the early 1980s, those early years on the World Cup were no picnic. At times it was a real slog. Some resorts and hotels treated us well. Others, taking into account our status as relative unknowns, treated us to European chauvinism at its worst. Even though we paid our bills like everyone else, they would try to tuck us into unobtrusive corners.

Team resources were so limited in 1974 that Scotty's wife, Sully, acted as video cameraman. We also had an assistant coach, Bob Donnelly and a physiotherapist. Against us the Austrians, the Swiss, the Italians, and the West Germans sent well-oiled machines, which included as many as a dozen coaches, and a battery of servicemen to take temperature readings, record section times and provide boxes of videotapes.

To those who did not know him well, Scotty appeared to be a laconic man. He was shy and formal with outsiders. Within the team he was never garrulous, but he imparted a very "rah, rah" philosophy that belied his quiet public face. He told us we could match the achievements of the other teams only if we agreed to support each other. Every scrap of information was to be shared. The only way to negate the European advantage was to trade information. To succeed we had to be much more than friends.

Irwin and Murray were on Head Skis at the time, and usually had a serviceman of their own. The rest of us had to forage for ourselves for equipment and for help with our ski waxes and boots. The situation was so bad that, although Steve and I were using Fischer skis, it was not until late in the season that we were able to secure from them a pair of race skis. Fischer's position was that, because we were not Europeans and had no contract, our needs should be taken care of by their office in Canada. The little equipment they did provide was second-rate, and of almost antique vintage. All the skis with the newest bases went to racers in their European stable.

But it wasn't just skis. Plastic suits were introduced in December, 1974, but the Austrian manufacturer refused to give or sell us any, although it did provide us with old, slower, blue-cloth ones. At first we could not figure this out, but in very little time we realized that we were being shafted, because we were not part of the European skiing establishment.

At the first race of my World Cup career, the *Critérium de la Première Neige*, or "Test of the First Snow," at Val d'Isère, France, we were rudely introduced to some of the capabilities of the new technologies just then sweeping the sport. There was much talk of little plastic sheets, like foils, to cloak boots and bindings in an aerodynamic shield. More telling was what the young Austrian downhillers had to say. They told us excitedly that, by reducing wind resistance, their new suits made them go much, much faster than before. Scotty scoffed at this. "Talent makes the difference, not equipment," he growled. We hoped he was right.

With a start number in the fifties at Val d'Isère, I had plenty of time to listen to the radio and to find out how Hunter, who was in the first seed, had done. From Collombin's Bump Scotty had little to say about Hunter's run, but plenty to say about the new suits. "My God, they make an incredible difference," he reported. "You should see these guys! They're rocketing all over the place. They've got so much speed they don't know how to handle it!"

The news stunned me. As I readied myself for my first World Cup race, I was being told that try as I might, I would probably be four seconds behind everyone in the first minute, even if I skied perfectly. There was nothing I could do except step out on to the mountain and do my best. I ended up thirtieth, almost five seconds behind the winner, Austria's Franz Klammer, but only two places behind Hunter. Podborski and Irwin tied for thirty-first.

There was, of course, a tremendous fuss made over the new suits. Plastic on the outside of the suit was immediately banned, because a racer wearing such a costume would bounce and slide to eternity when he fell.

At Val d'Isère, on that day in 1974, the spirit of *camaraderie* and fellowship which made the Crazy Canucks special, was truly born. As we stood together in the finish area, we shared a common thought: under the right conditions, with good equipment, we could defeat anyone.

The first half of the 1974-1975 season was frustrating. Hunter won a couple of training runs, and we skied at the level our seed numbers indicated, but there was no breakthrough. At Garmisch, for example, Hunter was the training leader and I had a pair of top ten times, but on a soft track, on race day, I slipped back to twenty-ninth, more than four seconds adrift of Klammer. I was annoyed at myself, but the Fischer service rep came up to me and put the result in its proper perspective. "You started sixtieth and finished twenty-ninth. That's pretty damn good."

Equipment deficiencies continued to hamper us. A week after the Garmisch result, at Wengen, an Italian first-seed racer, Guiliano Besson, who also used Fischer skis, looked over at me and my gnarled boards and asked, "Are you using your Ms or your Ws today?" I didn't have a clue what he was talking about! I was using the only race skis I had.

At the next race, which was at Kitzbühel, the season began to fall into place for all of us. That winter the Hahnenkamm track was especially intimidating. With marginal snow cover, only forty-nine men were brave enough to enter the race.

I ended up with a good pair of skis more or less by accident. A Fischer rep, who was waxing skis for Americans that winter, had given a choice pair to a US racer, Karl Anderson. But Anderson had fallen in training and was forced to withdraw from the race. As the result of a binding problem, I had broken my museum pieces at about the same time. When I related my misfortune to the Fischer man and asked for help, he told me his cupboard was bare. But an American Salomon rep, Dave Lennon, who overheard my plea, said to him, "What about

Karl's pair? They're not being used." With extreme reluctance, the Fischer rep handed me Anderson's W skis.

On race day, from start position forty-four, I rode those boards into the top twenty. David Murray had been fourteenth, Irwin fifteenth, I was nineteenth and Hunter was twenty-first. The Europeans congratulated us on our progress, but the clippings my parents kept for me at home showed that, according to Canadian journalists, we had done poorly. A week later, at Innsbruck, in the pre-Olympic race, Irwin placed sixth, Hunter tenth; I was sixteenth and Steve was nineteenth. At the next and last stop of the season, Megève, it was my turn to be best Canadian with an eighth; Murray was eleventh, Hunter, twelfth, and Podborski fifteenth.

I was on quite a roll. Back home, at the Canadian Championships at Tod Mountain, near Kamloops, I concluded my season by winning the downhill by three and a half seconds. This title would be the first in an unbroken string of five Canadian downhill championships, one of my proudest accomplishments. This result, which was achieved on new skis, gave me such low FIS points that, when it was combined with my World Cup eighth at Megève, I had a points total which vaulted me into the first seed.

That summer, in Argentina, in a downhill race with the Italians, I solidified my first-seed position with a second place finish, one hundredth of a second behind Dave Irwin. The result ranked me thirteenth in the world. Dave was fifteenth, and all the rest of the Crazy Canucks were in the first thirty.

Our eventual success in downhill has created the false impression that we were only chosen for, and trained by, Scott Henderson as downhillers. Nothing could be further from the truth. We ended up emphasizing downhill because that was what we did best, but in my first few seasons on the World Cup, Scott insisted that we train and compete in the other disciplines, too. It was the technical base we acquired by skiing slalom and giant slalom gates with Scotty that stood us in such good stead when we did finally concentrate on downhill.

Try as we might, we were never able to do better than thirtieth or fortieth place in the technical events. To chip away at the European advantage in these disciplines would have taken us years. Yet, we popped into the first twenty in downhill in one winter. It was clearly the way for us to go.

WORLD
CUP
BREAKTHROUGH *CHAPTER FIVE*

T HE RESULTS OF THE 1974-1975 season, our greatly improved start numbers (which were directly tied to our improving FIS rankings) exceptional fall training at Zermatt, and a much better, if not perfect, attitude on the part of our suppliers, had us brimming with confidence in December, 1975, when we checked into the Kandahar Hotel at Val d'Isère.

As a team, we did not necessarily always live, eat, and sleep together, but from the beginning of the day until dusk, Scotty insisted that we do everything else together. Hours were spent sideslipping courses and training pitches, arguing over the smallest details about where to proceed and where to brake. It was a heady time for the young bucks from the New World. Every day revealed new secrets to us about the sport and the ski world.

Dave Irwin and I had fallen in together. We worked as a single engine. It was a style of race training that I subsequently established with Steve Podborski and, years later, with Todd Brooker. We knew that such collaboration was not the European way. The Austrian and Swiss teams were so competitive that sharing information could cost a racer his place. But for us, in Europe on a shoestring, there was no other choice.

Our collaboration was necessary in another way. Unlike the Europeans, for whom the World Cup circuit was almost always close to home, we spent months at a time away from our families. We were obliged to learn to like, or at least tolerate, each other because we had little privacy, little chance for escape. We were on top of one another all the time.

In 1975 the course at Val d'Isère was particularly difficult because of thin snow cover. An intimidating ridge known as Collombin's Bump in honour of Roland Collombin, a former

World Cup champion from Switzerland who had fallen and broken his back there one year earlier, quickly began to exact a heavy toll. On the second day of training, poor Roland went for a second loop at the same spot. This fall broke his back again, and put paid to a remarkable career.

A second cloud hanging over the World Cup was the death two days before the race of the only obvious heir to Jean-Claude Killy, the young French racer, Michel Dujon. While testing skis a few miles away, on a glacier at Tignes, Dujon crashed head-first into a lift tower. Out of respect for their fallen comrade the French team withdrew from the race, but the rest of the White Circus carried on.

In the days before the race, indications were normal. I had been tenth, twelfth and fifteenth in training. The rest of the team did no better than usual, and no worse.

One month earlier, while training in Zermatt, I had jokingly told one of the women on the Swiss team that if I ever made the first seed, I would probably draw number one and win the race. She laughed at my joking boast and said that I could not possibly beat Klammer, or Switzerland's idol, Bernhard Russi.

Now, on the eve of my second season, as I did some sit-ups in the hallway of the Kandahar Hotel, Scotty bounded up to me and said, "Well, you've got the number you've always wanted. You're number one. The weather forecast for tomorrow is the same as it was today. Clear and cold. No change anticipated. It should be a good number."

The Fischer Skis headquarters in Austria had finally become formally involved with the Canadian team. I had a contract for $3,000. Dave Irwin had switched from Head, joining Steve and I, and we had a serviceman all to ourselves. We were given the vaunted M and W skis. But they had also come out with another series of skis, the MW, which was said to be better adapted for a range of different snow temperatures. However, instead of receiving two pairs each, one for racing and one for training, as the Austrians had, we received only one pair each. We were advised to try the new skis in training, but not in a race. Our race MWs would arrive the following week.

Unlike most other World Cup coaches, Scotty was still heavily involved in ski preparation and selection. In training, we found the MWs went very well, so he told us to use them in the race. Our rep threw a tantrum because he had been ordered by Fischer to leave them in the wax room. The battle escalated until Fischer's race service director, Gerold Krims, came over to insist that the skis not be used. But Scotty was adamant. We would use them, and that was that.

Sunday, December 7, 1975, was as clear as had been forecast, but the temperature had eased up a few degrees. Morning warmup passed without incident. My skis felt good. The turns I carved were crisp and smooth. I was enjoying myself so much that I took a little too much time. On my way up the mountain, the lift stopped and I had to walk the last 100 yards to the start. With ten minutes until my turn, I quickly dropped my outer clothes, affixed my number and got my bindings adjusted. I had time for none of my usual pre-race deliberations, but then I had no time to be nervous about starting first for the first time in my life, either. I had my new skis and was ready to tackle the Oreiller-Killy course for the twenty-first *Critérium*.

It wasn't pretty, but I somehow survived Collombin's Bump. In the meadow which followed, I could feel that I was tracing exactly the line I wanted. I also realized that the track I was travelling on was far from the track that had been established by the forerunners. A compression where many had come to grief in training was next. It scared me a bit, but I got through it easily, with a spectacular, aerodynamic leap. The key was to stay on line and, at the critical moment, relax and let gravity do its work. My landing was rough, like a jet fighter smacking on to a carrier deck in high seas, but I was still on my feet and tucking for the finish. My time was 2:04.97, faster than anyone's training time, but a good chunk slower than the course record of 2:03.19, that Klammer had established the year before.

Being number one involved more than racing first. It also involved an agonizing wait while everyone else came down the mountain. Dave Irwin, skiing fourth, had a good interval time, but made a mistake in the compression, and came home in second place. His good interval placement only lasted a moment because Russi, with start number seven, came through the intermediate timer even faster. My reaction was, "Now things are falling into place — this is the beginning of the European onslaught. But Russi lost it badly at the bottom, to take second place, two thirds of a second behind me. It was the first inkling I had that my time might actually stand.

I was still in first place with two first-seed racers to go, and I was ecstatic, but I couldn't let it show for even a moment because I was convinced that Klammer, with start number fourteen, would vanquish me.

"*L'autrichien Franz Klammer, vainqueur de Val d'Isère, Schladming, Kitzbühel, Garmisch, Wengen, Val Gardena, St. Moritz,* Jackson Hole *et la descente pre-Olympique à Innsbruck, est sur la piste. Der Kaiser von Oesterreich, Franz Klammer ist jetzt unterwegs,* Franz Klammer, the Austrian superstar and current World Cup champion is now on course," the public announcer screamed. The crowd, anticipating his victory, squealed its delight. Journalists and photographers braced themselves for the scrum with Klammer.

At the interval timer, which was on a section known as the *Bosse à Jean,* but known to us from video sessions as the "Tunnel Bumps," Klammer was four-tenths of a second behind me. Maybe it was possible for me to squeeze this out, after all. In the compression, he foundered momentarily, but righted himself. Classic Klammer. In the finish schuss, I was gauging his time by watching the scoreboard clock and his progress past the gates. It was going to be very close, indeed. Then, suddenly, not 100 metres from first or second place, he caught an edge in a hole and fell. This unexpected development left me experiencing a jumble of conflicting emotions. My arms went up in the air in triumph, but quickly came down as I looked to see if Klammer was hurt. I had to find out if Klammer was all right. He had taken a hell of a fall, but he did not seem to be badly hurt.

The last racer in the first seed, René Berthod of Switzerland, crashed at exactly the same spot, and I knew absolutely for certain that victory was mine. Irwin ended up fourth, behind Italy's Herbert Plank and Russi. Hunter was ninth, Podborski tenth, and Murray thirteenth. Canada had a ski team to be reckoned with and, like it or not, Alpine Europe knew it.

The Europeans reacted with respectful disbelief. Downhill had been the last bastion of Alpine supremacy. Slalom and giant slalom and all the women's disciplines had occasionally fallen to outsiders, but not the downhill. The only non-European to achieve a World Cup downhill victory had been the Australian, Malcolm Milne, in 1969, but that was somehow explicable because he had trained with the French. As soon as he won, he was kicked off the French team and never won again. Canada's victory was different. It was stamped, "Made in Canada." The racer was Canadian and so were his coaches.

The German television announcer, Harry Valerian, explained to his countrymen that I had won because I was not afraid to attack the mountain. World Cup founder Serge Lang, writing in *La Suisse* said, "This massive Canadian result gives one cause to ponder. Val d'Isère was much more difficult this year than usual, but the Canadians left the racers from the Alpine countries naked. They will represent a primordial factor in future races.

"Ken Read's run was impressive in its perfection. His bib number, one, was a small disadvantage, but he ignored it and the much faster course conditions and won the day."

A few days later, in another column in *La Suisse*, Lang added, "We've waited a long time for this, the time when the accursed or damned Canadians arrive. Read, Irwin, Murray, Hunter, Podborski, they represent the new strength of Alpine skiing. They are the ones willing to give absolutely everything to downhill."

John Samuel, sports editor of the *Manchester Guardian*, and an erudite Alpine journalist of decades' standing, called it a "breakthrough long threatened. With five Canadians in the first thirteen, it was no one-off fluke."

In all my years of skiing, I only telephoned my parents from Europe twice. The first time was after I won Canada's first men's downhill World Cup race at Val d'Isère. I couldn't get through because they were up at Banff for the weekend, skiing with my younger brother, Jim, but I asked my sister, Janet, why she thought I was calling. She said, "You're hurt?" I told her I'd won. She told me she was astonished. My parents rang the next day to congratulate me.

The only other time I called home was after winning at Chamonix, several years later. In all my years with the team they never again called me. It wasn't our way to be telephoning around the world, but I always knew how much they cared about how I was and how I was doing because, before every significant race and after every victory or disappointing result, they would send me a wire with a smart rhyme or a limerick to make me smile and boost my spirits.

Gian Franco Kasper, the secretary-general of FIS, watched a race on television from Kitzbühel in 1982, with my parents.

He told me he found the experience "totally backward" from what he had experienced with other racers' parents. My father was the nervous parent, twisting and turning with me all the way down the course. My mother was calm and relaxed. Gian Franco described them just the way they are. My mother, the former racer, saw my progress as a matter of course. My father was always on the edge of his seat, waiting for the dreaded call from Europe with news that I had been hurt in a fall. Fortunately, in all my years overseas, the telephone only rang once with such news. And it wasn't so bad. It was a knee that had popped. My head was all right.

FIVE DAYS AFTER WINNING at Val d'Isère, at a rare World Cup downhill at Madonna di Campiglio, Italy — the town usually hosted slalom races — Klammer gained his revenge, returning to the podium as winner. But Canadians once again excelled. Irwin was fourth again, I was eleventh, Murray was fifteenth, Podborski sixteenth, and Hunter seventeenth.

A week later, on December 21, with a Fischer advertising poster celebrating my Val d'Isère victory on all the doors of Austria's *Vereinsbank*, 30,000 Austrians came out to Schladming's Planai course to see Klammer smite the new boys. But it was not to be. Irwin, who had been the best in training twice the previous day, tucked most of the way down the track, which is known unofficially as the Autobahn. His winning time of 2:00.84, was almost two seconds and four places better than Klammer. Murray was seventh, Hunter fifteenth, and Podborski twenty-sixth. I made the mistake of trying new ski boots and could only place seventeenth.

It was around this time that the name "Crazy Canucks" came into usage. I believe it was first penned by French journalist Patrick Lang. My co-author believes that Patrick's father, Serge, was responsible. Whoever it was, the first phrase was something like, "The Canucks, they ski like crazy." Headline writers figured out the rest.

What (one of) the Langs meant, in a roundabout way, was that we were prepared to take unacceptable risks to win. Okay, we'd won a couple, but at some point soon we'd self-destruct and be removed from the downhill equation. It was a sentiment that had broad appeal in Europe. "Crazy Canucks" was an easy, slightly dismissive handle, a breezy way to describe our success. In no time at all, journalists everywhere were using it.

But I shouldn't sound like I'm complaining. We revelled in our new status and the name that went with it. We thought it captured nicely our brave mood. In downhill racing, there are much worse things to be called than "crazy."

Ours was the first generation of Canadian racers to train year-round on snow. The magic of television had given us a glimpse of European competition. The impact of the federal government's contributions also cannot be overstated. Until the early 1970s the national team operated on a shoestring budget. Ask Nancy Greene, who was obliged to return to Canada in mid-season in 1967 to raise funds to keep the team in operation. It almost cost her the World Cup title. While the government's initial outlay was small, it helped alleviate some of the financial pressure, allowing the team to slowly expand, and add extra coaching staff. For the first time Canadians could think about competing on a nearly-equal basis with Europeans. Full equality was still a few years away — the servicemen, wax, and downhill suits would make the difference.

Why did the Crazy Canucks succeed, when so many before had tried and failed? The answer is simple enough: Scott Henderson. He took a gang with very different personalities, but with a common will to succeed. Through hard work and dedication, he moulded us into winners. His theory was: "Give me the chargers. I'll drill in the basics."

But as a coach, Scott unfortunately had one serious flaw. While he had a remarkable talent for identifying, teaching and inspiring young racers, he had difficulty keeping up with, or taking seriously, the technological developments that were helping other teams to improve. Scott's answer to any setback was to work us harder. This was fine when dealing with raw novices, but it was not necessarily the best approach to adopt with a world-class team. Partly as a result of his inability to deal with technological advances, we had a string of atrocious results during the 1976-1977 season.

That winter, Steve Podborski was coming back slowly from his first serious injury, and it was a tough, lonely slog. Hunter was on his way out. He'd finished third from last at the Hahnenkamm, and was devastated. Irwin had not recovered from his crash at Wengen the year before, or from several more recent crashes. He was consulting doctors in Canada about problems with his memory and his vision. Steve and I had two lonely successes that year. I won a FIS downhill (that is, it was worth FIS points, but was not part of the World Cup) in Cortina, Italy, which established the highest downhill average speed ever: 117 kilometres per hour. Steve placed third in a FIS downhill at Lenzerheide, Switzerland. Beyond that, our best placing on the World Cup was a dismal thirteenth.

Our Italian downhill suits were a problem, too. They were subsequently tested at the National Research Centre in Ottawa and found to be wanting, costing us more than three seconds per two-minute run. The team became fractious, with Hunter, Irwin, and me at Scott Henderson's throat. At times, it seemed as if the group would disintegrate in anger and despair. We had all expected so much after the triumphs of the previous year. Instead, we ended up with heartache. Were we one-year wonders? The team had reached its nadir.

The summer and fall camps of 1977 were tense. Most of the racers lined up against Scott and his you-must-work-harder approach. We made our views known to the Canadian Ski Association.

The ideal solution would have been to keep Scott in the program as the director of junior development to tap his nurturing talents. Unfortunately, feelings at the time were too raw. The Canadian Ski Association dismissed him.

Perspectives change when a developing team blossoms into a winner. We had grown beyond the point at which work and practice would significantly improve performance. Now the little things, like waxes, skis, and equipment, made all the difference. Scott's solutions were no longer enough.

For several years, relations between Scott and me were very strained. But in 1981, while I was hobbling around on crutches at the Las Vegas ski trade show, Scott approached me. We ended up having a long talk about the past and present. That broke the ice. I can now say that we are close friends.

THE FIRST CANADIAN downhill victory came in 1975 but, incredibly, it was not until 1980 that we were able to compete as equals against the Swiss and Austrians. It was a long, trying scramble to reach the point where our equipment was as good as theirs.

Ski racing is a European game. Most of the tour takes place in the Alps. The major ski manufacturers are found in the five main Alpine nations. They were not very keen on sharing it.

Like Scott Henderson, we innocently believed, for a time, that hard work could overcome our technological disadvantages. This was the right strategy when we were trying to shave seconds off our time, but it never worked when we sought to shave hundredths of seconds off. Getting the best equipment was, for many years, our biggest problem. We had to twist the arms of ski manufacturers for service, and beg downhill suit suppliers for the same materials they were supplying to the Swiss and Austrians. By 1978, we thought we had our equipment problems solved. We were wrong.

A week before the season opener, which was held at Schladming that winter, our Austrian supplier, Dolomit-Ender, delivered our downhill suits. A new factor had been introduced. New standards of air permeability — fifty litres of air per minute per square metre of material — had been set, ostensibly because this would help racers "breathe" through the suit. But this slowed the suit down. It was also becoming apparent that fit was as important, or more important a factor in downhill aerodynamics than permeability. The suits we had been provided with didn't fit worth a damn.

The CSA's program director, Andrezj Kozbial, found us an alternative. We were offered thinner, snugger suits by our Italian clothing supplier, Lafont. We opted to use them and presto! Four Canadians finished in the top ten at Schladming, and we had a one-two finish: Read before Murray.

But even the Lafont suits weren't a perfect fit so, over the Christmas break, I imposed upon my mother to improve mine. With her sewing skills, she made small tucks and folds, and turned the suit into a second skin. In a high tech game, where millions of dollars are put into ski and wax technology, it was amazing to me that such an important ingredient in the equation was improved on a home sewing machine.

Upon our return to Europe in January, 1979, for a race at Morzine, France, a Japanese clothing manufacturer called Descente approached us to use their new downhill suit. They provided us with four, bright-yellow outfits, already emblazoned with maple leafs. Since no one else was giving us a secure supply of fast suits, we agreed to give them a try. Mine was perfect. Never in my life had I put on such a snug suit.

The only hurdle we faced was official approval from the FIS, but the portable testing machine they brought to most races was nowhere to be found. Without approval, we could use the suits, but if another team protested their use we would be obliged to submit them for testing after the race. David Murray and I elected to use the new suits immediately. Steve chose to use an old suit. His new outfit was too tight a fit.

Mur and I were not alone that day. The Australians and the Japanese also wore Descente's new suit, but they were not to be part of the ensuing controversy, because they didn't win the race. Canada did.

It was another one-two Canadian sweep. This time it was Read-Podborski. But there was a catch. To the surprise of our coaches, and of the FIS technical delegate at the race, Hans Kung, the Italian team protested my victory. My suit was to be sent to St. Gallen, Switzerland, where the Swiss standards institute, EMPA, would test its perocity. Kung apologized to me: "I'm sorry but rules are rules, and I must sign for your suit and send it," he said. "I'm sure there is no problem."

Forty-eight hours later, the suit was tested and failed! I was disqualified. Twenty-five World Cup points were lost.

Later, Bernhard Russi asked me why I hadn't stretched the suit in the twelve hours between the end of the race and Kung's arrival at the hotel to pick it up for testing. I could not, in good conscience, have done so. We also truly believed that the suit was legal, or I would not have used it in the first place.

Ironically, the two suits that were not used at Morzine were tested on the portable machine at the next World Cup stop, Crans Montana, Switzerland. Each was passed and was given the FIS *plomb* or "seal." This was probably because there was a discrepancy of standards between the portable machine and EMPA's machine. A research team from the University of Calgary's engineering faculty was prepared to travel to Europe to investigate, but this offer was refused by the CSA.

Events such as this demonstrated who my true friends were. For example, although Pod was awarded the victory, to this day he calls it a mistake. He proudly holds up his first at St. Moritz, two years later, as his first "real" World Cup win. The Austrians, their coach Charlie Kahr, and many of his racers such as Uli Spiess, and Werner Grissman, were sympathetic to my plight. So were the Brits and the Americans. Kahr was quoted in the press as having said: "The suit didn't matter.

Ken Read would have won Morzine if he had worn a business suit."

Our new friends at Descente were terribly embarassed by the outcome. It is certainly not the Japanese way to cheat or even even to appear as if they had cheated. Descente felt it had let us down. To this day it remains a staunch ally of the Canadian team. And it still supplies the yellow downhill suits that became our trademark.

As I told *Zurich Sport*'s Stefan Oswalt, moments after learning from our coach, John Ritchie, that the victory had been taken away from me, I wanted to cry out in rage at what had happened. For once all the elements — skis, wax and suits — had been equal. I felt brutalized, robbed, stripped naked by a bureacracy that wanted to keep the world "right."

But I muted my anger as much as I could. What else could I do? To accuse the Italians of foul play for protesting the result would only have served to lower myself to their level. Far better to bottle up the rage and express it in results. That's what I did in the next race (I was a good third at Crans). But the game was over.

The furious debate which followed the disqualification *débâcle* distracted the team. After Crans, only David Murray managed to climb to the podium again that winter, with a third place result at Lake Placid, in the pre-Olympic downhill. The 1978-1979 season, which had begun with promise with victories at Schladming and Morzine, was lost in bitterness and controversy.

TOP: *Skiing was always a family affair.* Left to right: *me, my brother Ron, and sister Janet.*
JOHN READ

BELOW: *My first exposure to international competition was in the Pontiac Cup at Mt. Norquay, Alberta in December, 1969.*
KEN READ

TOP: *My first World Cup victory at Val d'Isère, France, on December 7, 1975, came just twelve months after my first World Cup race.*
JEAN-PAUL MAEDER

BELOW: *I felt mixed emotions when World Cup downhill champion, Franz Klammer, fell near the finish. Fortunately, he wasn't hurt.*
KONRAD BARTELSKI

TOP: *For Scotty Henderson (right), coach of the Canadian team, Val d'Isère was the realization of a dream. Five Canadians finished in the top thirteen.*
SKI CANADA

BELOW: *Team Canada — ready to take on the world!* Left to right: *Ken Read, Jim Hunter, Dave Irwin, and Dave Murray, at the Innsbruck Olympic Winter Games in 1976.*
CANADIAN OLYMPIC ASSOCIATION

TOP: *The Olympic downhill in 1976 was the greatest ski race ever. 70,000 people lined the slopes to watch Klammer win. The number ten on my helmet remains a cherished momento of the day.*
CANADIAN OLYMPIC ASSOCIATION

BELOW: *My mother, Dee, met me at Calgary International Airport after my World Cup victory at Chamonix, France, in February, 1978.*
BILL SIMPKINS/THE CALGARY HERALD

My father, Dr. John Read, was with me in April, 1979, when I was named Calgary athlete of the year.

RICHARD PITMAN/THE CALGARY HERALD

Roughly $25,000 went to the Canadian Ski Team as a result of this promotion with Gillette and Saab. The racers, myself included, received $1,250 each.

SKI CANADA/GILLETTE CANADA

TOP: *On January 6, 1979, I mounted the top step of the podium to claim my fourth World Cup Victory at Morzine. Steve Podborski (left) finished second, and Herbert Plank third. Forty-eight hours later, because of the "illegal" suit, the victory was taken away from me.*
PIERRE MICHEL

BELOW: *Always the clown: Werner "Grizzly" Grissman of the Austrian team ribs "Baby-face" Read after a fast training run. Grissman: "You're too fast on the bottom for me!"*

TOP: *On January 19, 1980, I won at Wengen, completing the "classic double" in what a Swiss TV commentator called "ski racing's greatest, most exciting moment."*

INSET: *With Peter Müller after the race at Kitzbühel, January 12, 1980. We traded victories throughout the 1980 season in a chase that went right down to the wire, at Lake Louise.*
CARL YARBROUGH/TEAM RUSSELL

BELOW: *I was proud to carry the Canadian banner in the Opening Ceremonies at the 1980 Lake Placid Olympic Winter Games.*
LAKE PLACID OLYMPIC ORGANIZING COMMITTEE

On February 14,
1980, at the Lake
Placid Olympics,
photographer Robert
Riger asked Swiss
star, Bernhard Russi
where to watch the
race. Russi told him
that the race would
be won or lost at the

*op. His pictures
show how a ripple in
the snow lifted my
inside ski. As it
came down again,
the sideways
momentum knocked
it away. For me, the
race was over.*
ROBERT RIGER

ABOVE: *Our greatest team success at Val d'Isère in December, 1980, when five team members placed in the top seven. Left to right: Dave Murray, Ken Read, Steve Podborski, Dave Irwin, Chris Kent, Robin McLeish.*
SERGE LANG

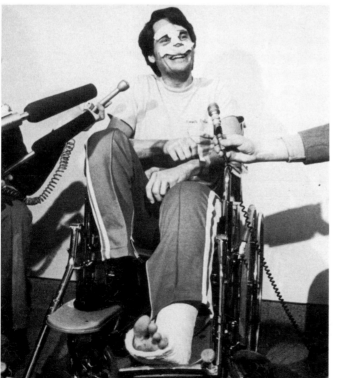

LEFT: *Two days after I fell at Garmisch, Dr. Pat McConkey put my knee back together. Media interest was so intense that, two days after the operation, on January 15, 1981, a full press conference was called.*
CANAPRESS PHOTO SERVICE

TOP: *Our European success often attracted the interest of leading politicians.*
Left to right: *Steve Podborski, Ken Read, Gerry Sorensen and fellow skier,
Prime Minister Pierre Trudeau.*
JEAN-MARC CARISSE

BELOW: *The Canadian Ski Team, 1981-1982 consisted of (left to right) Ken
Read, Steve Podborski, Dave Irwin, Doug Kerr, Bob Styan, Dave Murray,
Robin McLeish, Chris Kent, Todd Brooker, Brian O'Rourke.*
CHRIS SPEEDIE/SKI CANADA

ABOVE: *The comeback confirmed: in the season following my knee injury, I had three successive third-place finishes; two of them at Kitzbühel.*

RIGHT: *Kitzbühel, January 16, 1982; the owner of The Londoner pub helped us to establish a Canadian tradition by offering free champagne to the racers whenever an English-speaking skier won the Hahnenkamm. We were happy to accept the offer four years in succession.*

TOP: *With Franz Klammer, January 20, 1983, we "hurry up and wait," as bad weather leads to the cancellation of downhill training (again!).*
CANAPRESS PHOTO SERVICE

BELOW: *With Steve Podborski (centre) and team trainer, Terry Spence, at Aspen, Colorado, in March, 1983. Terry's experience and on-hill manner were highly-valued.*
CANAPRESS PHOTO SERVICE

ABOVE: *With Nancy Greene at Whistler, BC. Known as "The Tiger," Nancy influenced almost every young skier of our generation.*

RIGHT: *In action, in 1983. The World Cup title eluded me, but I retired as the top-ranked Canadian skier in the World Cup standings.*
DESCENTE

ABOVE: *After ten years on the circuit, and seventy World Cup downhills, new priorities took precedence in my life, Lynda chief among them.*
JAKE ROBBINS

LEFT: *"King Killy": Jean-Claude has been extremely successful both as a skier and as a businessperson.*
JOHN RUSSELL/TEAM RUSSELL

With one World Cup Victory under his belt, Rob Boyd (right) leads the new generation of Canadian ski racers. The spirit of the Crazy Canucks lives!
KURT SCHORRER

III
THE
WORLD
CUP

SERGE LANG

O NE MAN HAS LOOMED LARGE over the World Cup since its inception in 1966, and that man is Serge Lang.

Serge is a huge, gruff, multilingual, French journalist from the Alsace, with a great and abiding affection for Yorkshire terriers which I have never been able to understand. Twenty-one years ago, while the winds howled through the Andes at the Portillo World Championships, it is said that he and a few others had time for a long, long chat about the sorry state of Alpine racing.

Until then ski racing had almost no focus. It was a hopscotch mishmash of a few races such as the Lauberhorn at Wengen, the Hahnenkamm on Kitzbühel's Streif, and the Arlberg-Kandahar, a race that was moved from resort to resort every winter in central Europe. International rankings were a joke, and public interest in the sport was tepid, at best, although it was widely noted that the sale of skiing equipment and the development of posh resorts in Europe and North America were accelerating.

Holding the world championships in the Andes in August was obviously not the answer. But what was? Was it possible to marry ski racing to the commercial development of the sport?

As the blizzard raged, the idea grew that in order to drum up interest in the sport the world's best racers had to take their show on the road. Serge and the US coach, Bob Beattie (who now works as a commentator with ABC Sports), undertook to strong-arm a few resorts into taking races and to make arrangments for press facilities so the news could be sprung on an unsuspecting world.

That first winter, despite the reluctance of some resort operators who preferred the custom of high spending tourists to
impoverished ski racers, Serge cobbled together a mini-tour
for men and women which took in Kitzbühel, Wengen, Adel-
boden, Megève, Sestrière, Franconia, Berchtesgaden, Grindelwald, Schruns, Oberstaufen, St. Gervais and Jackson Hole,
Wyoming. The first stars thrown up were France's handsome
archetype of Gallic urbanity, Jean-Claude Killy, and Canada's
irrepressible fire-plug, Nancy Greene.

The birth of the World Cup coincided with a world-wide
skiing boom. Over the next decade, old resorts flourished and
new ones sprang up. Television executives saw what the middle class was doing and decided that ski racing made good
entertainment. Televised races meant a bonanza of free publicity for ski towns, and the reluctance of hill operators and
hotel keepers to host races disappeared. Suddenly, they stum-
bled over one another to be included.

Ski manufacturers had also been sceptical. Now they wanted
to get on board, too. What better way to advertise and test
their wares than with the best racers?

In those early years, Serge ran the sport like a Ruritanian
fiefdom. If at times he played Machiavelli, pitting resorts and
nations against one another, he did it both for the sport's good
and his own amusement. He was both the helmsman who
steered the course and the engine whose power made it work.

As a journalist for the French sports daily, *L'Equipe,* he had
followed the *Tour de France* bicycle race, and he knew about
the colossal media coverage it generated. He was the first to
understand that ski racing had comparable potential. Today,
as a result of his vision, the World Cup girdles the globe, and
is a model for other sports. There are now World Cups for
ski jumping, cross-country skiing, bobsledding, luge, speedskating and track and field.

Whether at the top or the bottom of the World Cup standings, every racer bumped into Serge in his trademark navy-
blue greatcoat. He was a larger than life presence. Unlike the
many on the circuit who only want to cozy up to the winners,
Serge wanted to have contact with everyone. Even when we
were young, unproven Canadians with a short, unflattering
record, he sought us out, peppered us with questions and offered
counsel with a wag of his immense fingers. Long before others

had cottoned on to our potential, he was singing our praises, telling the world we were introducing a new dimension of risk and fun to the sport. One day we were going to be winners.

With Killy long gone, only the Austrians and Swiss were winning the glamour event, the downhill. This had choked interest in the sport. The Canadians were needed to make it interesting again. Our success would help prove that Serge was the master of a truly *World* Cup. We enhanced his creation and he treated us well because of it.

But Serge was not only a pal and defender of the Crazy Canucks. He was also close to Sweden's incomparable and incomparably shy slalomist, Ingemar Stenmark, and to the Russian skiers, who represented an opening to the East.

As a proud Frenchman, his heart was very much with the French team. After the joy of watching Killy hoist the tricolour three times at the Grenoble Olympics, it pained him to see Killy's successors screw up, year after year. Some of his most savage reporting in later years was reserved for the hapless French team.

Serge and his wife, Ann, a refugee from the destruction of Berlin, settled after the war in the northern Swiss village of Riehen. Most of the family income was derived from work for the Swiss German-language tabloid, *Blick*, and the French-language broadsheet, *La Suisse*, so he also wrote frequently about the great stable of Swiss racers.

During the summer, when he wasn't chasing cyclists or convening World Cup committee meetings to decide the next year's skiing calendar, he and his son, Patrick, assembled a ski magazine under the trade name *Biorama*. In much the same way that the *Sporting News* serves as baseball's Bible, *Biorama* became an indispensable compendium of data for ski racing fanatics.

The success in the late 1970s of Stenmark, the Crazy Canucks and the American technical experts, Phil and Steve Mahre, put pressure on the World Cup organizers to go beyond their European borders more often. Leading the movement for change was the "racer's union," an unofficial grouping of first-seed racers, most of whom were from the traditional Alpine nations. The union demanded that regular World Cup fixtures be penciled in for Scandinavia, North America, and Japan. Opposing the union were most of the racers' federations.

Serge, as World Cup chairman, was not at all supportive of the burgeoning racers' movement because it represented a challenge to his authority, but he was always a pragmatist. He saw the value of our suggestions and quickly adopted our views on expanding the calendar and making a global circuit. He took them to his committee as if they were his own, becoming a leading proponent of the internationalization of the sport. But he encountered strong resistance from hidebound Europeans, especially the Swiss and Austrians.

The Europeans, who controlled a majority of the votes, saw the universe from a very narrow, nationalistic perspective. It was like the National Hockey League in the early 1960s. Blind to a world beyond their own borders, the spokesmen of the Alpine nations argued that they alone possessed the knowledge and the mountains to stage world class events. There were complaints about the high cost of travel to remote skiing outposts like Whistler and Aspen, and worries that if the circuit left the Alps for more than a few days at a time, interest there would dwindle. The racers' union challenged these myths, and insisted there was a need for a cohesive world schedule. But, for the longest time, the central Europeans refused to see beyond their own parochial concerns.

It was deeply resented that whenever the World Cup left the Alps, Serge and Ann, and their son, Patrick, who had no status except that of a journalist and family member, were treated like visiting royalty. Laying on first-class meals, hotel suites and limousines for the Lang family became the custom in North America, Japan, and eastern Europe, while the other European ski barons got no special attention whatsoever.

Sometimes, I'll grant you, the organizers did get a little carried away, but this was not Serge's fault; it was the fault of would-be or first-time sponsors. Their overwhelming displays of affection reflected their gratitude for efforts few in Alpine Europe were prepared to make. After all, whatever his reasons, Serge was one of the few Europeans willing to extend the frontiers of ski racing beyond the Alps.

It took time, but Serge won most of the skirmishes over scheduling. Sometimes he achieved his victories by subtle negotiation, quietly trading races and promises with a fluid coalition of marginal European nations such as Norway, Yugoslavia, and Czechoslovakia, and political featherweights such as Canada and Japan. More often he simply seized the initiative and said, "Like it or not, *meine damen und herren*, this is how it is going to be."

Rather than fight all night with the wily Alsatian, the European powers usually threw their arms up in disgust or despair, and surrendered. In this way, Serge developed a World Cup tour for men and women that included annual fixtures in Scandinavia, eastern Europe, and North America, and biennial excursions to Japan. As a result Whistler, Panorama, and Lake Louise became known not only in Canada, but around the world as great places to ski. And, for the first time, we had a chance to compete in high-quality races on our own snow.

It was not that Serge didn't like racing in central Europe. He understood that the Alps will always form the axis around which the White Circus revolves. And he was careful to favour a few rinky-dink resorts there with a race or two in order to soothe hurt feelings.

But Serge Lang could also see the whole scenario. He realized it was wise to toss the Warsaw Pact countries a few bones, even if they were dead broke and couldn't organize a very pleasant weekend. The Scandinavians had long been keen fans of skiing, and deserved to be dealt in. The reason for including the Japanese and the North Americans was more compelling. These markets were definitely worth including in the tournament for their vast growth potential.

Although the European-based ski industry hadn't any official say in World Cup deliberations, North America is where their sales people wanted the tour to expand. Sales in Europe were stagnant. The Mahres, the Reads, and Podborskis provided an opening to the New World, and Serge was more than happy to follow through.

The results of his scheduling experiments were simply spectacular. As many as 30,000 Swedes and Yugoslavs turned out for slalom races at towns such as Åre, Maribor, and Ljubljana. Bulgarian and Czechoslovakian races also received an enthusiastic welcome from entertainment-starved Slavs, and from East German vacationers who were forbidden to travel to the West, but became fans by watching all the races on West German television.

In North America, races at Aspen, Vail, Whistler, and Sunshine Village became the focuses of a year's advertising dollars.

Tens of thousands showed up for Molson, Husky, and Subaru World Cup extravaganzas. With a few humbling exceptions, the United States and Canada are now home to the best-staged races on the circuit.

And no one, *but no one*, was willing to throw as much money and television coverage at the World Cup as the hospitable Japanese. Racers and coaches loved going over the pole because chartered 747s were sometimes laid on for *en route* parties. After being fêted at Bacchanalian soirées, they would return home laden with booty, such as expensive electronic gadgets, flashy skiwear and luggage, and tales of bathhouses that were nothing like those in Europe or North America.

Serge was also an innovator. He fought for improved safety on courses and, unlike some, never stood in the way of racers making a fair buck. He introduced the super giant slalom, a hybrid discipline combining technical elements from the giant slalom and the speed of the downhill, in an effort to regain some of the traditional features of ski racing — working the terrain of the hill. Many of the racers are still not sold on it — Phil Mahre of the United States, in particular. Ironically, with his technical skills and his capacity to handle high speeds, I think he would have been one of the best at it.

Love it or hate it, the "Super G" quickly acquired recognition as an Olympic and World Championship discipline. It has added hours of television coverage to World Cup events, and the revenues that go with it.

Throughout his career as president of the World Cup, Serge was clearly often in a position of conflict of interest. He would float a tentative schedule or rule changes in his newspaper columns, formally present them to the World Cup committee, and then defend them in the newspapers. Once they were passed, he would steal a march on his journalistic colleagues by announcing them to the world.

He was also the chairman of the AIJS, the Association of International Ski Journalists, which had three members on the World Cup committee. Always handpicked by him, they were his chorus once the season was underway, and the meddlesome federation members were back in their offices. When spur-of-the-moment decisions were required it was not necessary to convene a meeting. He knew his colleagues would agree with what he had decided.

To North Americans, the idea of someone wearing as many hats as Serge is virtually insupportable. The media would have been after his scalp years ago. It would be as if international hockey potentate and player's union boss, Alan Eagleson, had founded the National Hockey League, become its first president and chairman of its Board of Governors, headed its writers' association, was lead columnist for three major dailies in Canada and the United States and editor, publisher, and lead writer, of the *Hockey News*.

Europeans do not seem to fret over such questions as we do. Although they would often quarrel with Serge, it was convenient for the other World Cup Committee members to have a journalist in charge. He'd create the myths and fill in the personalities of the racers and then, on the fly, arbitrate scheduling disputes when bad weather shut the Circus down. From the journalists there was some hostility, but if they wanted inside information they had to play ball. Serge was always willing to share news. Once he'd used it himself.

I never envied Serge his peculiar role as both godfather to, and leading critic of, the World Cup. He had to contend with the constant jockeying for advantage by the national federations, television networks, and resort operators. I admired his willingness to keep at it, indeed to thrive on the everyday controversies that were created by weather, technology, and national interests. He walked a precarious high wire, balancing shrill competing interests, and satisfying most of them. If he'd caved in, allowing each country to host as many races as they thought they deserved, the World Cup calendar would have been a shambles.

In May, 1980, Steve Podborski and I were mucking around Europe, testing equipment, and making contractual arrangements for the coming season. With Serge's help, Lake Louise had just successfully staged Canada's first men's World Cup downhill. Steve and I thought it wise to consolidate that gain, and discuss the racers' rights movement informally with Serge.

He met with us at his new summer residence, across the border from his Swiss home, in the rolling hills of his native Alsace. When we arrived, he and his dogs gave us a tour through an old-style structure made of barn beams and mortar. As he directed a few workmen who were completing the construction, he complained good-naturedly about the poor quality and high cost of French workmanship. But it was obvious that he was immensely proud of his new dwelling.

Serge and Ann, and Patrick and his wife, took us out to lunch in Serge's Second World War US army jeep. It fascinated us, but so did most of the memorabilia in the Lang home. Serge was mesmerized by the United States and things American. There were souvenirs from cowboy bars in Jackson Hole and Aspen Mountain, and a history of ski racing at Vail. He lamented the passing of the oldest North American ski race, the Harriman Cup, in the 1960s, and wondered why no one in Sun Valley, Idaho, was willing to revive it.

We pressed him about his ambiguous position as a prominent ski journalist and World Cup boss. He put on a very humble face and amused us with a brief answer that was totally at variance with the facts.

"I'm a simple Frenchman who happens to be chairman of the World Cup," he said modestly, his body trembling gently the way John Diefenbaker's did. "It's the committee that decides. I really have very little to say about what goes on. I'm, how do you say it in English? a minor player in this theatre."

During the summer of 1986 Serge's various conflicts of interest and his imperial style finally became too much for some members of the World Cup Committee. The coalitions he had forged during his twenty years as World Cup president suddenly collapsed and he was dethroned. But he remains a man of great influence. Through his columns, and through his presence at every men's World Cup race, he continues to have a say in the White Circus. No one of consequence in skiing can afford to ignore him.

Think of it. From a confused series of ski races in central Europe one man created, in two decades, an exciting, living, global carnival which employs as many as 1,000 people directly, and tens of thousands of others indirectly. Through what the French call *le petit écran*, or "the little screen," he touched millions of lives every winter. As a ski racer, and someone who loves ski racing, I will always be in his debt.

"DER KAISER"— FRANZ KLAMMER

FRANZ KLAMMER IS UNQUESTIONABLY the greatest downhill racer ever. He entered 115 World Cup downhill races between 1972 and 1985. He won twenty-five, and in fifteen others he finished second or third. He also won the Olympic downhill at Innsbruck in 1976. No one else has come close to matching these achievements.

The next biggest World Cup winner is Peter Müller. By the end of last season the dogged Swiss racer, once my greatest rival, had sixteen downhill victories in eleven seasons. In nine years of World Cup racing, I stepped to the top of the podium six times (if my victory at Morzine, where I was later disqualified because of the "illegal" suit, is included).

I first heard of Klammer before I joined the Canadian team. He burst into prominence in 1973 when, in his second season on the World Cup, he came from the third group to finish second at St. Anton, Austria. Then, on the heels of that stunning performance, he finished third at the pre-World Championships event at St. Moritz, in a crazy race that saw another Austrian, Werner Grissman, come from the fourth seed to steal victory. The next winter, Klammer won an infamous downhill at Schladming, Austria. During the week a *foehn* (Mountain German for a chinook, or warm breeze) haunted the low-lying valley, and turned the Planai course into slush. On the eve of the race it turned bitterly cold, freezing the piste rock-hard. It was terribly intimidating, but Klammer skied the pants off everyone. He nosed out the World Cup champion, Roland Collombin and the world champion, Bernhard Russi, ending several years of dominance by the two great Swiss racers.

At the time Klammer's coach, Charlie Kahr, and the Austrian media were hungry for a star of their own. Klammer was immediately anointed as the chosen one. I am sure they hadn't any idea how prophetic their assumption was. In 1974-1975 Klammer turned the Alpine world topsy-turvy, winning eight of the nine World Cup downhills. The race he did not win was at Megève, where he lost a ski. It is true that Jean-Claude Killy swept all the downhill races eight winters earlier, in the first season of the World Cup, but there were only five races that season.

Except at Kitzbühel, where Klammer won by one-hundredth of a second after recovering from some incredible errors, no one came close to challenging Klammer's superiority. At Wengen, for example, he won by more than three and a half seconds, the largest margin of victory ever. At Jackson Hole, he was first by over two seconds. To finish so far behind a winner usually meant a thirtieth- or fortieth-place result, not second place. The only qualifying factor in these wondrous results is that Klammer achieved them using Fischer skis. It was a perfect combination: the best racer and the best ski manufacturer of the time.

What is often forgotten is his role as an innovator. Jim Hunter said to me at my first World Cup, at Val d'Isère, "Watch him: he'll not only win the race, he'll win all the training runs, as well." Until then, this had been heresy, but Franz did it. He was the first star to approach training runs as though they were races. He learned more about handling the courses than anyone else, because he always pushed himself and his equipment to the absolute limit.

Klammer's all-out, or "total downhill" style was a harbinger of things to come. When we came to the fore the following winter, with victories at Val d'Isère and Schladming, we carried the same message to the rest of the racers. We went for broke in training, and it improved our chances on race day. For this they tagged us "world training champions" and "Crazy Canucks." It was argued that we took unacceptable risks. All we were doing was copying Franz. The difference was merely that he was better!

Klammer was born in December, 1953, in the village of Mooswald, in Carinthia, in southeastern Austria. His childhood was like something out of a Heidi movie. His parents were farmers, scratching a meagre living on marginal soil near the Yugoslav border. Franz skied to school every morning. There were no lifts, so he climbed back up the mountain again to get home when classes were over. It was as simple and traditional an Alpine existence as could be found in the early 1960s. It would make a wonderful film today.

I think much in Franz's strength of character came from being a Carinthian. This made him an outsider on the Austrian team, which was dominated by those from the country's two most powerful skiing provinces, Tyrol and Salzberg. For the longest time, the big kids on the block did not want Klammer to join them. When he was eighteen they relented, but apparently only because the Carinthians agreed to pay all his expenses. A year later, he was in the first seed and people were falling all over each other to pay his bills.

Klammer might have been custom-built for downhill racing. He stands about six feet tall, and has a stocky frame which is slightly heavier on the bottom than on the top. His attitude was also perfect. He loved skiing and feared nothing. As the result of all those youthful years when he trundled up and down mountains by himself, he picked up the rare, intuitive sense of when and where to place his skis. Proof of his proficiency as a technical racer came in 1974, when he was ranked in the top fifteen in the world in giant slalom. Later he concentrated on downhill.

To his everlasting credit, whether a winner or a loser, Klammer remained an approachable country boy, without affectation. In my first season with the Canadian team in Europe, I was ranked 101st by the International Ski Federation, but Franz flattered me by acknowledging my presence. He took note of a few creditable results, offered me cheery hellos and the odd word of encouragement. I wouldn't pretend that we were pals, or even acquaintances, but he made me feel we were colleagues in the same fraternity.

Like many of the greatest athletes, Klammer was a notorious carouser. I don't say this in a malicious or irresponsible sense. He just loved a good time. This was not always easy to find in Austria, where his every move was observed and chronicled. It is one of the reasons he and his running mates, Werner Grissman, and later, Leonhard Stock, particularly enjoyed competing in North America. Here, where skiing's profile is nothing like so great as in Europe, Klammer could shed for a few days the mantle of the beloved superstar. He could be anonymous in a bar, just a run-of-the-mill guy, which in out-look he was. If a pretty woman caught his eye, he would chase her just like anyone else. In the New World he did not have to worry that photographs of his grinning, gap-toothed coun-tenance, and that of a momentary acquaintance, would dom-inate the front pages of the tabloids *Neue Kroenung Zeitung* or *Der Kurier* the next morning, and become the talk of all Austria that night.

The first time I came into close contact with Klammer, and the top end of the huge Austrian team, was at St. Moritz in 1974. The week before, at Val d'Isère, Grissman has used a sponge cushion as an aerodynamic foil in front of his body, and had placed second. (The apparatus was immediately banned.) Before training began at St. Moritz, Jim Hunter swiped Griss-man's cushion. This caused Grizzly to behave as if he had been mortally wounded. Once mollified by the return of the foil, Grissman and Klammer teased Jim mercilessly about resorting to such tactics in an attempt to win his first race. We were all amused by such jibing.

In the second training run that week at St. Moritz, I sat back going off a bump on the lower part of the course, and did a face plant. I cut my chin, broke several teeth and mangled my tongue so badly that it required four stitches. (At least I wasn't alone: the great Russi came to grief at the same spot, and was knocked from competition for several weeks.)

As I lay in a heap after the fall, Erwin Stricker, a German-speaking Italian racer who was also injured, happened upon me, and proceeded to drag me away from the track. He asked me to open my mouth. I did. "Eeeeuch!" was his only response.

On race day, when I got to the top of the hill, there was Stricker, a great raconteur. He was regaling the Austrians with the story of how awful my mouth looked after the crash. Again, I was asked to open my mouth, and again I obliged, revealing a pulpy, swollen mess of stitches and flesh. Everyone howled in commiseration. They advised me to sit this one out, to save myself for another day.

I was starting fifty-fifth that day, so Klammer had long since been declared the unofficial winner when I steered myself on to the track. I apparently caused a small stir by becoming the only non-Swiss or non-Austrian to post a top ten, first-interval time. I fell back progressively after that, because I did not yet have the experience to deal with the mountain. What has stayed with me, though, was that Stricher, who was providing commentary for Italian television, pointed out that on exactly the same pitch where I had crashed two days earlier, a radar gun picked me up going 131 kilometres per hour. Only Klammer was faster.

It was this kind of little drama which helped bring all of us to the attention of the Europeans. Lovely tongues or not, we were becoming known as chargers and a coming force. From that day on, Klammer was by turns chiding or complimenting us for challenging the Austrians, Swiss, Italians, and West Germans of the Alpine heartland.

Klammer and "Klammermania" probably reached their zenith at the Innsbruck Olympics in 1976. Before 70,000 spectators and a television audience of millions, Klammer bore the hopes of the entire Austrian nation in "their" event, the men's downhill. He won the gold medal in what I think was the single, most spectacular, downhill run ever.

Innsbruck's 3,100 metre Patscherkofel course was not particularly suited to Klammer's flamboyant, non-stop style. There were stretches where racers could reach speeds of 140 kilometres per hour, but it also included many very icy turns which could cause injury to even the best technicians. Erwin Stricker and Anton Steiner, a sixteen-year-old Austrian technical specialist, had already confirmed this by spinning out on one such turn, a brutal ninety-degree right-hander known as the Bear's Neck, 400 metres above the finish.

In practice runs at Innsbruck I had been running a secret line. Serge Lange, who always kept up on such things, was badgering me to reveal why I was taking a direct path through the Ochsen Schlal, a tricky series of sweeping turns in the middle of the course. Doing this caused me to take additional air before landing and adjusting for a compression, and a sharp, ninety-degree, fallaway turn. However, if this stretch was successfully negotiated, interval timers we set up showed it would shave precious hundredths of a second. Unfortunately, on the second-last training run, I didn't execute it properly, and fell.

I had number ten that fine, sun-splashed morning, when ABC television immortalized Klammer's descent on videotape. Through the first section time I was third, but instead of following my heart, I skied a conservative line. My problems in training influenced my decision. I finished third, soon to be pushed back to fourth by Switzerland's Philippe Roux and then, finally, when Klammer was finished, to fifth place.

With the highest-ranking Austrian, Sepp Walcher, lying eighth, all eyes were focused on Klammer. The day before, "Der Kaiser" had carried the Austrian flag at the Opening Ceremony. Now he was the eastern reich's last, and best chance. Everyone waited expectantly.

Starting fifteenth, Franz knew that the leader, Bernhard Russi, who had started second, had knocked almost nine seconds off the course record Klammer had established the previous winter, in the pre-Olympic World Cup. He also had to be aware that the skis of each racer were slowly eating away at the track, causing it to deteriorate. As the winner of the three previous World Cup downhills, and ten of the previous thirteen, Klammer was the overwhelming favourite. However, there had been seven training runs at Innsbruck, and seven different racers had clocked best times. For a change, Klammer was not one of them.

Out of the start hut, which we had taken to calling "the Execution Chamber," Klammer plunged like one possessed. After only ten seconds he made a major error, catching his ski in a rut on the first tough turn. He swung hard and wide to avoid augering in. By the first interval clock, he was behind. Because of his error at the top, he knew he had to try something daring. At the second timer he was still adrift, but he had made up some time by taking the quick line I had introduced, but for which I no longer had the stomach. The tricks continued from there to the bottom of the course. Lunging and lurching across the course, Franz frantically windmilled his arms from side to side, and above his head, to maintain his balance. Everywhere, he cheated the course of a few centimetres of its length, and got away with it. As he hove into view above the finish area, he continued to overtake the demon of defeat. Rather than go around the last bump as everyone else had, he went straight over it! Sure enough, when the final line was reached, his time was thirty-hundredths of a second faster than Russi's.

At Innsbruck, Klammer faced pressure of a kind which few athletes have ever faced. He mastered it with talent, bravery, and audacity. When it was over, Austria's greatest sports celebration ever could begin.

FOR MOST OF THE two seasons which followed the 1976 Olympics, Klammer continued to be the racer against whom we all measured ourselves. He won at Aspen, Val Gardena (twice), Garmisch, Kitzbühel, Wengen, Laax, Val d'Isère and Laax again. Then, towards the end of the 1977-1978 season, his results began to slip. At Garmisch, where he had won before, he was only fifth in the World Championships — making this the only downhill prize that ever eluded him.

Chinks in his armour began to appear. There were rumours that he was going to turn professional. He quashed them by saying that the World Cup was the only test for a serious downhill racer. There were difficulties with Hans Stroi, the senior race technician at Fischer. Franz bolted the company, taking up with another Austrian firm, Kneissl. His younger brother, Klaus, was paralyzed from the waist down in an accident in a downhill race at Lienz, Austria.

I first noticed his absence from the front ranks of the World Cup at Schladming, in December, 1978. Going into the first World Cup downhill of the new season, three racers had training times which suggested they were contending for a first-place finish: my great Norwegian friend and occasional training partner, Erik Haaker, was one; Franz Klammer and I were the others. But Franz came down with an extreme case of the flu, and couldn't race. I won, David Murray was second, Dave Irwin was seventh and Steve Podborski was ninth. After a year in the Alpine wilderness, the Canadians were back, and Klammer was gone.

The next week, at Val Gardena, a course on which Klammer enjoyed many of his early successes, Haaker won the first and only downhill of his career. Klammer slipped to fifth. At Morzine, Klammer didn't finish. At Crans Montana he was twenty-ninth, three seconds behind the leader; at Kitzbühel eleventh, two seconds back; at Garmisch he didn't finish again; at Villars he was fortieth; at Lake Placid nineteenth.

For the next two seasons, wherever we went, we were asked to name our favourites for that week's race. I'd always try to to give an educated guess based upon recent performances, strengths, and weaknesses vis-à-vis course conditions, and other factors such as equipment and mental disposition. Quite often I wouldn't mention Klammer, and the Austrian journalists would be all over me for an explanation. I always gave them the same response: "Never discount Klammer. He may not be running well, but he is certainly capable of pulling out of his slump, anytime."

After suffering the ignominy of exclusion from Austria's team in the 1980 Lake Placid Olympics — there were only a few positions and his World Cup results had been terrible — Klammer went to the first World Cup downhill to be held at Lake Louise. In training there, at the entrance to the Cannonbarrel, he caught an edge and went down, tearing ligaments in his knee.

In addition to his competitive slump, continuing difficulties with his suppliers and the immeasurable psychological impact of his brother's tragic accident, he now had a physical problem. The Austrian media and public urged him to retire gracefully. He was their hero and they wanted to remember him at his best.

But this was not Franz's way. As tenacious as ever, he declared that he still loved skiing, and wanted to continue competing. Before beginning the long and painful rehabilitation required to make his knee sound again, he switched ski firms for the third time. Kneissl had gone bankrupt, so he joined forces with an emerging Austrian success story, Blizzard.

Through all these tests, Franz put on a brave front. He never once complained or used any of his problems as an excuse. Outwardly he remained as friendly and relaxed as when he was the toast of Austria.

The season after the Lake Placid Olympics did not see him back on top again, but after a slow beginning at Val d'Isère, where he was twentieth, he provided us with sporadic indications that his mind and body were on the mend. There were several first-seed results, including a seventh at Wengen.

In 1981-1982, he re-emerged as one of the leaders by winning the *Critérium* at Val d'Isère, becoming the first racer ever to win there twice. A few weeks later, he placed second to Steve Podborski before his once-again reverential countrymen at Kitzbühel. Franz no longer dominated as he once had, but after almost four years adrift, he was back in the first seed.

The next winter there was another victory, at Val Gardena, and four other top-eight finishes going into the final race. This put him second to Conradin Cathomen, of Switzerland. If Franz could place in the top three, and finish ahead of Cathomen, he would win the World Cup downhill title for the first time since 1978. Fittingly, the downhill finale was at Lake

Louise, the course on which he tore his leg in 1980. Once again, he had his lucky start number, fifteen. And down he swooped to place second to a much younger teammate, Helmut Hoeflehner. Once again, Franz had won the big prize. I'm not sure if church bells pealed across Austria when news of his feat reached home, but many a beer stein and glass of schnaps must have been raised in his honour.

But the fairy-tale of resurrection and renewal didn't end at Lake Louise. The next winter, his twelfth on the White Circus, he had five more top-ten finishes, including a victory at Kitzbühel, where he spearheaded an Austrian sweep, finishing more than half a second ahead of Erwin Resch and Anton Steiner. It was the same, ineffable Klammer, whom we all remembered from the 1970s. From top to bottom, he skied like a kid. Umpteen times it looked like he was beyond it, on the verge of capsizing. But somehow, as in days of yore, the Kaiser kept his pins and won.

Three weeks later, Klammer was included in the Sarajevo Olympic team but, after more than 100 races, he had shot his bolt. He placed tenth, a second and a half behind the American gold medallist, Billy D. Johnson. Then, as though on a victory lap, he cruised across the Atlantic one last time for races at Aspen. His results were undistinguished, but, as I know Franz, he enjoyed himself, mightily!

MONEY _____

CHAPTER EIGHT

A CCORDING TO THE NARROW DEFINITION found in most dictionaries, I lost my "amateur" status at the age of fourteen, when I decided to become a ski racer.

The concept of the amateur, as one who does not engage in athletic contests for money, is an anachronism. It is used as a moral standard by the keepers of the flame. According to these purists, amateurs are more honourable and worthy than those who dirty their hands by accepting money or competing for cash.

In the early years of the modern Olympic era, amateur sport was practised by gentlemen. According to Richard Gruneau of the University of British Columbia, there was a time when the receipt of money for athletic proficiency was thought to be not only "ungentlemanly," but also vaguely threatening. It offered members of the working classes the opportunity to challenge their social superiors on an equal footing. The Olympic movement originally opposed any such subversive possibilities. The purity of sport-for-pleasure was codified in an Olympic ideal that was effectively for the upper classes only. Professional sport was for the lower or working classes. Things have changed, of course, but it was not until 1981 that the International Olympic Committee moved away from the old definition of an amateur athlete (the infamous Rule 26) to the more benign definition now in force.

Today, the gates are swinging wide open. The new "Athlete's Code" proposed by the IOC should allow any athlete, professional or non-professional, to compete in the Olympics. So the romantic idea of the amateur athlete is almost dead. The public wants winners.

I was raised in this new, more pragmatic environment. I was one of a number of ski racers who would train and compete twelve months of the year in an effort to win world-class races. On hundreds of occasions we were told that the country expected nothing less.

Yes, we earned a very good income from our skiing exploits, but we did it within the rules. As recently as 1984, Wayne Parrish, then of the *Toronto Star*, wrote a National Newspaper Award-winning *exposé* about the millions of dollars Canadian skiers earned from races. Implicit in the underlying tone of these articles was the sense that some of these payments were illicit, that we abused the system, accepting money outside the rules. This simply was not so.

THERE IS NO SET FEE for a World Cup victory or a strong finish. Various factors influence how much money may be earned. It is a very complex subject.

The sum agreed upon between a ski supplier and a racer is most often determined by the racer's achievements in the previous season and his present condition. Other significant considerations are his competitive record, his injury rate since he joined the circuit, and his perceived appeal — whether he is thought to be sympathetic, articulate, or handsome. Also taken into account are the number of languages he speaks, and whether the racer is from a country or geographic region that has a strong ski, and ski-tourism, market. If the region with which the racer is identified is already well served by other strong, high-profile racers this, too, will be a factor. For example, Russians earn much less than West Germans or Americans for similar results — and most of what they earn is given to the federation, not the racer.

Canadians had a tough go of it initially, because the Europeans looked at the balance sheets of their Canadian subsidiaries, and saw problems. Our market was actually number five in the world, but because Canada is so big, marketing is difficult. The European companies were reluctant to add to their already high costs by giving us large sums of money.

Over time, the Canadian racers managed to change that. We were abetted by the excellent relations we maintained with the American ski commentators, Frank Gifford and Bob Beattie of the ABC television network, Billy Kidd and Tim Ryan of CBS, and Greg Lewis of NBC. It was a marriage of convenience. They gave us a lot of attention. We gave them downhill racers who spoke English fluently. Unlike most of the other top North American racers, we as a team had the additional advantage that almost all of us could communicate in French and German. Because we seemed to be everyone's second choice in Europe, behind the home country favourites, we were acceptable fodder for advertising campaigns across the continent. No matter how good and personable a Swiss racer might be, to sell him to the Italian or Austrian markets is difficult.

The Canadian Ski Association was seldom involved in this contractual process, beyond insisting that every ski supplier also contribute a certain amount of money to the team pool. They also provided us with a trust fund in which we could park our earnings. We negotiated contracts directly with the various suppliers and sponsors. In return for a fee, and the use of the suppliers' goods, we promised to endorse the product, and do a certain amount of formal advertising, for posters and what not.

Ski industry contracts are generally for a two-year period. Bonuses are closely tied to success, with fixed sums on a sliding scale for first-, second- or third-place finishes in the World Cup downhill standings, and at individual World Cup races. There are also sometimes much smaller payments for each World Cup point earned.

It is estimated that last year the ski industry spent in excess of twenty million dollars on competitive racing, covering the whole spectrum of activity, from the World Cup to provincial or junior levels. Financial payments to racers actually made up a tiny portion of this total. The twenty million dollar figure included research and development, supplying the product and servicing it, and that, in turn, meant paying the salary, room and board of the travelling servicemen.

How much is a World Cup victory worth? From virtually nothing to $25,000 or more. Only the top fifty men and a handful of women on the World Cup receive significant income from ski racing.

Canada has fifty racers at all levels on its National Ski Team. Perhaps three of them make enough money to live away from their parents' home or buy a car. Most of the rest don't make enough to buy an extra dessert for themselves, once or twice a week.

Men generally receive more money than women for similar results, because their races attract much larger on-hill audiences, and higher television ratings. For the same reasons, downhill specialists usually get paid more money per win than slalom and giant slalom skiers. However, the legendary slalomist, Ingemar Stenmark, was a huge exception to this rule. The quiet Swede won more than seventy-five World Cup races. He took out a FIS "B" card after the Lake Placid Olympics, which meant that he could strike any deals he wanted. The price he paid was that he was no longer allowed to compete at the Olympics or World Championships (although the rules may be changed to allow him to compete at the Calgary Games).

The press in Sweden said Stenmark's annual income in the early 1980s was well into seven figures. Who knows? For tax reasons, he has lived in Monaco for many years.

The Crazy Canucks were in a much different situation. True, we were winning downhills, but even collectively we had only sixteen victories altogether. Speculation in the media over our earnings was almost always overblown. None of us was even close to being a being millionaire, that's for sure.

Payments to racers by ski manufacturers became an issue in the late 1960s and early 1970s. It had long been suspected that there had been under-the-table payments to top racers, even before the time of Karl Schranz and Jean-Claude Killy. A lot was made of International Olympic Committee (IOC) president, Avery Brundage, and his opposition then to Alpine skiing, because of suspicions about the existence of these payments. It was said that he had a list of fifty racers, who were accepting money illegally.

The controversy came to a head because Schranz challenged the IOC to exclude Alpine skiers from the Sapporo Olympics in 1972. On the eve of the competition, International Ski Federation president, Marc Holder, successfully argued that skiing was clean. But because Schranz gave the impression that he thought himself larger than the Olympics, Brundage ruled that he was ineligible for the Games.

Schranz may have been in disgrace in the eyes of the Olympic movement, but he was accorded a hero's welcome in Vienna. And the IOC's action did nothing to stop the increasing commercialization of Alpine skiing. At the next Games, in Innsbruck, competitors were ordered to surrender their skis the moment the race stopped. They were not allowed to raise them before the television cameras. This resulted in a remarkable scene in which the downhill winner, Franz Klammer, was involved in a brawling set-to with officials after the race. He wanted to protect the best pair of skis he had. They wanted to protect the television audience from the sight of them. The ski police won. The hottest boards in the world were wired together and tossed on to a sled.

Today, Brundage's dream of sporting (and skiing's) purity lives on, but in a much reduced form. Racers at World Cups, World Championships, and the Olympics, must cross a red line drawn in the snow in the finish area before taking their skis off. Five years ago, Switzerland's Toni Buergler forgot the rule in a World Cup race at Val Gardena. He was disqualified. Luckily for him, his result on the day was not worth advertising.

As recreational skiing boomed in the 1960s and 1970s, the World Cup mushroomed into a major international business. The ski industry took note of the increasing public interest and substantially increased its involvement. Out of its growing financial commitment came the Alpine ski pool. National ski teams set up these pools and obliged manufacturers to pay a fee; in return, manufacturers were given the right to use team logos and to supply products to racers. The idea was to allow a range of products into the pool to help support the team.

It was the responsibility of each racer to test the various brands of equipment and decide which one suited him best on the hill, and in the pocketbook. Although many kinds of gear were included in the pool agreements, by far the most important to both the team and the racer were skis, boots, and bindings. These are the tools of the trade. They have the most influence on performance.

Another important function of the pool was to make high-quality ski equipment available to the most talented twelve and thirteen year-olds. No money changed hands in these deals, but the manufacturers hoped that if the material was good, and the racer improved, he or she would be loyal to the supplier when the big time beckoned.

When I first became a Canadian team member in 1973, there was an understanding that our earnings were to be paid into a trust fund administered by the CSA, until we decided to take it out. This arrangement fell within the rules of the FIS and the IOC. We were really professionals, but we weren't labelled as professionals.

The arrangement was both simple and ambiguous. What caused the confusion was that each federation set its own guidelines for the administration of the funds. The rules varied greatly.

In Canada we were given a relatively free rein. We could establish our own trust funds or investment portfolios, but the money was to be held until we retired. The Swiss did not set up trust funds, but established a system of broken-time payments. In effect, these were annual salaries to the racers based on their previous year's performance. From very early on, the West Germans instituted victory payments. The racers got what they'd earned almost immediately after the competition.

In the late 1970s, a new factor further confused the money scenario. As the World Cup grew in popularity, more and more non-skiing interests clamoured to participate. Athletes began to receive offers to endorse products which were not covered by the pool agreement. Until then, the pools used a minimum of three athletes to endorse products on radio and television, and in print. This was in compliance with an IOC requirement that no athlete be seen to be *personally* endorsing a product.

The question of outside endorsements quickly became a sore point with the more successful racers. They were being asked to perform for their pools for little or no compensation. At the same time, they were obliged to turn down direct approaches to endorse products for large sums of money.

Every World Cup racer knew his days as a big earner from the sport had real limits. A downhiller who avoided injury might go ten years on the World Cup. His results would be good enough to earn a reasonable income for perhaps half of that time. Any day, an injury could rip his livelihood out from under him. Poof! Obliterated! Gone in the time it takes for a knee to unwind at 140 kilometres per hour.

In 1979, the Canadian ski team participated in an ad for Gillette razors. Four Crazy Canucks (Podborski, Irwin, Murray, and I) appeared in a thirty-second commercial which announced a Gillette contest in which four Saab automobiles were to be given away. (Saab supplied us with vehicles in Europe and in North America at the time.)

For each entry received in the contest, the companies donated twenty-five cents to the ski team's "Quest For Gold" fund, for the 1980 Olympics. The program netted in excess of $25,000 for the team. It gave Gillette and Saab positive publicity. The four of us, around whom the commercial was built, received $1,250 each — slightly above minimum union scale — for two days of work in Toronto, in the middle of a brief vacation.

The team's defence was succinct. It takes between $40,000 and $50,000 to keep one skier on the road for a year. Agreed! The team naturally wished to protect its share of the revenue. But athletes, too, needed to capitalize on their brief success. A compromise between these points of view had to be struck.

The first personal endorsement I undertook was for McCain's orange juice. The commercial was to be shot in Toronto in English with figure skater Tracy Wainman and in French with speedskater Gaetan Boucher. For two days, wearing winter clothing in the thirty-degree heat and 100 per cent humidity, we bravely acted out our roles.

Despite the sweltering conditions, we had a delightful time. Believe it: negotiating my share of the proceeds with the Canadian Ski Association was a much more draining experience.

At stake was roughly $25,000. The CSA insisted that I was not Ken Read in the commercial, I was Ken Read of the Canadian National Ski Team. I required their permission to do the ad and I could have it, if the revenues were split 75 : 25 in their favour.

This was unacceptable. The sponsor had approached me. In discussions with McCain's' advertising agency the CSA was never mentioned. They wanted me. A 75 : 25 cut was outrageous. My position was that it had to be a 50 : 50 split or I'd walk away from the deal. The CSA reluctantly accepted these terms. Since then, the athlete's short earning span has been recognized and a 75 : 25 split — in the athlete's favour — has become standard.

My own little war over agents did not go very well. When I was racing, the CSA would not allow racers to have agents. Mike Halsted, a vice-president for Mark McCormick's worldwide company, International Management Group, which represented retired ski racers such as Bernhard Russi and Rosi Mittermaier, gave me his card once and urged me to get in touch with him. We soon came to general terms, but I was

obliged to have the CSA ratify the contract. The CSA decided
not to. A racer's allegiance had to be to the team, they said.
Ironically, one month after I retired, in 1983, the CSA caved
in to pressure: racers and agents are now allowed to establish
their own contractual agreements.

I don't subscribe to the free enterprise philosophy of most
North American professional athletes, that anything they can
earn belongs solely to them. I believe that the club teams and
schools which supported their development should receive
something for their time and trouble. I'm all for the ski team
keeping a reasonable share of what their athletes earn. We all
came from somewhere. My somewhere was a program that
supported me for several years, while I gave back nothing but
my heart.

If a skier becomes successful, he ought to try to repay his
benefactors so that others, in turn, will get the same opportunities. There are many ways to help out. For example, a
strong racer's presence in the pool acts as a magnet for ski
suppliers. When the Crazy Canucks went to Europe together
for the first time, our pool was worth $50,000 a year. When I
retired in 1983, the pool was valued at $1,000,000. I think all
the Crazy Canucks were responsible for much of that growth.
As racers at the peak of our game, we were called on to attend
dozens of team fund-raisers. Our job at these cocktail parties
and dinners was to squeeze a few dollars for the team out of
every handshake. We never expected or got more than a drink
or a meal in return, but we made a significant contribution,
often flying cross-country during our brief, off-season vacations to represent the CSA.

Some critics have decried government subsidies to the ski
team, and public appeals for donations, because we are professionals. But these funds are used to run the whole ski team,
while the ski manufacturers continue to be associated with
only the best athletes. Pull the system down and it won't be
the top skiers who are hurt. They can support themselves from
endorsements. It is the other forty or fifty members of the
team who would suffer. These racers would suddenly face a
$40,000 or $50,000 annual bill to remain on the team.

There is a perception in Canada that for certain, high-profile
amateur athletes, there is a pot of gold at the end of the rain-
bow. The reality is different. After retirement, very few racers

earn more than a few thousand dollars a year from endorse-ments. Once you're no longer racing on television every week-end, your value to advertisers drops quickly, unless you have been a particularly dominant and celebrated performer, such as Nancy Greene or Jean-Claude Killy. In the entire skiing fraternity, I can only think of about ten skiers who have done well by endorsements in retirement. Other than Greene and Killy, some of them are Switzerland's Bernhard Russi, Aus-tria's Franz Klammer and Toni Sailer, and the American, Billy Kidd.

Perhaps it is just as well: instead of living off their past glories, most athletes have to apply the same energy and deter-mination they displayed in sport to other challenges and objec-tives. From the Canadian ski team, there are many examples of those who made the difficult transition successfully. Today, former racers such as Bob Miller and Mike Irwin are stock-brokers. Dave Irwin is the marketing manager for Sunshine Village, near Banff. David Murray operates one of Canada's best recreational racing programs — the Molson Canadian Masters Alpine Series. My wife, Lynda Robbins, graduated as the gold medallist in her physical education class at the Uni-versity of Calgary. And former racer and coach, John Ritchie, is an executive with a brewery.

As a former ski racer I have, in the past, only been associated with products that were used in my sport. But this year I broke what, for me, was new ground. I agreed to do work with Coca-Cola and Birks Jewellers.

Skiing, in a way, continues to be a part of our livelihoods in retirement. Several of us have set up consulting companies. In my case, as president of K.J. Read Consulting, I am involved in sport marketing and promotion, broadcasting and writing on sports subjects and, increasingly, drawing on my years of experience on the White Circus, in ski-area design as part of Canada Ski Consultants.

THE
MEDIA *CHAPTER NINE*

M OST CANADIANS KNOW LITTLE about so-called amateur sport,
but a great deal about a few professional sports. Professional hockey, baseball, football, even basketball, are presented to them through long seasons within a continental
media framework which includes extensive coverage on TV
and radio, and in newspapers and magazines.

How has this imbalance come about? Why the comparative
ignorance on one hand, the intensity on the other?

The media of Canada accords little time or space to amateur
sport beyond the few weeks before, and the fortnight during,
the Olympic Games. People in the media have decided, for
various reasons, that the "pros" merit immense coverage, but
amateur sport does not. One explanation for this fixation may
be the simple, widespread conviction that the pros are tops.
Other explanations are related to the long, pre-set schedules
of North American pro leagues, circuits, and tournaments,
which make media coverage cheaper and easier, and the calculated provision of stars and personalities and statistics, which
form a common pool of material that all media can draw on.
And the particularly Canadian element comes in the reach
into so many homes of a profusion of American TV channels.
Canadians, arguably, from a sporting point of view, are quasi-
Americans.

If those media with a popular reach — millions of listeners,
viewers, and readers — pay only random, or cursory attention
to amateur sport, the consequences are unavoidable. But those
of us in amateur sport have the right to ask if this neglect is

justified. Is there a shortfall in quality, excitement or competitive fire in our sports? Or could there be a lack of understanding, a vision block, even a bit of laziness and snobbery, among those who report upon and interpret sport?

Let me emphasize this: I have no enemies in the media. I haven't any need, let alone urge, to get back at any reporter or broadcaster. My focus is on the situation as it is, and what has to change if it is to become a happier one. I do appreciate that we're discussing something much broader and more complicated than a handful of sports departments in newspapers or TV stations.

Canada has a more sophisticated communications system than any other country in the world. I mean, in terms of TV and radio networks and stations, and of press services that knit a number of daily newspapers together, the organization of news media is very highly developed. The majority of newspapers are "chained" to large, prosperous corporations. One hardly needs to have read the reports of the several royal commissions which have investigated the media to know that the Canadian communications system is dominated by large, powerful, profitable, and technically competent operations. Take a few examples. No capital city in the world has access to as many television stations as Ottawa. Few major cities in the world have as many well-heeled newspapers and TV stations competing with each other as Toronto. Ten minutes after a politician speaks in Ottawa, you can hear the gist of it in Calgary or Moncton. In short, we have a sturdy, able communications system. The reporters and broadcasters who supply this system with information can easily fill the sports pages and the radio and TV slots available to them.

One of my first observations as a skier was that, almost always, a junior reporter was detached to cover my sport. Senior reporters, particularly columnists, covered the pros.

I saw this in my home base, Calgary. A reporter for *The Albertan*, Eric Duhatschek was a "cub" when he began to report on skiing. Over the next few years, Eric learned the basics about us and the sport. In time, *The Albertan* folded and Eric joined a new paper, *The Calgary Sun*. Eric became very knowledgeable about skiing. When he switched to the larger, more prestigious *Calgary Herald*, the ski portfolio remained his. Then NHL hockey came to Calgary from Atlanta

— the Flames. Able Eric got the top beat, covering them. He wanted to keep his hand in skiing. Permission was refused. Either he reported on hockey, or nothing. Ski reporting simply wasn't worthy of his growing status. Even though our team was having unprecedented success, the ski beat in Calgary reverted to another junior reporter learning the ropes.

This happens all the time. It's almost always the inexperienced reporters who cover amateur sport. It frustrates me that a competent reporter, who knows the amateur side from A to Z, hasn't really made it until he or she has covered the pros.

To an irritating degree, the Olympic Games are an exception. They're on US television by the hour, so they must be important. Top story! And so the stalwart leaders of the sports media fraternity (and it is still largely a fraternity) smother the Games with coverage, whether they've got much notion of what's transpiring or not.

Isn't this bizarre? Viewers and readers get blanket coverage of the Games from journalists who, in the main, have paid no attention to amateur sport in the preceding four years. Someone might say that editors do the same for a major political party convention or a federal election campaign, but that's not quite so. Politics in Canada, in almost all its aspects, and certainly in its international aspects, gets steady coverage, not merely saturation for the big deals.

Our journalists and editors obviously see all the elements of great sport in the quadrennial pageant. Surely, at least a few of the component sports, particularly those in which Canadians are competitive, deserve some steady, serious coverage? Surely there's a national interest to be served, presently and prospectively, by supporting our athletes when they compete on the world stage? It would be foolish to expect for amateur sport the immense and detailed attention which any hockey star's sore shoulder is given, as if it were as serious as a cabinet minister's heart attack, but some regular notice by experienced reporters or commentators would sustain amateur athletes, and build the following which both nourishes and revels in the Olympics.

Every year when I was skiing, on the third or fourth weekend in January, a small regiment of Canadian journalists left the icy North to join more than a thousand American colleagues for football's Super Bowl in southern warmth and sunshine. Meanwhile, at Kitzbühel, another battalion of sports journalists gathered to watch and report the world's most celebrated and dangerous ski race, the Hahnenkamm.

Both events attracted television audiences of more than 100 million. For Canadians, however, there was a marked difference. The pack of Canadians in the American South filed few, if any, Canadian stories and interviewed no Canadian players. How could they? None of their countrymen was playing. The Canadian writers, most of them veteran "experts," were covering an American cultural extravaganza.

At Kitzbühel, however, a Canadian journalist would have had something Canadian to write or comment about. Since 1980, Canucks had beaten the best of other skiing nations four times in a row, a feat only matched, but never surpassed, by the host Austrians. When not winning, the racers from Canada provided another kind of excitement, by cartwheeling off the course.

Although the stars of our sports journalism and their editors were not very concerned with what our boys did in Austria, much of the rest of the world was. There were reporters present from the United Kingdom, Scandinavia, and Japan, nations not traditionally devoted to downhill success. For those Canadians who were interested in the skiing results, there were the short reports and items taken from the wire services. Not until 1984, did one staff sports reporter from a Canadian daily newspaper see a Canadian racer compete in a World Cup downhill in Europe. By then, the men's and women's teams had won almost thirty races, including all the big ones.

Until very recently, TV coverage of skiing in Canada consisted of the Olympics, ABC's coverage of Kitzbühel, which was aired on CTV, and occasionally, the Canadian Championship. After our first successes in Europe in 1975, I asked Pat Marsden, then a CTV commentator, what it would take to get World Cup skiing on TV in Canada. He said: "You win a couple more races, and there'll be a build-up of excitement. We'll have to televise your races."

Well, it took another four years, and another five World Cup wins, before our European races were beamed home to Canada. And this came only because a ski fan, CBC producer Jim Thompson, needed a staple for the new CBC program, *Sports-*

weekend. He got a fabulous debut with a victory in the first race, and a second and third in the second race. A World Cup race has been shown every weekend of the tour since, and has been an incredible boon to our sport. Many racers have become household names at home as a result (years after we became winners) but more importantly, the coverage has broadened the base of skiing participation and interest in the sport.

Television was a factor for years in our inability to hold World Cup races in Canada. We couldn't get races without sponsors; we couldn't get sponsors without TV; we couldn't get TV without races.

But aside from Alpine skiing and figure skating (which some consider to be more aesthetic entertainment than sport) there is still hardly any coverage of Canadian amateur sport from overseas. Only the Olympics, the Commonwealth Games, and the World Track and Field Championships attract attention. It's a travesty which amateur sport lives with every year.

One needn't go back to the time of the Crazy Canucks. The media continues to ignore the Olympic sports, while printing millions of words, and giving thousands of TV-hours, to American sporting activities. Flip through the sports pages or recall recent sportscasts. With the certain exception of ice hockey, most of the prime space and air time goes to the heroic deeds, thoughts, and ultimately, the cultural values of Americans such as Refrigerator Perry, Dwight Gooden, and John McEnroe. The video clips shown every night are mostly snippets from dozens of stateside basketball, baseball, and football games. They are packaged and readily available, instantly and cheaply, to any Canadian TV outfit with a satellite dish.

It's not as though Canada does not have winners. In recent years, sprinters Ben Johnson and Angela Taylor, and swimmers Victor Davis and Alex Baumann have led the world. At present, at least a dozen Canadian individuals or teams are ranked in the top three or four in the world in Olympic sports. Several are world champions or world-record holders.

We still haven't taken as many Olympic or world championship medals as either the public or the athletes would like. And every Olympics, the journalists clamour for improvement. But we do have world-class swimmers, ski jumpers, field hockey players, speedskaters, sprinters, hurdlers, high jumpers, rowers, kayakers, canoeists, cross-country skiers, divers, figure skaters, shooters, rythmic gymnasts and synchronized swimmers. This is not insignificant. For a country of twenty-five million, it's remarkable, especially in one so plugged into American pro sports — sports, incidentally, at which few Canadians do well.

If there's an unfairness, even a scandal, in all this it's because most of the Canadian sports media marches in lockstep with the American professional sports machine. Canadians are consequently denied much chance to see, read about, honour, or identify with Canadian athletes.

When Britain's middle distance runners, Sebastian Coe and Steve Ovett, were careering around the world setting world records, their every move and thought were reported by dozens of British journalists. Today, Canada's Ben Johnson is the world's fastest human. He could set a world record anytime, anywhere. But Ben doesn't get the treatment from Canadian writers that the British gave their two running stars. There's rarely a single Canadian journalist on hand for a Johnson race when he goes to meets in the US and overseas.

Gaetan Boucher won two speedskating gold medals at the Sarajevo Olympics. ABC was there. So was CTV. So were about fifty Canadian print journalists. They fêted Boucher. He was a hero. Two weeks later Boucher was a favourite in the World Championships in Oslo. Not one Canadian journalist was there. No one telephoned him to ask about his prospects or results.

Canada's Olympic team defeated the world and Olympic champions, the Netherlands, in women's field hockey at Amsterdam. A huge crowd was there. Millions watched it on Dutch television. The event got two or three sentences, at most, in Canadian newspapers. The same thing happened when the men's volleyball team defeated Japan in Tokyo. Millions there watched the national humiliation on prime-time TV. Hardly anyone in Canada ever discovered that the game took place. It happened a few weeks before the Los Angeles Olympics.

What other country allows teams composed entirely of foreigners, such as those who play for the Toronto Blue Jays and the Montreal Expos, to live in their land and get paid in a foreign currency to compete against other foreigners? European, Asian, and South American countries restrict foreign players in hockey, basketball, volleyball, and baseball to two or three per team.

My argument is not with US pro sports. Lord knows, it's interesting, and mostly of high calibre. My argument is with the Canadian sports editors and producers who believe that their readers and viewers only want hockey and US pro sport. They have decided that our interest in amateur sport erupts, incredibly, for a mere two weeks every two years. Then the appetite is so fierce it must be fed with extra sections and "specials."

I know all amateur sport is not riveting. Much of the Canadian activity and results do not merit extensive coverage. It is still true, however, that Canadians cannot possibly become excited over our many successes as long as editors refuse to cover them.

Canadians have been keen on international competitions where there has been some chance of Canadian success. The TV ratings here for Olympic coverage are high. As the CBC's Brian Williams has told me, the show he hosts and which I appear on regularly, *Sportsweekend*, often has its best ratings when it's showing World Cup downhill races. And take a single game: in 1983, viewers at home were mesmerized by CBC's prime-time telecast of our men's basketball team playing (and beating) Yugoslavia at the World University Games.

After victories outside Canada by cyclist Steve Bauer, *The Globe and Mail* assigned a freelancer, Robert Zeller, to cover the *Tour de France*. I know beans about the sport, despite a little exposure to it in Europe, but through Zeller's reports I've become keen about cycling and Canadian cyclists. Now I like to know whether Stephen Roche or Charles Mottet has the yellow jersey. It's sad we've had so few similar journalistic assays into the realm of international sport.

Two years ago in Brazil, an audience gauged at 25,000,000 watched a Canada-Brazil basketball game that was played under police guard because of threats to the Canadian team. This and the other matches in the series were available to evening audiences across Central and South America. None was shown in Canada. In fact, not once did any of the games by the Canadian team earn more than a two-sentence mention in a Canadian newspaper.

I've seen the problem from two sides. As a broadcaster, with CBC, I have an appreciation of some of the difficulties journalists experience in getting information from the amateur sport world. And I know the time and financial commitment that is required by a network before it can produce a small documentary or televise an event. Working with *Sportsweekend*, which carries more Canadian amateur sport, by far, than any other Canadian sports show, has also taught me that amateur sport can be presented in an interesting way to Canadians. For example, it was *Sportsweekend* that brought Canadians same-day satellite coverage of the the Canada-Netherlands women's field hockey World Cup finals from Kuala Lumpur, Malaysia, in 1983. It was a bold, magical stroke, which showed the power and glory of Canadians competing at the summit. But such ventures must be more than experiments. With every passing day, I realize that much, much more can be done in this sphere.

Surely there's an irony in the usually polite, but endemic anti-Americanism of so many Canadian nationalists about so many things — acid rain, softwood lumber, shakes and shingles, Arctic sovereignty, B-52 overflights, cruise missile testing, and so on — everything but sport. Daily and weekly, defenders of our "cultural" interests such as Robert Fulford, Mavor Moore, and the Edmonton publisher, Mel Hurtig, warn and cajole us about American threats to our distinctiveness and values. And there are vigorous, institutionalized lobbies, vigilant in protecting us, like the Canada Council and ACTRA and the Canadian Council of the Arts.

Shouldn't there be a similiar sense of public responsiblity for showing and reporting the feats of our amateur athletes in a steady way?

In pro sports, the competitors usually represent a city or a region. When you're a national team athlete, you represent your country. There can't be many times when we are more bound together than when following fellow Canadians as they compete and succeed in international sports contests. Few of us over twenty-five have forgotten the 1972 hockey series with the USSR.

But where are the natural allies of Olympic sports in Canada?

The federal government has backed high performance amateur sport. It has also helped provide some media coverage by picking up all the travelling expenses of freelance journalists, Mary Hynes and Randy Starkman, who report regularly from abroad on Canadian activities for CBC Radio, the Canadian Press news agency, and several major Canadian dailies.

But it's clear to me that few sports reporters or editors think they have any duty to make Canadians better informed about the accomplishments of their countrymen. They obviously feel that most Canadians are uninterested in non-professional athletic competition. But I think they're wrong. Given a fair chance, Canadians do care.

IV

A
SKIING
LIFE

OUR
LIFE

TO ARRIVE AT VAL D'ISÈRE every December for the *Critérium de la Première Neige*, or "Test of the First Snow," was something I always looked forward to.

The White Circus was back together again after an eight-month hiatus. After the tough off-season grind of work-like-hell days, which began at 5:30 a.m., and seemed never to end, life was about to become bearable again. There were friends to see and races to race! The monotony of training and waiting was over. A summer's worth of questions was about to be answered.

After installing ourselves in a hotel — over the years we stayed in several in Val d'Isère — we'd hustle off to the Taverne d'Alsace on the town's wide main drag. There, in the company of our peers, we'd share gossip. Who was wearing what colours? Who was dating whom? And most of all, who had the fast skis?

It was a small fraternity and that made us proud.   The feelings and sentiments we shared were exactly like those which came across in the book and film, *The Right Stuff*. We felt like young jet- and rocket-engine test pilots gathered in the 1950s in a bar, in the hot California desert, to talk bravely about punching the far side of the envelope. Only a handful of people in the world could handle the mountains and we knew it. We were confident, even cocky. But like the joystick jockeys, we were always respectful of our enemies: weather, the mountains, and time.

In my first few years on the tour, Val d'Isère was more fun than it is for racers today, and not only because the men's and women's tours meshed there for a few glorious days. It was a better time because less was at stake.

With every passing day, technological and financial considerations play a bigger role in the sport. Today's racers often have agents in tow, and an eye on the stock market. They must also prepare more seriously for every race, because the new technologies push them ever faster down the mountain. To avoid becoming an advertisment for a life insurance company, they must always have their wits about them and train, train, train. There is no time for mucking about. It's just as well that the women's calendar seldom coincides any longer with the men's.

Looking back through rose-tinted glasses, in the good old days of the 1970s, there was space on the World Cup tour not only for earnest young men, such as the Crazy, hardworking Canucks, but also for rowdy men such as Werner Grissman, a sybaritic Austrian with an eye for the bottle and the ladies. Today, it seems, most of the racers have adopted our sober example.

Grissman was a lovable rube and a fine skier. He won a downhill race at St. Moritz, in 1973, and a medal at the 1978 World Championships, and little else. But, somehow, he seemed to make the Austrian team every fall. A chubby, unshaven, unkempt life-of-the-party sort, he answered to the name "Grizzly," and spent a decade among us, parlaying his excellent interval times, but thin finish results, into fabulous party invitations and scores of hilarious, front-page stories.

Perhaps Grizzly's most celebrated escapade was in St. Anton, where he attached Roman candle-like rockets to his ski boots for a training run. He said he needed them because he always ran out of gas after the second interval timer (which was true). Everyone except his coaches was amused. He was suspended for a few days. I'm sure he spent the time dreaming up new tricks.

Gone, too, is Switzerland's boisterous Roland Collombin, who was seen returning to his hotel at Kitzbühel in 1974 after an all-night foray. Three hours later, the celebrated lady's man defeated the world's most dangerous mountain.

Today, coaches would kick their racers to kingdom-come if they tried to pull such stunts in mid-season. And they'd be right, too, because the technical situation today is so complex. With racers pushing themselves to the limit at all times, such entertainments are more likely to result in serious injury than in victory.

I was never one for pranks. I guess the closest I ever came to pulling one was at Whistler, in 1979, when we were obliged to race the world's first super-G after the Europeans pulled the plug on our downhill, because they said it was too dangerous. I took the first three gates properly, but from there to the bottom of the mountain I ran it as a downhill. I knew the crowd had come to watch a downhill, and I intended to race one. It was my message to the Europeans that there was nothing wrong with the hill.

Competing in God's great outdoors was wonderful. But we were at the mercy of the elements every day of our racing lives. As organizers found out last winter, during a full dress rehearsal at the Mount Allan Alpine Olympic site, many different factors may send a downhill race up the flue. Delays and cancellations can be caused by not enough snow, too much snow, high winds, rain, sleet, fog, driving snow, thaws, sudden heat-waves, sub-zero temperatures, poor course preparation, insufficient safety netting, and broken lifts. Throw in additional factors, such as which countries' racers have the most to gain or lose by a cancellation, or whether Eurovision, which transmits all the races to every country in Western Europe, would rather a race be held on a Friday, as scheduled, or be delayed from Friday to Saturday for a larger weekend television audience, and you've got some idea of what race juries are up against. And I have not yet mentioned that if a race is put off for one day, the White Circus may not have beds to sleep in that night!

Racers have a lot of time to get to know each other on the mountain. The sport's motto, "hurry up and wait," will endure forever. Small wonder I spent half my racing career waiting in crowded mountain lodges or restaurants for the word to go or, as often, to go home.

When zipping off to South America or New Zealand or the glaciers of Europe during the summer and fall, Canadian friends would rib me about our exotic lives of freedom, adventure, and romance. The reality was something else. We weren't going to pad through the back lanes of London's Soho, or sit in cafes on the Left Bank, in Paris. We were off to training camp and it was going to be pure drudgery. Places such as Hintertux and Zermatt were the bane of our existence.

Glaciers, by their very nature, are found in the highest and most remote valleys of Europe. The high seasons for these resorts are July, August, and the winter months. When we visited them in September or October they were bereft of tourists. Most of the hotels were shuttered, their Italian and Yugoslav *gastarbeiters*, or "guest workers," back home on vacation spending their pay packets. A deserted resort actually suited our purposes nicely. Fewer people meant fewer distractions, and no arguments with vacationers for hill space to train on.

If we were lucky, there might be another team around for training. Otherwise, it was us and 100 or 150 villagers for weeks and weeks on end. They were gentle, unassuming peasants in lederhosen or dirndls, always ready with a smile and a wave, but not very good at small talk.

By 6:00 a.m every morning, we would be on the glaciers. It was necessary to begin training so early because the heat of the day turned the snow to mush. By early afternoon these conditions always chased us into the valley. It might sound neat, but glaciers aren't fun to ski on. They're windy, and they always seem to recede, making for shorter runs each year. With each passing summer, they were rougher. Etching a short run out of glacier ice was difficult because of the crevasses, and the rock and dust particles that settled in them.

Afternoons at camp were spent playing soccer or doing the required dryland training. Beside us were fields which were always freshly manured to keep the grass growing for the cows, which sauntered around town clanging their bells. It seemed to us that they always kept a large quantity of manure in reserve, so they could spread a new coating every day during our stay. Not only did we get to appreciate the smell, but we also got to carry it home with us on our shoes and clothes, and in our hair.

To break the monotony, I always tried to vary my training regimen in the afternoon. I'd go on long hikes in the mountains, or run down to the next village which received the Austrian and German newspapers, the *International Herald Tribune* and the serious British newspapers, albeit a few days late. They were my link with the outside world. Through them I developed a fascination for the forces at work in international politics, and with the political games Europeans played within the Common Market, and with their poorer cousins behind the Iron Curtain — ominously, only an hour's drive to the north. In some respects, the Europe that I read about in newspapers reminded me of the World Cup. Everyone was jostling for advantage.

But the Europe of political intrigue and strife was definitely not part of our world at Hintertux. By 7:00 p.m. a cannon could be fired on the only street, and no one would be hurt. Zermatt, despite its reputation as a playground of the super-rich, was no different. Evenings in either burg were spent eating heavy mountain fare, and studying ourselves on video-tape. This was often tedious, but always essential, because it helped us to find and correct flaws of body position and line.

With the video out of the way, we'd adjourn to the hotel bar where perhaps the only eligible woman in town served us. Nothing ever came of it, but she would be courted shamelessly by some of the racers, coaches, and servicemen. It was often the only alternative to talking with one another.

A hot chocolate, an apple juice, or a beer were the highlight of our training-camp breaks. An hour's conversation in the bar, and we were ready for a few "zees." Unless we had the rare good fortune to meet up with a women's team for a few days, it was an ascetic life leavened by broad, male humour and coarse language.

There was an even more sobering side to life in such places. Glaciers are made for disaster and, regrettably, we saw a few in our time. A good friend, the American racer, Ron Bieder-mann, caught his foot in a crevasse, and it almost ripped his leg off. Another year, a teenage Finnish racer followed several teammates into an unmarked area that looked safe, but wasn't. She skied into a crevasse and landed many metres below on a snow bridge. A Canadian team doctor, Dave Millman, and a glacier rescue worker were lowered down to her. She was still alive when they reached her, but before a stretcher could be rigged to lift her out, she died of internal injuries.

Conditions in the mountains can turn harsh at any time. There are crevasses and switchback roads with no guard-rails, white-outs, avalanches, and broken cable cars. We had to be vigilant. More than one tour member died as a result of bad luck with the weather or a vehicle.

Skiing training camps, like military boot camps, or oil rig bush camps, formed an environment in which it was essential to adapt to the strengths and foibles of others. For four to six weeks at a time, there were often as many as ten racers, and five or six coaches and servicemen, living in extremely close quarters. Such confined circumstances can grossly exaggerate the conflicts and delights of normal life. It did not take long to find out whom you liked and whom you didn't. And who didn't like you.

Some of the guys were on their way up; others were on their way down. A few were infuriatingly lazy. One or two were lost in their own worlds, ethereal presences, impossible to figure out.

There were journeymen playing out the string. There were youngsters with talent and gumption galore, but no expertise. The journeymen were bad news, because they were often careless, not totally committed. The youngsters were extra baggage to those of us at the top, but you had to be tolerant, because they were the future of the team. They needed us as examples, as role models.

Among the best of my training experiences were the occasions when we trained with the Norwegians. They had a small group of five racers and two coaches. When we joined forces, we had two extra pairs of eyes to watch us on the hill, and give us feedback. There was strength in numbers. When Canada and Norway both asked an operator to block off a run for downhill training, he was much more likely to comply than if Canada had asked alone.

The Norwegians had a few duds on their team, but they also had exceptional racers, in particular Erik Haaker and, later, two younger talents, Evan Hole and Arnt-Erik Dale. During the months leading up to the 1977-1978 season Haaker helped lift us from the mess we'd gotten ourselves into during the previous season. We had had a miserable season, and had taken to bickering with each other and with our coach, Scott Henderson. With our confidence in shards, we needed a powerful outside force to measure ourselves against. Erik was our rabbit.

Erik was blond, blue-eyed, and indecently handsome. He was a droll fellow with a store of information about the early years of the World Cup. He was close to many of the legendary racers, because he was extraordinarily outgoing, and fluent in about half a dozen languages. He was also a fine technical skier who, in the twilight of his career, had gravitated from giant slalom to downhill, for the thrill of it. When I watched him carve a very difficult downhill turn, I could see how much more work I had to do before I had the movement down pat. If I beat him, I knew I was on the right track.

The major Alpine nations — Italy, West Germany, Austria, and Switzerland — had no need of temporary alliances to boost themselves through training, but for smaller teams such as the Canadian, American, Swedish, or Japanese, it was often imperative. There wasn't any point in throwing your lot in with just any team, but the right country, with the right program, at the right time, could help a lot. With the Norwegians it was an easy fit.

After training camp, what the racers hated most about life on the White Circus was the need to move to another venue at the end of each week. For six days, the upcoming race was the focus of life. If it worked out well, a little steam was blown off on Saturday night. If the week had been a failure, that was also an excuse to have a good time. But even while celebrating, winners and losers alike never forgot that Monday was moving day.

The Canadian team was responsible for moving about three tons of equipment every week. Big fish or minnow, everyone watched everyone else like a shark during the moves, to make sure each man pulled his weight. God help the racer who was conveniently away when the process of packing the van took place. He might find all his taped music had disappeared.

Once the packing of the van was completed, I always tried to get the *de luxe* ride, in the right-hand seat beside our serviceman, Hans Rammelmueller. He had a fast car with ample leg room, and a heater that worked.

Steve Podborski usually wanted to travel in the van with the world's youngest forty-year-old, our masseur, mascot, and start coach, Terry Spence. With the tape deck blaring, they'd head off into the wild blue yonder, sometimes scaring themselves silly because the vehicle was dangerously overloaded, and tended to bottom out or slide. It wasn't my idea of a nice day in the mountains.

As in the fable of the tortoise and the hare, Hans and I stopped *en route* to eat or to visit friends, while Terry and Steve plodded on. They would frequently be waiting for us at our destination. Waiting, I must say, for us to help unload the van!

Terry was a remarkable man. He held it all together for us in a mental and psychological sense. He was known as "Toulouse," after the French painter of similar, distinctive stature.

Like me, Terry had gone prematurely grey. Before dropping into our world, he had gone through several careers. He'd grown up in the Lakehead, in northern Ontario, become an account executive with IBM, and then chucked it for a low-key life at Whistler.

More than anyone on the White Circus, Terry had a cheerful, outgoing nature. Although he never managed to learn more than a smattering of German or French, he had chums everywhere. In his inimitable fashion he was able to break down barriers with other teams and racers that we couldn't. To this day, when I see Franz Klammer, his first question is always, "How's Toulouse?" When we were on the massage table every evening, Terry was our sounding board, the outlet for all our gripes about each other and the coaches. He'd always listen patiently to what we had to say and then give practical, fatherly advice.

We went to bed every night at about 10:00 p.m. And then Terry was a man transformed. No longer the wise old sage, until the wee hours of the morning he was on the prowl for fun and games. The Friday night ritual was the "weather antidote." If someone didn't go out to test the local nightlife, the weather would be atrocious in the morning. Needless to say, Toulouse always volunteered for this duty. But whatever transpired, he was always up at dawn, preparing like the rest of us for a day on the mountain.

The social life of the Crazy Canucks was never what most Canadians imagined or hoped it would be. Early in the race week, when we might have had some time for gadding about, the resorts were generally deserted. Later, when they filled up with spectators, we hadn't the time for socializing, because we were preoccupied with race preparations.

Almost nothing of a social nature ever happened between us and what you might call ordinary Europeans. There were, however, occasional relationships between male and female racers, especially in my early years on the circuit, when the tours frequently ran in tandem. Such romances evolved because the young men and women shared common interests and goals. Even with the language barriers, we had more in common with the racing women from Czechoslovakia or Italy than with the public.

Proof of the enduring nature of some of these pairings are the marriages of Switzerland's Peter Luescher and France's Fabienne Serrat, Austria's Harti Weirather and Liechtenstein's Hanni Wenzel, and Kenneth John Read and Lynda Robbins, of the Canadian men's and women's teams.

I had known Lynda vaguely for several years — she was from Toronto and I had skied briefly with her brother Derek — but it was not until my last season on the tour, in 1983, that I began to go out of my way to see her. Sometimes the detours were enormous. One time, late in the season, I flew from Sarajevo to Ljubljana, and then drove all night from there to Les Diablerets with two journalists, to spend a day with her at a women's race. The fog near Milan, as I approached the Saint-Bernard was terrible, and I had a wretched cough from Sarajevo's polluted air, but I made it. Twenty-four hours later, after watching her race in teeming rain, I was on the road again, driving to a race of my own.

AT THE *ÉLITE* LEVEL in any sport, there always seem to be group-ies and hangers-on. A few wanted to sleep with us. Most just wanted to be our friends or companions.

A difference, I think, between our circumstances and those of say, professional hockey players, is that we spent most of our competitive days in sleepy Alpine villages, not in big cit-ies. There were simply fewer people around of any kind.

I honestly never gave much thought to the girls and women who followed our team. I was so consumed by ski racing that I was always being razzed by my teammates. "If you want to know your result three weeks ago at the second interval timer in the fourth training run, just ask Kenny," was the way David Murray liked to put it.

At the same time, it was hard for me not be aware that some European fans of the Canadian team painted their cars white and red, with the maple leaf on the door. Others would write silly letters, or show up in hotel lobbies to ogle us, or try to hand us gifts. They were often not particularly good-looking young ladies, and some weren't young at all.

Not that he ever had any truck with them — most assuredly he did not — but Steve Podborski, in particular, seemed to attract these lonely souls. There was the "enigmatic Swiss blonde" (as we called her) from St. Gallen, who hung around finish lines, and in hotel lobbies, just to gaze at him. She is captured forever on celluloid in the documentary, *Thirteen Minutes to Wait*, taking a photo of Steve with her lens cap on!

Our attitude in these situations was to be as dignified and as aloof as possible. If corralled in a public area, we bantered in a jocular Canadian way about the weather, or something equally mundane, and then tried to extract ourselves from the encounter.

After a while, a few of our admirers would become too bold and persistent, checking into the same hotels, or showing up at the next table in a restaurant. At this point someone, usually one of the coaches, would raise hell with them. The ladies were told bluntly that support was appreciated but these chaps had a job to do. Good-bye!

My social life on the Circus was not something that caused anyone to speculate much. I never liked chasing a good time. It wasn't part of my nature then, and it is not part of my nature now. I'm not into what is called *après-ski*. It made me uncomfortable and was a distraction from the task at hand.

My idea of a good time was a nice dinner or a beer, and few hours of conversation with someone connected to the tour. Often it was with my friends, Mike Irwin and Robin McLeish, who were on the Canadian team in the early 1980s, or with Britain's Konrad Bartelski, whose career spanned the same years as mine. Today it's dinner with my wife and a few good friends in Calgary or Toronto. At a banquet or cocktail party, my guard goes up. I go to many of them and I think I make a fair fist of them, but I'm never relaxed. I prefer to meet with people one-on-one.

I always felt I was a self-contained sort. I didn't want victory to be lost because of other people, so I tended to spend a lot of time on my own. I didn't want to be driven crazy by the hurry-up-and-wait aspect of World Cup life. I sought my escape in books. My tastes run to Michener, Clavell, and Uris. I like sweeping historical novels that are entertaining and informative. I can't read a book for sheer pleasure like John Le Carré's. There was always an echo in my mind: "Ken, you're wasting your time. Try to learn as much as possible."

Others used different devices. David Murray strummed his guitar. Steve Podborski read science fiction, obsessively. Jim Hunter reviewed the Bible.

Several times in the Alps we hooked up briefly with the great Canadian Grand Prix racer, Gilles Villeneuve. Steve and I also travelled to Belgium and California to see him race. These meetings meant a lot to us. A strong bond was quickly formed because we were Canadians competing abroad, in sports that meant more to Europeans than Canadians. We also shared sports where many calculated risks were involved. We implicitly understood the passion of competing at the razor's edge. His death, in a racing accident, grieved all of us.

There weren't too many occasions when we had free time to enjoy the Europe that Canadian tourists get to see. However, from time to time, during training camps, or at the beginning or end of a long trip, we would have a couple of days to break out of the mountains and savour the other European experience.

I look back very fondly on the memories I share with David Murray of a week we spent between training camps on the Aegean Sea. We wanted to go with the flow, so we left for Greece without an agenda, and stopped at an island near the Turkish coast. We stayed at a ratty, little hotel, on the island of Samos, near the quay. To maintain conditioning, we would run in the clear waters of the Mediterranean. We explored a Greek Orthodox Church, sat out for dinner in uncovered restaurants to enjoy the view of the evening sea, and learned to appreciate the foul-tasting Greek wine called retsina, with moussaka and baclava. There was also time for the short sea voyage to the island of Kos, which is said to have been home to Hypocrates, and on to Rhodes to inspect the castles built by the Hospitaler knights.

I could never sleep in a car when we were travelling on the World Cup. I enjoyed staring out the window as history rolled by too much.

I have many favourite vistas and drives in Europe. One is through the Brenner Valley, which connects southern Europe to the north through a cleft in the mountains, in northern Italy. This is part of the German-speaking South Tyrol (the Italians call it the Alto Adige). When the Austro-Hungarian Empire collapsed during the First World War, the land and the people on it became Italian. To this day, German is widely spoken, and the architecture is very Austrian — but the telephones and the postal system, which aren't very good, are Italian!

I like the Brenner best in the spring or fall, when the expressway, on the valley floor, is bereft of snow, but the peaks are coated in white majesty. Castles guard the route, and my imagination runs right back to the time of the Romans, who used this path and others, to spread their sphere of influence to the other side of the mountains.

It is this kind of knowledge, so much of which was picked up haphazardly as we made our way across the continent, that stays with me today. In the same way, I acquired a good, working knowledge of German and French, and a smattering of a few other tongues, and the ability to understand and appreciate the cuisines and customs of more than a dozen countries. I can differentiate between a dozen tasty wursts, and can understand why the men who run the *heisse maroni*, or hot nut stands, do such a roaring trade at races such as Kitzbühel.

Many Europeans opened their hearts and even their homes to us. For an autograph, a customs agent would volunteer to let us jump the queue, and an innkeeper would offer me his best wine and his best room. We got to meet royalty, such as the Crown Prince of Liechtenstein, and celebrities from other sporting realms like race drivers, Villeneuve, and Nicki Lauda, cyclist Eddie Merckz, tennis stars Björn Borg and Henri Laconte.

For all the hours of misery and isolation in faraway training camps, these were the privileges of life on the tour that are hardest to measure and forget. They are the great, intangible benefits of a decade spent on the White Circus.

THE
SERVICEMEN _____

CHAPTER ELEVEN

S ERVICE REPRESENTATIVES aren't known by name to most ski fans, but to racers and coaches they are the glue holding the White Circus together. Without a good serviceman, a racer hasn't a chance. An association with the very best of these generally quiet, self-effacing Europeans can sometimes make a good racer unbeatable.

For a European from a town or village near or in the Alps, work on the World Cup as the representative of a major ski company is a highly desirable job. It confers a social status and local celebrity similar to that which attaches to a lad from hockey-mad Kirkland Lake or Prince Albert, if he becomes equipment manager or trainer with a National Hockey League team.

The responsibilities of a ski rep are much greater than those of an equipment manager or trainer in most other professional sports. To paraphrase British ski journalist, John Samuel, for something so simple-looking, a ski is a complicated piece of machinery. It is the serviceman's job to make sure it works.

He is the company man's mechanic for ski racing's version of the pit stop, responsible for last-second adjustments to the racer's wheels. He is part chemist and part walking encyclopedia. He must know how dozens of different waxes, and more than a dozen different pairs of finely-sharpened skis, will respond to different kinds of snow and snow temperatures. He must also serve as a consultant and strategist on the hill, helping to coax an extra few hundredths of a second out of a reluctant mountain.

In the winter, the serviceman's days are much longer and more demanding than anyone else's on the tour. They begin with 5:00 a.m. or 6:00 a.m. wake-up calls. Then the morning is spent on frozen Alpine pitches, clocking times, taking temperature, humidity and snow composition readings, and watching, always watching how the skis perform.

The mountain work is followed by quick, late lunches and long, lonely evenings in dank hotel cellars. There, amid the confusion of thirty or forty ski bags, and dozens of skis, standing over a long, narrow table not unlike an ironing board, the serviceman quietly works his magic. Under a small spotlight, in a thin fog of wood- and plastic-dust, and wax fumes, he usually spends four or five hours in his blue work-frock, sharpening, shaving, drilling, and sandpapering race implements. As the result of what he learned earlier on the mountain, he broods over and toys with a painter's chest full of wax. Finally, he applies different combinations and amounts of goo to the two pairs of skis per racer which have been selected for use the next day. This done, he blow-dries the ski, and cleans them up for action.

At week's end, when the training and racing are over, the skis are bagged, the board and a jumble of cords, heaters, files, and lathes are packed into crates for shipment to the next stop. There the process is repeated.

When time and geography permit, servicemen leave their teams for a few hours to visit their factories. There, the camber and base of the skis are checked and modified, or skis are exchanged for the next stage of the World Cup. Talks are also held with the scientists who design and make the skis. They furnish the servicemen with the latest computer-generated results from the test track, and give them informed opinions on the performance of their skis, and those of other companies against which they have been competing.

The best reps insinuate themselves gently into the fabric of a team. They act as friends and confidants to the most committed racers and coaches. If need be, they are father figures or honest brokers between feuding racers, or between racers and coaches.

Beyond their skiing lore, servicemen often possess treasure-troves of information about practical subjects such as: Which road do we take to Crans Montana if the St. Bernard Tunnel is closed? Do I need to put chains on the car this year to get over the Reschenpass? Where can I buy my girlfriend a nice ring? My mother a nice painting? Does this town have a good bakery? Is the area code for Salzburg 6222? Do I need a suit and tie to appear on *Sport am Montag* in Vienna? Everything.

In return for devotion to his company and his team, the serviceman is paid a modest salary, and provided with a liberal expense account. He may see little besides downhill courses and ski rooms, but from October to April he travels to the best, most renowned ski resorts in Europe, North America, and Asia. If he's with a winner, it can be a gratifying life.

During the off-season, the serviceman's world slows down. Except for occasional, fairly relaxed jaunts to Argentina, Chile, Australia, or New Zealand, one or two glacier camps in the Alps, and brief visits to the factory to speak with the eggheads about their latest creations, he sits at home, recuperating.

The best serviceman I've met is Hans Rammelmueller. After a series of hardworking, well-intentioned, but ineffectual servicemen, it was our immense good fortune to have him assigned to us in the autumn of 1977 by the Fischer Ski Company. Before that, he had been a Fischer representative on the Europa Cup, preparing skis for junior racers in regional and provincial programs in Austria. His work there had been good enough to put him on the World Cup when we badly needed a serviceman.

Hans had no idea what he was getting into when he joined us. After our great successes of the 1975-1976 season, when we had won at Val d'Isère and Schladming, and done well at several other World Cup fixtures, we had a miserable winter in 1976-1977. Our Fischer serviceman at the time was Colin Sanders, a Canadian. He was shattered by our lack of results. His inability to establish a good working rapport with the other Fischer reps, and with the factory, may have contributed to our poor showing. It wasn't for lack of effort on Colin's part; more than anything it was a language barrier. He was simply unable to get us the technical information we had to have. With Hans we never had that problem.

Rammelmueller is from Grieskirchen, a small farming community of perhaps 10,000 people and several dozen churches in conservative, hard working, Roman Catholic Oberosterreich. His home was about fifteen kilometres from the Fischer factory at Ried, and only a little further away from the West German and Czechoslovakian borders.

He is a tall, reedy man with kindly brown eyes, a ruddy complexion, and longish, brown hair that always seems to be askew, like that of a rebellious boy. His father had worked for Austrian Railways as a train switcher. His mother was a housewife. Despite a few English lessons at school he was, then, almost unilingual, and very shy. I'm not at all sure that he had ever spoken with a non-German speaker before he was assigned to our team. In our first weeks together, all our conversations were in German.

It was lucky that at the time Hans joined us, the Canadian team also engaged a brilliant new downhill coach, Heinz Kappeler, of Switzerland. Like so many of his countrymen, Heinz spoke three or four languages, including good, idiomatic English. His German was an opaque Zurich dialect, while Hans spoke another form of Low German, complicated by influences from the Alpine provinces of Tyrol and Salzburg. When together, the men spoke stilted High German while we, the racers, muddled through with a mishmash of English, and what we called "Mountain" German.

Until Hans and Heinz signed on with us, the Canadian team had only English-speaking coaches and service representatives, so this new situation took some getting used to. But, with Heinz's linguistic skills, and goodwill all around, we quickly became comfortable with one another.

At the time the Europeans were still unsure about our technical capabilities. They thought we won because of the foolish risks we took. Hans seemed to share this opinion. But he changed his mind after watching us closely for several hours one day in Hintertux, while we trained slalom and giant slalom gates. When we came down for lunch he was bubbling with enthusiasm.

"You guys actually know how to ski!" he told us.

After lunch we started into our specialty, the downhill, and he became even happier. A bond was formed that was to last until the Sarajevo Olympics in 1984.

The Austrian and Swiss teams treated their servicemen as peons. Of course, they had a different situation. Half a dozen first-rate servicemen, each from competing companies, travelled with them at all times. It was impractical to include a mob in all team activities and decisions. We had a much smaller, more cohesive unit, with only one or two servicemen, so it was much easier for Hans to feel like one of us. The goal, as our head coach, John Ritchie, put it to us that fall, was to fool him into believing he was a Canadian.

The best way to please him was to perform well on the hill, but we also tried to include him in our other activites. If there was a party, he was invited. When he came to Canada, he stayed with us in our homes. When we had a rare day off in Europe, we often spent it with him and his family.

Whenever I had the chance, I sought to drive with Hans, and not just because he had the nicest car. (It *was* the nicest car, though.) Although he was probably the most naturally humble and introspective man I've ever met, on long drives through the Arlberg and Brenner passes — the main avenues from Austria to Switzerland and Italy — he would loosen up and spin long, convoluted yarns about his country and his place in it. I would hardly call him a gossip, but he had a store of lore about the Austrian psyche, and the arcane world of ski racing. He was tuned into Fischer's high tech world, and could confirm or debunk the stories which spilled out of the Austrian camp every few days, about exciting new technologies and the latest personal tribulations of their racers. As our German improved so did his English. The relationship bloomed.

Two incidents illustrate the special position Hans came to occupy on the Canadian team. In 1978, our coaches included him in our delegation for the Opening Ceremony at the World Championships in Garmisch-Partenkirchen. I'm sure he was the only ski rep in the parade. In 1980, when Steve Podborski and I joined several of the best European racers at a gala in honour of Olympic medallists, Hanni and Andy Wenzel in Vaduz, with the Crown Prince of Licchtenstein presiding, we insisted that Hans join us. Dozens of the best racers in the world were there but, once again, the train switcher's son from Oberosterreich was the only serviceman present.

Once we began to win, it was not easy for us to keep Hans with the Canadian team. Within a year or two of his arrival, it was widely acknowledged that he had become one of the leading servicemen in the world. Inevitably, the Austrians wanted him for their big team. The Austrian team was the Fischer Ski Company's biggest ski racing advertisment. Such a move would clearly be a promotion for Hans. But he resisted all approaches until the last of the Crazy Canucks had retired. Even then, he wanted to stick with Canada, but Fischer and the great Austrian racers, Erwin Resch and Harti Weirather, insisted he switch. Because Canada no longer had any first seed racers on Fischer skis (Todd Brooker was with Head Skis)

Hans could refuse no longer. To this day he remains a Fischer rep with the Austrian team.

During his seven years with the Canadian team, Hans tried to keep as much as possible of what he was doing in his head. He wanted feedback from us about how his experiments were going, but he felt for us to know too much about the process by which he reached his selections would be counter-productive. Ski selection and preparation were his lookout. As he told me so often, the athlete's job was to take care of himself, to show up in good time, and be physically and mentally prepared to wrestle with the mountain. That was challenge enough. The serviceman would take care of the rest. Whatever decisions he made, and he made hundreds for us every day, we believed in them. We trusted him with our lives.

We had to be interested in the technologies being introduced, because to ignore them could be perilous, but none of us became really familiar with such things as the compounds that went into making waxes. Our task was to keep abreast of larger developments, such as the move to poles that were custom-fitted in wind tunnel tests to curve around each racer's tuck position, and to skin-tight downhill suits. Both developments made for a more aerodynamic, and therefore faster, ride.

Hans did offer us a few insights into the practical applications of technology during the long hours we shared with him at the Fischer test track at Tauplitz. To get things just right was a terribly time-consuming process. It often meant long evenings under arc-light, testing skis as much as fifteen times in temperatures of say, minus ten degrees. The next day Hans and the scientists would be hoping for minus-fifteen degree temperatures, so they could try some other skis or waxes. Why, one time, we waited until midnight to get minus-twenty degree conditions.

Tauplitz was the first test track custom-built by any ski firm. It revolutionized the way ski manufacturers approached the sport, but life there was monotonous. The village was nothing more than a couple of forlorn hotels situated on the top of a little hill, in an out-of-the-way valley about an hour east of Schladming, in the province of Styria. There was no place where I could go for a run. There was absolutely nothing to do but test skis. It drove me stir crazy. I couldn't stand the place, but every time I returned from there to the World Cup, I had good results. It served us well.

By the spring of 1978, both Steve and I were progressing well. We were both in the first seed and, as a team, we had managed to make up most of what we had lost in 1976-1977. We weren't at the top of the world, but we were close enough to feel good about our chances for next season. When we flew home from Europe, we were looking forward to a special series of slalom and giant slalom races at Fernie and Kimberley, British Columbia, and on my home hill, Lake Louise, Alberta.

This was the first time Hans crossed the ocean to be with us for the spring series. Although the races were of little consequence, they gave him a chance to get to know us better, and to learn a little about our roots. We'd seen Europe through his eyes. Now we wanted to show off a bit of our Canada.

I remember meeting him proudly at the spanking new Calgary International Airport, and then taking him around town to see the gleaming office towers and high-rises, which oil and natural gas dollars had recently built.

Hans' first impression was one of surprise. Calgary was my hometown and, yes, on a clear day you could see the mountains, but the mountains weren't on my doorstep, as they were for all the Austrian racers. He marvelled that World Cup racers could be born and raised in such an urban setting. As this jibed with our own proud assessment, we were pleased by the observation.

From Calgary, we set out by car for Fernie, breaking for lunch at a truck stop in the Crowsnest Pass. Over a hamburger, someone asked Hans what he thought of Canada now that he had travelled cross-country for a few hours. His English was still fractured. His enigmatic reply sounded something like: "Not bad, better a little maybe than Italy."

Italy! We always ate well there and the people were unfailingly kind but, except for the Ladino- and German-speaking southern Tyrolean valley of Val Gardena, it was the most disorganized and least prosperous place we visited in Europe. We were shocked for a moment. We took his comment to heart, as if it was a mean joke or a reproach. But as we talked later among ourselves about his response, we began to understand. That particular corner of the country is very beautiful, but its buildings are not the newest, nor are its inhabitants the most affluent. It is not Whistler, brash and booming, or Banff, staid and prosperous. It is a slice of Canada that has not yet been fully assimilated into the modern world.

Hans was from a nation re-built from the ashes of the Second World War. It had an abundance of postcard-perfect, well-developed Alpine locales, bought and paid for many times over by tourists from West Germany and northern Europe. When he visited Italy, it was as if he was propelled back into the 1950s, or earlier. To him the Crowsnest was no different. It was also a backwater, not a full participant in the western economy.

He was never one for vacations in the south of France, or the beaches of Mombassa, or for hobnobbing with the jet-setters at Kitzbühel. As much as he travelled, Hans was always happiest driving home to Grieskirchen to spend a few days with his parents and his school friends.

Only once did I cross Hans. It happened after a very bad downhill race in 1979, in heavy snow, at Villars, Switzerland. The course played to my weakness. It was nothing but flats. In such circumstances, I counted heavily on my skis to bail me out. In this case they performed sluggishly, and I finished well behind the rest of the first seed, and twenty or thirty other racers as well. Without bothering to look at the score-board to confirm what I already knew, I stormed through the finish. I was furious at myself for having allowed a season that had begun well, to trickle away.

A few weeks before, I had had a victory seized from me at Morzine, France, because I had worn a supposedly illegal suit. The Villars results, my worst of the season by far, had now been twinned with my Morzine disqualification. As it was the final European downhill of the season, I had lost my last two chances at a result which would have won me Canada's first World Cup downhill medal.

I realized this the moment I crossed the finish line. Something within me snapped. Without removing my race skis, I bolted from the finish area for our hotel, a mile or two away. I was angry at my skis for having betrayed me. I didn't care that it was a gravel road that I skied on. By the time I reached the hotel, the skis were pocked and ruined. Not satisfied with this, I hurled them to the ski room floor and tromped upstairs for lunch.

About half an hour later, Hans arrived from the mountain. Because the skis had been slow, I expected an apology. Instead, when I looked up from my food, I could see from his face that Hans was agitated. Normally the most gentle and congenial of men, he was now in a rare rage.

"You must always respect your equipment," he shouted at me, and the team, and the whole restaurant. "Even if they didn't work for you today, they could work for you another time. They have been carefully selected and tested. I know they're good because I've spent hundreds of hours with them. They could have been winners at Aspen or somewhere else. Because of your childish tantrum, how can these skis ever do anything again? You have trashed them. This is unprofessional. This is unacceptable."

When Hans was finished berating me, I think I tried to excuse my behaviour, saying that a lot of different pressures had come down on me at exactly the same time, but he would have none of it.

Needless to say, I was chagrined. I cannot explain why I had not thought of the skis in quite this way. My fury at the result had driven thoughts about anything else away.

Hans had bluntly reminded me of the cardinal rule of downhill racing: a racer must treat his skis like a special girlfriend. Skis are to be handled with respect and affection. Meticulous care must be taken at all times to ensure that no harm — not even a nick — scars or blemishes the base of the ski. That's why we carefully laid plastic over the tips every time we finished racing. I had let my serviceman down.

FEAR
OF
FALLING _____ *CHAPTER TWELVE*

DOWNHILL RACING IS A SPORT which sometimes leaves competitors permanently maimed. On rare occasions, it is a killer. This knowledge is stored in every cell of every racer's brain.

Fear governs everything that happens in downhill racing. It is also the only taboo on the White Circus. No one talks about it. No one wants to think openly about it. It's stuck in the back of the subconscious, much like a horrible nightmare. It seldom surfaces. It never goes away.

Which racer can forget the Canadian Corner, the Austrian Hole, the Italian Hole, Collombin's Bump, the Camel Bumps? Each has abruptly destroyed the careers of several racers.

To defeat these demons and the fear they inspire, racers ignore them. When they crash, they try to forget about it as quickly as possible. When someone else crashes, lame jokes are made, or racers avert their eyes. There is a macho argot that sums up and trivializes what has happened. He did a "face plant." She "augured in." He "bought the farm."

If it is a teammate or a friend who has gone down, it can be terribly hard to deal with. But we were callous about it. We surrounded ourselves with an unreal sense of well-being, and tried not to relate to what happened across the way. At the bottom, or in the hotel, we might commiserate with a fallen rival. On the hill, we concentrated on not making the same mistake.

The mental goal of the downhill racer is to explore the outer limits of his mind and body, become comfortable with them, and then stretch beyond them to a new frontier. If he is ossified by fear, this is not possible. Some racers are never able to deal with it. They never attain the confidence that allows them to push to the absolute limits. This supreme self-confidence is what separates the best from the rest. Dancing on the razor's edge is the essence of downhill racing.

Some who watch downhill racing think it is incredibly dangerous, and that those who practise it are a little daft. But they only see a man in a skintight, plastic suit plummeting off a precipice. They do not see what he sees. If done properly the race is a controlled freefall, a stupendous, thrilling experience.

The danger varies according to the skill of the skier. A good recreational skier can be comfortable and exhilarated by speeds of perhaps fifty kilometres per hour, and a bump that launches him five or six metres. Double or triple the speed and the distance he is thrown off the bump, and he is lost. But put a skier with two or three times the strength, technique, and experience into this situation: it should work out all right.

The slalom and giant slalom events are straightforward. There is a pole. Turn around it as fast as you can.

In downhill, speed is also crucial, but the principle by which it is achieved is completely different. A racer must find the most direct trajectory that is also safe. To do this, he must memorize the course, and then react to it instantaneously, as it hurtles towards him. There is no place for foolish or risky maneouvres. If he does anything rash or ill-conceived, he'll end up down and out.

The downhill learning process is begun when a skier is about twelve or fourteen years old. At each step along the way, there are hundreds of little tests and lessons to deal with. They are about carving high-speed turns, maintaining aerodynamic body shape, and pre-jumping or beginning a jump so that the landing is controlled. These tests make good skiers become better skiers. Ultimately, they teach a skier his limits, so that there is no fear. Confidence is the password that permits entry to the next stage. Only a handful of athletes in the world develop the physical, technical, and psychological suppleness needed to complete the course, and advance to the first seed of the World Cup.

When standing in the starting gate, I always had in my mind's eye an idea of exactly how I wanted to ski. Every single facet of the hill, every ripple, bump, knoll, bend, sidehill traverse, drop-away, and fall-away, and each type of snow and ice to be skied above, on, or around was etched in my memory.

I could recall having passed small ripples in the snow, and pine tree boughs on the side of the course which I had noticed during inspection runs. I knew exactly how I intended to use them as guideposts to mark my progress down the slope. In the real world, on the actual run, there would be mistakes. I would miss a corner or fly off a bump a few millimetres too early or late. When I made an error, or my body failed to execute a command I would try, once again from memory, to adapt. The ideal trajectory became the actual trajectory. There was a surprising amount of time for the mind to identify and solve problems, because the body was doing most of the work by rote, reacting instantaneously to the course.

Even at 130 kilometres per hour I saw my way clearly. A slow-moving panorama would unfold before me. I saw all the guideposts I was looking for. It was often as if what my eyes were seeing was a slow-motion film of the run.

When a driver makes a turn in his car, he doesn't have to get out to figure out where the curb is. His brain has calculated its position and decided the proper margin for the turn. Negotiating a turn on skis is no different than spinning the wheel of a car. I knew were my body was and where it should be going. My mind analyzed the arc that was necessary so I could flow smoothly on to the next bit of track. My actions were governed by technical requirements. A tight turn, properly held, usually meant that I carried more speed and momentum on to a straightaway. But sometimes, like a truck hauling a semitrailer, the best way to get around a curve was to go wide and then jack-knife back in. I got information for these decisions from memory, even if the memory was only two seconds old.

Downhill racing involves anticipation. Look ahead, never behind. What's over is done with. If a big mistake had been made, I had to work my way out of it by taking a calculated risk. An automatic, unthought-of, unrehearsed reaction or adaptation would usually pull me out of trouble. There was an adrenalin rush after really close calls, but the mind and the eye were already scouting five or ten seconds down the course for new problems. It wasn't until I crossed the finish line, and stopped and relaxed for a minute or two, that I could recollect what had actually happened to me on the way down.

If some of this process is hard to follow, it is because it is almost impossible to explain. The skier is guided by instinct, almost by feel. Sometimes I felt that my senses had acquired an extra dimension. It was something that welled up within me. And then I knew when and how to take unplanned, but perfectly calculated risks. These moments were mystical. It was like being in a state of grace. They happened to me several times a year. It happened, for example, at Kitzbühel, in 1980.

About ninety seconds down the Streif, at the very moment when my legs and heart began to cry uncle, I was launched down an ice wall at 130 kilometres per hour. Despite the great speed, and the wild gravitational pulls that jerked me forward and to the side, and the certain knowledge that if I tumbled I would be in considerable distress, I let my skis run loose while tucking across a steep, rough, traverse. To the untrained eye I looked totally out of control. I wasn't. In fact, provided that my equipment performed properly, the risk was minimal. If I kept my skis as square as possible, and my hands outstretched for balance, I knew I would survive. I surrendered myself to the mountain. I knew I could do it, and I knew I had to do it, if I was to have a chance of winning.

A lot of people have the notion that falling in downhill is like stepping out of a fast-moving car. It is not like that at all. The racer is usually on an incline, which means that if he does fall, his body momentum is pushing him forward. Gravity pulls him in the same direction along a path which also happens to offer the least resistance. Snow, even at 130 kilometres per hour, is much more forgiving than it looks. You just slide on it.

Falling on a flat is more hazardous because the slope of the mountain is against you. It's like the difference between throwing a rock down a water slide and skipping it across water. There is a lot more impact on the flat surface.

Worse yet is to crash into a compression, with your momentum carrying you up the hill. You decelerate quickly. It's like hitting a brick wall.

But most falls are less perilous than they look to outsiders. Resort operators on the tour have to meet high safety standards before a race can take place. There are nets, fences, and "willy bags," which absorb the impact of a crash. It is almost impossible for a downhill racer to run into a spectator or a tree stump or a rock. The track is a secured area. The enemies that can ensnare and hurt you are most often your own equipment or a gate.

There are certain hazards, however, that create the possibility of a very serious injury. High speed bumps are often dangerous. If they are not properly pre-jumped, a racer can be launched the length of a football field. At St. Moritz one year, half a dozen racers were hospitalized because of such a bump. A crowd of photographers, alerted to the possibilities by the first crash, gathered below the bump to shoot award-winning pictures. Some German-language newspapers loved to run headlines describing such multiple accidents as *sturzfest,* or "crash parties." The racers never shared their enthusiasm for such occurrences.

Every downhill racer, no matter how competent or careful, will fall at least once or twice a year, in training, in timed trials, or in races. What a racer wants to avoid, if possible, is a high-speed or low-speed accident. If a racer goes down at high speed, the sheer impact of his fall, and the distance it tosses him, mean that he is going to be banged up. Slow-speed spills may cause the body to be twisted and slowly torn apart. There is often less danger in a medium-speed crash, because the body only bounces a little and then stops.

When a racer crashes it is almost always because he has made a mistake. It usually happens so quickly that there is no time to think about it. When I fell, my mind would go blank because the plan wasn't working. Then, automatically, a trained reaction took over. I forced my body to relax. I simply let things go because there was no use fighting. To fight, the body must be rigid, and to be rigid is to invite trouble. Skis and bindings were usually blown away in an instant by the sheer force of the impact.

If I was sliding I couldn't get hurt. A tumble was more problematical, but if I relaxed, the odds were that I'd simply roll like a ball down the hill. It might seem strange to allow oneself to become a rolling human ball at 100 kilometres per hour, but it is amazing how much abuse a rolling body can endure, and still get up again to walk away normally. Only one in twenty or one in thirty crash victims needs to be taken away in what we called "the meat wagon."

My first thought when I came to a stop was whether all the parts of my body were where they should be, and whether they felt the way they should. My next reaction was to bail out quickly from wherever it was I had come to rest. Unless it was a straightforward crash, I was always a bit disoriented: I would have no sense of the time that had elapsed. In timed trials, racers are launched at thirty second intervals. I had no desire to have the next skier land on top of me.

The worst part of dealing with a fall was the morning after. I was often sore and banged up. The damage was generally slight: bruises and strawberries; muscles and ligaments that had been slightly overtaxed. But every twinge and ache reminded me that I had screwed up.

The best way to deal with a mishap is to get back up the mountain and run the course again. This was most difficult to do when the crash occurred on the eve of a race. Then, I not only had to ski the course again, but I had to try to push myself to the limit to win it.

I was fortunate. I seldom crashed on the World Cup tour. But I hated it when it happened. At the place where I fell, I would almost feel that a psychological block had been created. Was I up to it or not? Moving to the next venue was always a relief because the memory of a crash could then be put behind me. By the time I returned twelve months later, I had had lots of time in the off-season to think about what had happened and why. By then the barrier was dissolved. I always felt confident that I had found a solution. It wouldn't happen again.

I prided myself on keeping all my parts intact. But my luck ran out on me, at a race in Garmisch-Partenkirchen in January, 1981. I made a mental error and I paid for it with my knee.

I had had the fastest interval times as I swung into the final corner, a left-hander, a few metres above the finish line. I leaned in on my uphill ski to make the gate and, as I did so, the uphill ski tracked out. I didn't have my weight sitting on it properly. The inside ski hit the outside ski and down I went, face first. I could think of nothing except that the finish line was only five or six seconds away, and that I wasn't going to make it.

The impact of the fall knocked me out. When I came to, a few seconds later, I knew that something was very wrong. I had had the wind knocked out of me, so that I couldn't drag myself off the course without assistance. I almost couldn't move at all. I knew that I'd cut my forehead, and that my nose was smashed, because blood was splattering everywhere. Course helpers pulled me out of harm's way almost immediately. I had the wherewithal to take my other ski off (the binding had not let go) and I sat in the snow, trying to collect my thoughts.

Someone told me in German that I had a bad gash on my forehead, and that I'd probably broken my nose. It was slightly askew. Those injuries sounded survivable. What troubled me was that, when I took my ski off, my knee buckled. Ominously, there was was no pain at all.

In the ambulance, I kept running through a checklist of what could be wrong. Everything was fine except my knee, which felt funny. At the hospital, they released a statement saying that I had facial lacerations, but would be able to compete seven days later, at Kitzbühel.

The Canadian physician, Dave Ellis of Nanaimo, BC, was not so sure. He said there was evidence of at least third-degree tears in the knee joint. He advised me to fly home to meet with his colleague, Pat McConkey, in Vancouver.

In fact, the anterior cruciate and the medial collateral ligaments were torn in the left knee. When both ligaments rip, there is no pain. Until a few years before my accident, the technology to repair ligaments sufficiently to allow a skier to return to competition was still primitive; the medical solution to the problem was retirement. Now they staple one ligament back on and find replacement material for another (the semitendinosis, in my case) and, presto! it is possible to ski race again six or eight months later. If there had been damage to the cartilage I would have been in big trouble.

I'd fallen. I'd hurt myself fairly badly. I'd lost the rest of the season. Now I had to deal for the first time with the frustration of sitting on the sidelines, and watching others compete. And that wasn't the worst part of it. At the time of the injury, I was in superb shape. Watching my body wither away in a hospital bed was one of the most disheartening experiences of my life.

The operation at St. Paul's Hospital, in Vancouver, took place on a Tuesday evening. Twenty-four hours later I felt chipper enough to do a few chin-ups. Within two days I was into twice-a-day mini-circuits in my hospital room. It was all new to me, but I was determined to come back and face my fear.

Re-building my body after surgery was a long, difficult, painful process. For several months, the knee was very fragile. To avoid re-injuring it, I had to be very careful about what I did. For a minimum of three hours a day, for the next ten months, I did what is jokingly referred to as the "Tahoe Marathon" because it was created at South Lake, Tahoe, by the US ski team physician, Dick Steadman, who operates one of the world's leading rehabilitation clinics.

For half an hour at a time I pumped away at a Cybex machine, working with various levels of resistance, and at different tempos to re-build the fast- and slow-twitch muscles in my thighs and hamstrings. With my knee weakened, they would have to take on additional tasks. The routine also involved running in water, cycling and pharatic, or electrical stimulation of some of the muscles that had atrophied. On top of all this, I tried to stick as closely as possible to my usual off-season training regime. The rest of my body had to be able to handle ski racing again, too.

By late August, 1981, I was on skis, albeit cautiously, at a training camp in New Zealand. Four months later I was racing at Val d'Isère.

At a dinner in Annecy, France, several days before the season opener, Robert Nylander, international competition director for Salomon made me a bet. While sampling the Beaujolais *nouveau* and cheese over dinner, I had jokingly said that the only reason I kept ski racing was that the organizers at Val d'Isère had neglected to give me the traditional fifty kilo wheel of Beaufort cheese when I won there in 1975. I kept coming back, I told him, because I wanted to win the cheese — which happens to be my favourite. Robert countered with a challenge: if I finished in the top fifteen, Salomon would buy me the wheel.

I thought it would be easy. After several training runs in which I finished no better than twentieth, however, I wasn't so sure. But after eleven months of rehabilitation, I intended to make my return to competition successful. I didn't win, but my fifth-place finish showed my competitors, and myself, that I was back. Salomon duly came through with the cheese and, with the addition of a case of the new wine, we had a fine celebration. We were joined by most of the English-speaking crew on the White Circus, and by happy coincidence, the Swiss and Canadian women's teams, as well. In all, it was an evening to remember.

V
THE
SEASON
OF 1980

KITZBÜHEL_____ CHAPTER THIRTEEN

S OME VISITORS TO KITZBÜHEL say that the residents there have
an arrogance and conceit unmatched by the citizens of any
other World Cup resort. The detractors claim this haughtiness
shows at times as outright hostility towards the tens of thousands of outsiders who provide the town with most of its
income.

Although this assessment may be too sharp and simplistic,
I cannot disagree: some Kitzbühelers are conceited over the
gift God bestowed upon them.

But what a gift! Kitzbühel possesses what is widely considered to be the best downhill course in the world. The towns-
people did not seek the honour, but like residents of Wimbledon
or Wembley, they must share their living sports museum with
the world.

Whether they come from the Alpine provinces, the rolling
grasslands of Upper Austria, or the farming region of Burgen-
land on the Hungarian border, the Hahnenkamm holds a very
special place in all Austrian hearts. Over the years it has been
tested and tamed by downhill's most celebrated heroes: Toni
Sailer, Karl Schranz, Roland Collombin, Jean-Claude Killy,
and Franz Klammer among them.

The racers see the Hahnenkamm Streif course as the most
difficult of the downhills because it incorporates all the elements of ski racing. There are steep pitches, flats, high- and
low-speed traverses, rough terrain, wild bumps, deep compres-
sions, rollers, and icy pitches. Parts of the mountain intimi-
date. Others are almost too easy, lulling competitors into
inattentiveness. Lake Placid is a glider's course, and the straight
run at Schladming is made for speedsters, but Kitzbühel gives
no racer an absolute advantage. Technical skiers are fastest at

the top. Gliders are best through the middle, and the most confident, daring skiers are the quickest through the last third of the course. The best skier wins.

And there is also the historical factor. Kitzbühel occupies a special place in the history of skiing. The Hahnenkamm and Wengen's Lauberhorn are the only classic downhill courses. They follow trails that were first marked out for ski racing in the 1930s. Kitzbühel's course has been widened a little, but everything has been done to preserve its original character. The only significant change is the speed with which racers now navigate the mountain. Where once it took almost five minutes, it now takes racers less than two to reach the valley floor.

Spectators enjoy Kitzbühel because so much of the course is accessible. A ten-minute cable car trip lifts to the top of the mountain those who wish to watch the unparalleled thrills and spills in the Mausfalle or the Steilhang. Those with strong legs can climb up the side of the hill to the Hausbergkante or beyond, and view the action from a pasture or meadow. The less ambitious can watch from almost anywhere on the southwest side of town, as racers cross the last, wild sidehill traverse and drop into the compression that propels them across the finish line. The view from this huge, natural bowl lasts about thirty seconds. No other course puts a racer in full view of tens of thousands of spectators for more than the blink of an eye.

Kitzbühel is more than the home of the best, most storied downhill race. It is a ski pageant, played out every year in a town that is much older and more interesting than any other ski resort I've visited.

The old town is still partially walled-in. Everywhere, ancient archways and buildings have been protected and preserved. Interspersed with relics of the days when Austria was a nation to be reckoned with are fragments of the modern Kitzbühel, a glittering Las Vegas of discos, casinos, raunchy bars, and subdued five-star hotels, pricey jewellery and skiwear shops, overpowered cars, and overdressed ladies and gentlemen.

A natural advantage Kitzbühel enjoys over most Alpine resorts is its location, smack in the middle of Europe, close to high speed autobahns and rail arteries which run west into the German heartland, north to the Iron Curtain, east to Vienna, and south to the Mediterranean.

A train track bisects the valley, running within fifty metres of the mountain. From the main station to the finish line is a ten-minute walk. From a small station by the tramway entrance it takes only three minutes to find a prime viewing place. And drivers can easily get into Kitzbühel, too. A tame road — without so much as a single switchback turn — brings spectators up from Wörgl and St. Johann in Tyrol. Innsbruck is less than an hour away by road or rail; Salzburg is two hours; Munich, two and a half hours. Only a little further afield are other major cities like Stuttgart, Frankfurt, and Nuremberg. Amsterdam, Brussels, and Milan are just a day's drive away.

Even the timing of the Hahnenkamm is convenient. It is usually held in late January, making it sort of a mini-festival between Christmas and New Year's celebrations, and the Bavarian and Austrian winter holiday, *Fasching*.

All things considered, it is not surprising that the World Cup race at Kitzbühel has one of the highest television ratings in eastern and western Europe for a downhill race. And, unlike most other races, the Hahnenkamm is also shown to a huge international audience in Canada, the United States, Australia, New Zealand, and Japan. For TV programmers in many countries, it is the focus of their annual downhill coverage. For example, Sweden, which has virtually no downhill team, always celebrates the Hahnenkamm as something special. Why, the great slalom champion, Ingemar Stenmark of Sweden, broke his personal vow never to run a downhill so he could join us there for a race!

Perhaps because of their success, the race organizers at Kitzbühel are sometimes reluctant to accept new ways of doing things. They have been slow at times to accept FIS-mandated safety improvements, such as the provision of "willy bags" for protection at hazardous parts of the course. They have also never acknowledged that in terms of marketing, television, and corporate sponsorships, the North Americans put together a better show. But this is also true of most European World Cup hosts.

Of course, traditions are not a bad thing. It's one reason Kitzbühel is perhaps the favourite stop for the racers, and for the growing number of Canadian, American, and Australian tourists who visit during race week. They've seen the race on television back home and have caught glimpses of the town. They've probably heard exaggerated tales of the great debauches there after Canadian victories. If there is one World Cup race an English-speaking person wants to see in Europe, it must be the Hahnenkamm.

For Kitzbühelers, and for many Europeans, the mountains have a traditional, and even a spriitual significance. Much as hockey in Canada remains a small-town game, with thousands of volunteers putting in millions of hours to make dreams come true for youngsters, the men and women in places like Kitzbühel are truly the keepers of the Alpine flame. During the winter, when their animals are feeding in the valley, many of their spare hours are spent on the mountain with their families, skiing. During the summer, when the animals have been moved into Alpine meadows to graze, I've often seen them walking on the mountain in lederhosen and felt hats — while I've been out surveying the course and planning how to tackle it during the winter. In the fall of 1979 I made a special effort. I climbed the hill twice, once with Steve in September, and again a few weeks later, with Todd Brooker. Farmers told me that they, too, survey the course frequently during the summer while thinking about the race. The Hahnenkamm is the only downhill course I know of which has dozens of sign-posts to show hikers where the racers ski during the winter.

Many Austrian racers also have strong ties to the mountain. Peter Firtzinger, a member of the Austrian team when I joined the World Cup in 1974, was raised and still lives in a house beside the Hausbergkante, about twenty metres from the track. Another star, Hansi Hinterseer, grew up with his grandmother about fifteen metres from the inside turn of Seidlalm. Hinterseer was a good slalom specialist. Although he won the slalom segment of the Hahnekamm in 1974, I think it must always have bothered him that he was never able to qualify for the Austrian downhill team to race on his home course.

Regrettably, it seems to me that Kitzbühel, and most other big European resorts, are producing fewer world class racers than they once did. In the golden era, prior to the 1960s, the town was home to most of the Austrian Olympic and world champions: men like Toni Sailer, Anderl Molterer (known as "The Blitz from Kitz"), Christian Pravda and Hansi Hinterseer's father, Ernst.

As skiing evolved into a big business in the 1960s and 1970s, great numbers of vacationers invaded the quiet mountain villages. Instead of becoming racers, the boys and girls of these villages now became ski teachers, or the proprietors of businesses that make money from skiing. Even for those who want to become racers it is not as easy as it once was. The hills are now crowded with tourists who possess widely-varied degrees of skill. There is little space for local kids to let loose the way their parents and grandparents did.

Towns such as Kitzbühel continue to have racing programs for children, and occasionally families such as the Hinterseers produce some racers for the Austrian team. Six-year-olds from the local ski club are still to be seen whizzing through the Steilhang, but the focus of life in Kitzbühel is no longer fixed solely on the mountain. Today, the best European racers seem to come from smaller, more remote hamlets which are unknown to most ski vacationers. Kids in places such as Wängle in Tyrol, and Saas-Almagel in Switzerland's Valais, still haven't many distractions. They can either become farmers or hoteliers like their fathers and brothers, learn a trade and move to an industrial centre, or become ski racers like Harti Weirather or Pirmin Zurbriggen.

Austrians follow the fortunes of their ski team just as Canadians watch their national team play hockey with the Soviet Union: it is a matter of national pride. But in Austria, there is an additional factor. More than pride is at stake when a World Cup is raced. Ski tourism is a gigantic business in Austria. It employs about one-fifth of the population. Ski manufacturing is of almost equivalent importance. World leaders such as Blizzard, Atomic, Kneissl, Kästle, and Fischer have huge factories located within a few hours' drive of Kitzbühel. The world's second largest ski binding company, Tyrolia, is also set in western Austria. So are dozens of boot and skiwear manufacturers.

When all of these elements are put together, one can see why the pre-eminence of Kitzbühel's Hahnenkamm is of profound importance to Austria and Austrians. It is the best advertisement the ski tourism and manufacturing industries could possibly have.

January 12, 1980

KITZBÜHEL'S PARK HOTEL is a grand mansion in the old, imperial, style with large bedrooms and capacious public halls hung with magnificent chandeliers. In earlier times it must have welcomed counts and countesses from Vienna, and generals and their subalterns on leave from important, far-away posts. Now its days of glory are fading. It is the temporary refuge of swarms of boisterous, unskilled and underfunded ski enthusiasts, from places such as Manchester and Amsterdam. The aristocrats still come to Kitzbühel, but they now must mix with the new rich at more fashionable and far more expensive hotels and restaurants, like the Goldener Greif and the Tenne.

Dowdy it may be, but for us the Park Hotel is ideal. Unlike most modern, Alpine hotels, its long, wide corridors, high ceilings and oversized rooms give us lots of space for stretching and exercising, and for spreading our gear out. It is also favoured by a choice location in a small park, not two minutes removed from the town. More important, for downhill racers intent upon dryland training, it is only a couple of hundred metres to deserted country lanes. From the hotel each morning, I can easily escape Kitzbühel by jogging through quiet backstreets into the wilderness.

I love the way the Zielschuss, or the "run into the finish," looms above and dominates Kitzbühel's southwest side. In the semi-darkness of the early morning I always stop about seventy-five metres from the finish line. Before turning away to complete my loop back to the hotel for breakfast, I stare at this great white wall for a moment in absolute silence, imagining what it will be like to test myself again against the toughest ski mountain in the world.

Breakfasts on race day are different from those on any other day. During training there is some tension because we want to perform well. On race day there is little conversation. Those who trained well are confident, but too absorbed by the challenge ahead to talk much. Those who have not done well in training are still searching for pieces of the puzzle. Others, whose training has left them with doubts and fears, are by turns morose and unnaturally gay. They don't have a hope of doing well and they know it.

The ski company representatives and most of the coaches are gone by the time we make it to the breakfast table at 7:30

or 8:00 a.m., but their voices are very much with us. Every few seconds, two-way radios crackle with news from the mountain. Snow temperature and humidity readings are shouted out and jotted down, to be compared with those taken earlier in the week.

The reps have been up since some ungodly hour, living and breathing the weather. They are under intense pressure from their companies to deliver the right combinations of skis and wax. In the hours before a race, taking into account all the data they can gather, they make the decisions that are crucial to the outcome.

The temperature has remained the same — minus four or five degrees Celsius — but after a week of clear weather, a thin layer of snow has fallen overnight. It is a new factor and it makes us a little anxious.

While my rep, Hans Rammelmueller, frets, the coaches inspect the course for any small changes which the racers ought to know about. Was a corner iced last night by a blow-torch? Was a nasty bump shaved? Has a safety fence been moved? We won't see the course, except at a distance, until we're on it for real. We need every scrap of information. We need it to visualize the course. It is the small stuff of our waking dreams.

I PREFER THE PARK to almost any other hotel we stay in Europe because it is so near the hill. At Val d'Isère or Val Gardena, we have to squeeze into vans every morning to be driven to the lifts. But at Kitzbühel, with a pair of training skis on one shoulder, and a pair of race skis on the other, we can set off on foot for the cable car whenever we feel like it. In an hour or two the rep will bring a second pair of race skis up to us.

By the time we leave the hotel, the town has come alive. An ant-like procession of figures can be seen silhouetted against the snow, making the long, brutal climb up the side of the course to witness the race from one of many the spectacular cliffs or corners. Meanwhile, in the valley, traffic begins to back up on the approach roads, as drivers compete with each other and the *polizei* for any scrap of land large enough to park a car on. These late arrivals will never make it past the first turn on the course. Most will have to be content to watch the race in the natural amphitheatre which surrounds the finish area.

As we make our way through this pleasant, bustling mob, there is a lot of bantering back and forth. Shouts of encouragement are mixed with good-natured catcalls. Their supporters let us know how well the Austrians are going to do. But where are the Austrians? Or the Swiss? Except for a few competitors from some of the fringe nations, such as France, we seldom see any rivals so early in the morning.

Our theory is always to leave enough time to free ski and then, if time remains, to relax and wait for the race. Nine times out of ten we are the first team at the gondola. At Kitzbühel, we leave the hotel at about 9:30 a.m., three hours before the race. The Austrians and Swiss will catch up to us in about an hour.

Even at this hour, there is a long queue waiting for the ride. We are allowed to cut to the front, but that is the full extent of our privilege. In fact, we have to contend with the desire of the tram attendant to push us and our extra-long race skis in with as many as fifty spectators.

The three- or four-minute ascent of Hahnenkamm mountain provides those closest to the windows with a beautiful view of the finish area, and occasional glimpses of the course. What can't be seen from the cable car can be imagined or recalled. For a moment I think of the marvelous free skiing I enjoyed here, four days ago, when David Murray took Canada's World Cup Committee representative, Peter Andrews, and I to places on the mountain I have never been before. There were stretches of powder, and hard-packed moguls, and sunshine . . . it was one of the best days of recreational skiing I've had in my life.

By the time we have ascended the mountain, Hans will have decided how to prepare our skis. Before returning to the hotel to ready them, however, he will chat nervously, briefly, with the other technicians about the race. But they will all be lying to each other, or at least avoiding the truth about what they think. No rep reveals his preparations except, perhaps, to another rep working for the same company — if that rep happens to be a close friend!

WITH HANS, screw-ups on wax and ski selection are very rare, but a recent incident at Val Gardena, in which a senior executive from Fischer ordered him to apply a new wax, fresh from the factory, turned into a disaster. This interference from head office has added to the already complex equation by which the rep tries to choose the best waxes and skis.

This is what happened. At Fischer's running track at Tauplitz, Hans Stroi, the director of development, came up with what he thought was a wonder wax. Rather than have the racers test it there, or in training races on a World Cup course, he rushed it into service on race day at Val Gardena. Our Hans objected, but his complaints went nowhere. All Fischer reps were ordered to apply the wax and shut up. Fearing for his job, Hans told none of us about the switch.

To give Stroi his due, he was the individual principally responsible for the incredible technological revolution in downhill racing in the 1970s. He and his scientists were so successful in the development of new waxes and skis that, for a four- or five-year period in the late 1970s, Fischer absolutely dominated the field. But now Fischer is no longer the clear leader, and Stroi is desperately seeking new compositions to re-assert their supremacy.

What Stroi has begun to do is search for gimmicks. While other companies stick to the bread-and-butter fundamentals of bases and waxes, he has been putting holes in the tips of skis, and plastic balls along their sides. In theory these inventions are sound, but in practice they have not particularly enhanced performance. The new wax looked super on a fifteen-second test track, but in a two-minute race it was a disaster.

With tried and tested methods we had exceptional training results at Val Gardena this winter, but from the first moment on race day, from start position number one, I knew something was very wrong. It was as if glue had been applied to the skis. By picking up every possible hundredth-of-a-second by gliding and tucking, and being as light as a feather in turns, I was able to finish seventh. David Murray, who also skied well, was eleventh. Steve Podborski, with the same wax and good training results, placed forty-fifth. Dave Irwin was fifty-first and two other Fischer first-seed racers, Michael Veith of West Germany, and Toni Buergler of Switzerland, were fifty-third and sixty-second.

Stroi accepted full responsibility for the *débâcle* and promised that he would never again interfere with his servicemen's wax selections. But on the eve of today's Hahnenkamm, he has reversed himself and ordered his servicemen to apply the new wax again.

This time Hans, and the Austrian team's Fischer rep, Hans Bosch, with whom he has shared ideas, turn immediately to our downhill coach, Heinz Kappeler, and explain what is happening, that their jobs have been threatened. Kappeler's advice is to pitch the new wax into the garbage, but tell Stroi it's being used. The two servicemen reluctantly agree to his counsel.

I do not wish to suggest that Stroi wants to sabotage our efforts or those of anyone else. In fact, like all of us, he wants to win. But for some, inexplicable reason, he feels so supremely confident in this new compound that he doesn't think it necessary to test it thoroughly.

So, while I am at the top of the mountain, beginning my final preparations, Hans Rammelmueller is in the cavernous basement of the Park Hotel dying a thousand deaths, while he applies his own chosen wax to my second pair of skis. No matter how the race turns out, Hans is convinced he is about to be sacked.

I know about this little drama because Hans has told me. Rather than add to my worries, it gives me peace of mind. Things are as they should be. My coach and my serviceman are working together. Outsiders are not part of the process.

For my pre-race warmup I wear an old pair of downhill skis, race helmet, race goggles, race boots, race poles, regular ski gloves, a downhill suit, team parka and warmup pants.

The exercise begins with a very slow first run. By "very slow," I mean just that. I ski like a beginner, probably not exceeding ten kilometres per hour. The goal is to stand on my skis and find the right balance point, while getting a feel for my equipment, my timing, and the snow. As I become used to the conditions, I begin carving gentle arcs on the hill.

This morning there is a high haze, and a temperature of minus five, Celsius, at the top of the mountain. The snowfall overnight was light. Chances are the wind, and the activities of the race jury and the hill crew have pushed most, or all of it aside. Conditions are almost the same as they were in training.

The warmup slope I use is beside one of the old, single-chair lifts which farmers operate all over Hahnenkamm mountain. This is actually a cow pasture with the fences pulled back to give us some semblance of a run.

By now I am feeling my way through small bumps and practising little jumps. If something doesn't feel right, I go back and do it again. If there is a little kink in my body, I stretch and work it out.

At this point, I try to banish thoughts of the race for a few minutes. I don't want to dwell on problems I might have in the race. If I don't relax and just watch the world around me — there are thousands of others here getting in some leisure skiing before they watch the race — I could become emotionally tied up in the race long before I need to. This, I know, is dangerous. Such premature worrying can leave a racer worn out just when he needs his energy.

When the warmup is over I retreat to the privacy of the *bergstation*, the chalet-like building that houses the cable car machinery at the top of the hill. The Austrians have a room upstairs in the staff quarters — the best deal. Our room is in the attic. It is here, about forty-five minutes before the race, that I try to relax and get warm again.

This building affords me a chance to study the way Werner Grissman prepares for the downhill. The jovial Austrian veteran is having a merry old time, buzzing around the upper part of the lodge on a kid's tricycle. Others, including me, play darts for a few minutes, or smash a tennis ball against a backboard. Then, suddenly, with about thirty minutes to go before the race, the foolery ends and everyone starts into their race routine. The long johns, turtlenecks and boots come off, and the downhill suits go on. To have put the suit on earlier would have stretched the weave unnecessarily, which would allow air to penetrate and cause a small, but perhaps telling loss of speed. Even at this juncture, we wear only the lower half of the outfit, so we can put our boots on over them. The rest of the costume hangs loose. It will be done up at the last moment. Meanwhile, our masseur and start coach, Terry Spence, applies a brief back massage.

At this point I get some last-minute course information from our coaches. Now I start to think about the race again. I rehearse it in my mind exactly as I did when I was lying in bed this morning.

The first fifteen racers start at 100-second intervals — the timetable is dictated by the needs of television. With a little fresh snow on the track, I know those with the lowest numbers have no chance. The track will be fastest for those at the back of the first seed. I thank my lucky stars that I have drawn number ten. It isn't perfect, but it's a damn sight better than it might have been.

As I walk over to the start hut, I can see Hans standing nearby beside two pairs of my skis. The skis are buried in the snow so they'll be at snow temperature for the race. Every few minutes Hans takes a reading, checks the sky, listens to the radio, and then continues to agonize over which ones to give me.

The start hut at Kitzbühel is like a fish bowl. The racers, start coaches, servicemen, and timers are on the inside, behind a picket fence, surrounded by a semi-circle of spectators who seem to be in awe of the whole process. While the crowd gawks, we discuss strategy with our coaches. A study of the videotapes indicates a tighter line through the Mausfalle might be slightly faster, because the track is smoother and more direct. Another Calgarian, Mike Irwin, agrees to be the guinea pig. Although seeded well back, he is to ski before us, because the jury has decided to have a snow seed of half a dozen racers from the back of the pack run first, to run the track in for the first group. Heinz Kappeler stations himself beside the Mausfalle and calls up an immediate report on Mike's progress by radio. After hearing what he has to say — the new line does not seem to make much difference — we decide that I should stick with the route worked out for me in training.

Once our Mausfalle strategy is sorted out, there is a final problem to be solved before the race. Because I am nervous, I have to head for the trees for the first of several pees. There are people and television cameras everywhere. The skin-hugging downhill suit, and the bulky outer wear I'm dressed in, make these necessary excursions extremely awkward.

When I return to the safety of the enclosure, I find that everyone is facing the race in his own way. Franz Klammer, who won here in 1976, engages in a very vigorous warmup routine. Another Austrian, Uli Spiess, bolts a schnaps. Others merely perform a few squats and bends. My routine falls somewhere in the middle. I spend about five minutes rolling my head, stretching my hamstrings and moving my knees in and out. Then I go down on my haunches and into a trance.

I have found that once I am on the hill, I tend to be extremely aggressive. This can throw off my timing and cause me to

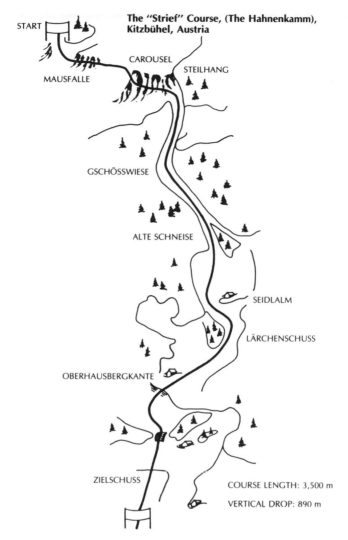

The "Strief" Course, (The Hahnenkamm),
Kitzbühel, Austria

START

CAROUSEL

STEILHANG

MAUSFALLE

GSCHÖSSWIESE

ALTE SCHNEISE

SEIDLALM

LÄRCHENSCHUSS

OBERHAUSBERGKANTE

ZIELSCHUSS

COURSE LENGTH: 3,500 m

VERTICAL DROP: 890 m

make mistakes. The purpose of the trance is to drain my body
of tension and aggression. Until the ski rep and bindings rep
appear to make final adjustments to my skis, my mind is a
blank.

With the skis on, and the start only moments away, I perform a little dance to make sure the skis are comfortable and
secure. As I enter the hut, I quickly imagine the course once
more, with special emphasis on the little touchstones I have
dwelt on in my dreams during the week. Where am I having
problems? How have I decided to solve them?

At this point, little psychological games are being played. I don't want to know how anyone else has done, but an Austrian coach walks by, his radio blaring out the times of those who have already finished. He knows full well that I understand every word. He makes sure I hear, by placing the source of the sound about six inches from my ear. . . .

Terry rubs my legs while I flex my hands and open and close my mouth in an exaggerated way. There is no time to relax now. Years and years of training are coming together to make my actions in the next two minutes automatic.

The race is as good as any dream I've ever had. Except for a small failure in the Carousel, where I push too hard to get into my tuck for the Steilhang, I am on my game. In training, I was seven-eighths of a second slower than the field in the Steilhang, but made up enough between there and the bottom to record the fastest time. With the rest of the field improving every day, I know that today I have to be better.

The problem in the Steilhang is that I haven't been turning fast enough, or soon enough, into or out of the second turn. After the last training run, Heinz Kappeler and I sidestepped the area for half an hour. He pointed out exactly what path I should follow, and what to look for in order to find it. His advice was simple: "Look for the fence and turn as soon as you see it."

As I come over a little rise, I see the fence for the first time all week. Immediately, I hit my edges as hard as I can. Why haven't I thought of this before? The extreme sidehill fall-away and the Steilhang falls into place. It seems so easy. One and a half minutes from the finish line, Kappeler's wisdom has won the race. Having executed his plan for the Steilhang, the rest of the mountain surrenders just as it had in training. The momentum gives me all the advantage I need for the Bruckenschuss and the Alte Schneise. Through the Seidlalm, the skis run smoothly. The Lärchenschuss, the Oberhausberg. No problem. I can tell the skis are gliding well. Hans has done his job perfectly. In the Hausbergkante I get my first glimpse of the finish area. The sides and bottom of the Zielschuss are black with tens of thousands of spectators. To them I am black, too; a black dot against a vast expanse of white, plummeting towards them at 130 kilometres per hour. Driving around the sidehill I struggle to hold an edge on the downhill ski while freefalling across the steep face. With only seconds remaining, the Zeilschuss throws up the final challenges: the incredibly steep drop into the amphitheatre, and the last, treacherous compression. Through the final 150 metres, I begin to brake. As I come to a stop, I catch a glimpse of the finish area timer. It reads 2:04.93. Looking back over my shoulder at the scoreboard, I see my name and nationality flashed across the top — in first place. Peter Müller of Switzerland, is now (temporarily) second with a time of 2:06.34. Twenty minutes later the emerging Austrian star, Harti Weirather, will narrow the lead to fifty-eight hundredths of a second, but that's as close as anyone gets. It is the fourth World Cup victory of my career. But winning at Val d'Isère, Chamonix, and Schladming was nothing like this. For just the second time (Buddy Wemer was the first in 1959), a non-European has won the greatest downhill test there is. A Canadian is on the podium.

FOR THE NEXT TEN HOURS I am fêted as I have never been before. After a few out-of-breath minutes with the print journalists, who are crammed into an enclosure next to the racers' pen, someone pulls me in front of the ABC cameras to talk to commentator, Bob Beattie. I spend an hour repeating myself in English, French, and German to radio and television announcers in small sound booths on the other side of the finish area. After that, the print journalists get another chance at me. I receive the first of what will be eight trophies, for having won the Jubilaeum Pokal, the fortieth running of the Hahnenkamm. I pose for victory photos with my skis, and then with Weirather and Italy's Herbert Plank, who is third. Another presentation awaits me in the press centre. My prize is a white rooster (Hahnenkamm does, after all, mean "rooster's crest") which will later be slaughtered and stuffed by the farmer who presents it to me. It squirms in my hands as photographers press in front of me, angling for the best shot.

Winning at Kitzbühel on an Austrian product brings with it special responsibilities. The day becomes a blur of handshakes, backslaps and toasts to my continued success. Pepi Fischer and his daughters preside over a wine and cheese party. There is little talk about the ski wax situation, and a lot about Austro-Canadian friendship. The team has a celebration at the Park. A dinner is held in my honour at the trendy Tenne. Among the beautiful people with fast cars, I feel lost. Fortunately, many of my teammates are with me to share the razzle-dazzle and keep me company. The press reviews begin to arrive, delivered by Turkish and Yugoslav news-agents. The *Kurier* says: "Ken Read risked everything and conquered the most difficult downhill in the world." The *Neue Kronung Zeitung* declares: "Finally! A Canadian! Ken Read, the handsome lady charmer from Calgary has won the biggest race of his career." West Germany's *Bild* proclaims: "The Canadian is the Olympic favourite." Later, I spend a few hours dancing and socializing at the Drop-In nightclub with sponsors. But there is one more affair I must attend to make my Kitzbühel night complete.

A few days before the race, the owner of the Londoner Pub, a chubby middle-aged Brit, Rick Gunnel, felt confident enough to offer a challenge: if an English-speaking racer won the Hanhenkamm, the drinks were on the house. About 11:00 p.m., my other social duties having finally run their course, I went to collect on the offer!

Making my way past a huge line-up of would-be celebrants, I squeeze through the door, and on to a small stairwell that looks down on the pub. Below me hundreds of people are jammed together under the amber bar light. They greet my arrival with clapping and singing and pop hundreds of champagne corks in my honour. They've been waiting for me for several hours. Now the party can begin in earnest!

It is, more-or-less, a closed gathering, but earlier in the evening a few of the most devoted fans — mostly hard-partying British and Australian kids who work in Kitzbühel every winter as chambermaids and waiters — have been allowed in. All the Canadian racers and coaches are here. (Some of them are acting as bartenders!) Here, too, are the American, Australian, and British racers and coaches. Many of the journalists and service reps, and a dozen or more of the better and more outgoing European racers like Franz Klammer, Peter Wirnsberger, Harti Weirather, Helmut Hoeflehner, Peter Müller, Toni Buergler, and Michael Veith are already well into the booze. So, apparently, is half of the Canadian Embassy staff from Vienna!

After a week of hard work and tension, everyone is ready for a blast. It is a riotous night of revelry both above and below the tables — a real gathering of the clan.

WENGEN _____

CHAPTER 14

January 14, 1980

O N MONDAY MORNING I leave with Hans Rammelmueller for Wengen, Switzerland. Kitzbühel wasn't our first victory together — that was at Chamonix in 1978 — but this victory is special. "Kenny," Hans tells me, "you make me really, really happy." I, too, feel like a million bucks. After weeks in which the elements and equipment seemed to conspire against us, wc are at the summit. The other classic, Wengen's Lauberhorn, a sidetrip to Megève, and the Lake Placid Olympics are ahead of us. There is so much to look forward to.

It is a lovely, sunny day for the six-hour drive west through the Arlberg to Wengen. Most of the weekend skiers are back at work in the industrial north, and the roads are clear except for a little truck traffic. As is our custom when travelling between Austria and Switzerland or France, we stopped for lunch at the Hotel Stern in Bludenz, in the province of Voralberg. The food is always good there, and the proprietor is a ski enthusiast. After we finish eating, he tells us the meal is on the house.

At the Swiss border we are waved through without so much as a cursory glance at our documents or possessions. This is extraordinary. The service vehicles, with their commercial markings and stacks of newish gear, are usually of great interest to the customs men. Hans laughs and says we should win more often.

If your images of Switzerland consist of spectacular mountain peaks and tilted meadows, with villages clinging precariously to the hillsides, you have probably been looking at photos of Wengen. It is located high in the Bernese Oberland, in what I feel is one of the most beautiful mountain settings in the world. Towering overhead are the Jungfrau, Monch, and Eiger, and their glaciers. Two thousand metres below is a valley, the Lautertal. Just behind the Lauberhorn, in a smaller valley, is the village of Grindelwald, which also has fine skiing.

To get to Wengen you must take a cog, or rack railway up from Lauternbrunnen. Its path was carved from stone by Swiss mountaineers. Passing Wengen, which straddles a narrow plateau, the train climbs past the Eiger and the Monch, issuing on to a crest which overlooks the Jungfrau Glacier. The view is unsurpassed, and all the more remarkable when you consider that it took over fifty years to complete the railway that carries you to it. Like everything else in Switzerland, the train trip is horribly expensive. Fortunately, ski racers are given a free pass that gets us most of the way up. The final leg is offered to us at half price.

Wengen is a world apart. It's chock-a-block with massive, immaculate hotels, expensive shops, graceful chalets, and narrow passageways. It has no vehicular traffic except for a small fleet of electric carts and trolleys which transports food and other supplies, tourists' baggage and, occasionally, some enfeebled tourists. Despite the absence of conventional traffic, it is always wise to walk attentively. The electrically-driven carts and trolleys can bear down almost silently upon inattentive pedestrians.

In the middle of town a small sports complex offers curling, pleasure skating, and the odd hockey match. My favourite recreation during Lauberhorn week is to leave the crowded centre and run along a trail that zigzags away from town to the finish area of the slalom and downhill races. There and back is about three miles. The scenery consists of a few farmers' chalets and a high stand of timber.

Unlike Kitzbühel, with its medieval lineage and architecture, its haughty style and social assurance, Wengen is very much a twentieth-century town. Its citizens take pride in their understated good taste. Wengen is a product of the first age of tourism, which brought British gentry to the continent to enjoy the mountains and, from a comfortable distance, see how the natives lived. Before the best of British society graced the Bernese Oberland with their presence, the region had been a sleepy agricultural hinterland. Sir Arnold Lunn, the gentleman who wrote the first rules of downhill ski racing, began skiing in Wengen and the neighbouring town of Mürren, with the Kandahar Ski Club. But it was Ernst Gertsch, a gregarious Swiss who passed away in 1986, who was responsible for developing the Lauberhorn course. He proposed the famous race in 1930 in a challenge to British racing supremacy.

The Lauberhorn race has continued ever since. The British, Germans, and Austrians all declined to participate during the Second World War, but this was no reason for the Swiss to stop. They were not involved in the fighting and had become much superior racers to their British mentors. As Britain's empire waned, so her small, informal skiing realm shrank. At war's end, some of the British returned to Wengen — they still do today — but it was no longer their private enclave. The Swiss controlled their mountains and their ski racing.

My sheer enjoyment of a week at Wengen tells me something about myself. The clean, austere-but-comfortable, and highly-organized environment to be found there appeals to me. After charming, but somewhat chaotic races in France and Italy, and the freewheeling, chauvinistic ways of the Bavarians and Austrians, it is a treat to sit back and watch a nation derive pleasure from quietly and ably imposing a precise order on ski life. Why, even the media rooms in Switzerland are organized like an army headquarters with quick, analytical result sheets, letter-perfect telex services, banks of phones that work as well as any in North America, and a phalanx of support workers whose array of languages would stagger the Pope.

Many people have told me they find it impossible to crack the prim reserve with which the Swiss protect themselves from outsiders. I think, as a community, they are reserved, but I always twig to the Swiss on a personal basis. Perhaps because I try to speak the local dialects, or because I spent a year among them as a teenager, I have always been welcomed like a friend in Switzerland. I have become fast friends with Heinz Kappeler and his wife, Andrea; the great and glamorous racer, Bernhard Russi, whose career is just winding down; and with the *Zurich Sport* newspaper's ski reporter, Stefan Oswalt, a quiet bookish man with a superb understanding of sport and his country.

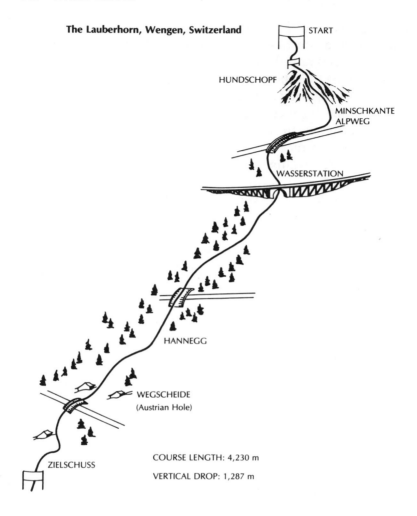

The Lauberhorn, Wengen, Switzerland

START

HUNDSCHOPF

MINSCHKANTE
ALPWEG

WASSERSTATION

HANNEGG

WEGSCHEIDE
(Austrian Hole)

ZIELSCHUSS

COURSE LENGTH: 4,230 m

VERTICAL DROP: 1,287 m

The Lauberhorn in Wengen, like the Hahnenkamm in Kitzbühel, has its distinctive quirks. After the long flats out of the
start hut, there is the Hundschopf or "dog's head." It is an
immense, two-pronged, sandy brown rock. From its middle,
or mouth, racers are catapulted down a steep pitch into the
Minschkannte, named after the Swiss racer, Jos Minsch, who
came to grief there in 1965. It starts with a bump, swings into
a compression turn, then falls away into a blind sidehill. This
is called informally the Canadian Corner, because Dave Irwin

bought it there in 1976, interrupting what might have been a brilliant racing career. Next is a long, narrow catwalk, known as the Alpweg. It's only four or five metres across, with a tight S-turn in the middle. This narrow section continues under a railway bridge known as the Wasserstation. Such quirky little features are only found on the two "classic" courses.

The Lauberhorn and Hahnenkamm courses are dissimilar. Kitzbühel's Hahnenkamm crams every element of downhill racing into two minutes of total downhill. Every centimetre of the course requires, on the part of the racer, a kind of blind faith. And past experience is often the racer's only weapon against its many challenges. Wengen's Lauberhorn has only a few hellish stretches, but it is still a formidable mountain. At four and a half kilometres — the longest of the downhill courses — it is downhill's marathon. An extra thirty seconds on a very long run make racers vulnerable to fatigue and disaster. Calves, thighs, and hearts scream for rest, but the eyes and the brain see nothing after the railway bridge except the high-speed Hanneggschuss, followed by the undulating terrain once known as the Wegschiede, but now known as the Osterreichischer Loch, or "Austrian Hole," because that's where most of the Austrians fell in the winter of 1954. Three tricky turns and the cliff of the Zielschuss are the last challenges. Thirty metres below this final precipice is the finish and relief.

Paradoxically, the Lauberhorn's length can also work to a racer's advantage. Mistakes can be survived, forgiven and forgotten. An early error or two is permissible, because there is time left to make up for it elsewhere.

To win at Wengen requires subtlety and intense concentration. It is an extraordinary course with its long, straight sections linked by tight turns. The top flats are vital because, if done well — with a perfectly flat, fast ski — speed can be carried into the lower sections, where giant slalom arcs give the best technicians an advantage.

January 18–19, 1980

IN WENGEN, CANADIAN TEAMS have always stayed at the Hotel Metropol. It is a swank but friendly establishment on the main drag, a baseball's throw from the sports complex and the post office. The view from the back of the fine restaurant, where we usually eat, looks south to the sun-drenched mountains and valley. Below the restaurant there is a splendid indoor swimming pool. Its large glass windows offer the same stunning vista. In the best of European traditions, a mixed sauna, regularly patronized by a bevy of beautiful women vacationers, is tucked in beside the pool. In the lobby is a comfortable coffee bar, where guests and racers mix. Beside the lobby is a large-ish conference room where we play videotapes of the day's events and discuss tactics for the morrow. Without question, the Metropol is our favourite hotel on the World Cup.

As I walk into the lobby with Hans, I am handed a stack of congratulatory telegrams from, among other people, Prime Minister Joe Clark, and Opposition Leader Pierre Trudeau. My parents, old girlfriends, former coaches, ski industry people, and others I don't know from Adam have also taken the time to wire me greetings. The upsurge in interest on the other side of the Atlantic pleases me immensely, but it is not altogether surprising. The American Broadcasting Corporation's *Wide World of Sports* carried the Kitzbühel race, and the Olympics are less than a month off. After an abysmal start to the season, during which good training times did not translate into strong race results, Canadians have suddenly been reminded of our existence. Indeed, our prospects of success at Lake Placid are soaring.

I have just two days to savour the Hahnenkamm victory. By Tuesday morning I am back in my usual routine. Fog cancels training, so I go free skiing for several hours with my usual sidekick, Steve Podborski. After a late lunch, I run out to the finish area by myself, and spend half an hour or so enjoying the fine mountain scenery. I know from my Kitzbühel result, and from the way I feel when free skiing, that I am on a roll. For once I am free of the the small aches and pains and traumas usually associated with downhill racing. Everything I try works. Physically and mentally I have never felt better. Oh, that it was always thus!

In training I am dreadfully slow in the upper parts, which favour the glider, but in the middle, which is a little more technical, and over the bottom, which is a maze of turns on glare ice, I am in my element. My slow time on the top flats is a puzzle that may never be solved. It isn't the skis: senior officials at Fischer have been warned to desist and leave Hans to his own devices. As Hans and Heinz proved at Kitzbühel, when left alone, they are without peers. Like me, they are in a winning groove. But the flats . . . . As good as I feel, perhaps I am just not finding the proper leg angle to ride a perfectly flat ski. It is a matter of millimetres and milliseconds.

During the time trials, Heinz Kappeler stations himself on a television tower, above the final turns. As Steve and I weave our way down, he analyzes our line and compares it to that of the other favourites. When we come down the mountain a couple of hours later, on our inspection, he is waiting there for us with an important message. To maintain our speed, and carry our momentum for as long and as far as possible, we have to hold a low tuck and delay initiating the first turn for a fraction of a second longer than the other racers. Then, when we are committed to the turn, we are to "reef," or slam on our edges as hard as possible. Heinz wants us to complete the last two turns by leaning into the gates as if we are in a giant slalom. It will take courage and supreme confidence in our turning abilities to make this gambit effective, but Heinz assures us it is possible, and that we are capable of it.

Wengen has two World Cup downhills this winter. The first race, on Friday, is to make up for one that had been abandoned because of rain and fog at Schladming, Austria. The extra race means we have one less day to prepare ourselves. There is the additional burden of trying to reach a psychological peak twice in the same week. The second race is to be run on Saturday.

Friday dawns sunny, bright, and warm in the Oberland. Swiss fighter aircraft entertain us for a while by playing tag across the sky. High on the other side of the valley, great blue chunks of breakaway ice separate from the Jungfrau glacier and thunder to earth.

The Lauberhorn track is in fantastic condition. I have drawn start number eleven, as good a start position as I had at Kitzbühel. My problems on the flats notwithstanding, I placed first and fourth in the final training runs on Thursday. So, when I launch myself from the start hut, I am feeling good about my chances.

Although I don't know it until later, I am still slow on the flats this morning. By the first section timer, I am almost one second behind the field. But the turns above the mouth of the Hundschopf and the wide, fall-away arc through the Minschkante, flow smoothly under my skis. The runs across the Alpweg, past the Wasserstation and through the tunnel under the railway tracks all go well. However, at the second interval timer, after I have accelerated down the Haneggschuss, I am still half a second behind.

I have thirty seconds of highly technical racing ahead of me. In addition to three hairpin turns, there is the Austrian Hole still to be negotiated. In normal circumstances these huge rolls would be comparatively easy, but at Wengen they are encountered after the body has endured two minutes of high-speed racing. The hillocks come up at me one after the other. I try to submerge the pain, remain as loose and flexible as possible, and rebound from each little bump, treating my legs like shock absorbers. I pass this mini-test uneventfully.

As the knolls disappear behind me, I make a slight direction change to traverse a small bridge. Now for the turns which Heinz told us to delay beginning. These turns were so badly damaged during training, by racers jamming on the brakes, that gas heaters had been applied to harden what was left of the rutted snow, turning it into ice as dense as that of any glacier. I follow the line suggested by Heinz. Throttling down at the last possible instant, I dance through the turns, and leap down the steep pitch to the finish. When I stop, I can't see the timer right away, but I hear the announcer scream and the cowbells clang. When I turn to look at the scoreboard suspended by the finish banner, I can only see my own time: 2:31.31. Then somebody shrieks that I have deprived the Austrians of a one-two finish. In a moment the board confirms it. *"Neue Best Zeit!"* I am three hundredths of a second ahead of Sepp Walcher. I averaged 102.06 kilometres per hour, and I've broken the course record by almost four seconds. Another Austrian, Peter Wirnsberger, has been bumped from second place to third. Few on the hill know it, but Heinz Kappeler's daring strategy has delivered another victory to the Canadians.

After six years on the World Cup tour I have, in six days, conquered the two best-known and most-difficult downhill tracks in the world. For an instant and forever, I am in the select company of Karl Schranz, Jean-Claude Killy, Roland Collombin and Franz Klammer. Like these Alpine masters, I have turned the coveted "classic double." I have conquered both the Hahnenkamm and the Lauberhorn.

But once again, as at Kitzbühel the week before, victory brings mixed emotions. I have beaten the world, but Dave Irwin, who had come back brilliantly to place fifth the week before — his best result in five seasons — caught an edge and lost a ski just above the Hundschopf. He went down at about 120 kilometres per hour, tumbling like a rag doll a few hundred metres before the Canadian Corner, where he fell savagely in 1976. This time, as four years earlier, he ends up unconscious in a mound of chewed-up snow beside the course. He is ferried by helicopter to a hospital ten minutes away in Interlaken.

So, back at the hotel, I have to field two lines of questions from the reporters calling from Canada. How and where did I win? How badly is Dave injured?

Fortunately, Dave's injuries are not too bad: a concussion, a strained neck and a multitude of scrapes and bruises. He is well enough, in any case, to receive comfort and solace from a Swiss lady friend at the hotel later that afternoon. Still, the cumulative effect of this crash and others at Wengen and Cortina d'Ampezzo begin to tell. Dave keeps racing for a few more years, squeezing out one last third-place finish in 1982, at the Molson World downhill.

ANOTHER THOUGHT SOON TEMPERS my jubilation: I have another engagement with the same mountain tomorrow. Neither today's victory nor Dave's crash has anything to do with tomorrow's race.

Switzerland's Peter Müller, who is leading the World Cup downhill table, was a disappointing seventh at Kitzbühel and fourth at Wengen. He is a gangly, bellicose man who sets very high standards for himself, and usually attains them. Wengen suits his coiled, aerodynamic style. I know that a few hundred metres away, he is already well into his mental preparations for the morrow's race. To get the kinks out, I stretch for a while, and then retire to the peace of my room to begin my own deliberations.

Saturday's Lauberhorn race falls on the fiftieth anniversary of skiing's oldest, continuously-run Alpine downhill. It brings out a great many more cowbell-toting Swiss than yesterday's did. It is another ideal day for downhill racing — still air, blue skies, mild temperatures.

When I am approaching the Minschkante, which I negotiated perfectly yesterday, I make a slight miscalculation. I don't press or pre-jump the bump as I want to. As a result, my right arm waves in the air, and is still up there when I land, causing me to hit my skis too hard. I go very wide on the following turn, almost creaming a battery of photographers in the process. As I recover my balance, I say to myself, "Damn it, I've blown it." From there to the bottom I curse myself and ski to the limit. An error of this magnitude can be decisive. As it turns out, I ski the last half of the course even better than I did yesterday, and set another course record. But I lost too much time on the Minschkante. Müller, a superb glider, good technician, and ferocious competitor is not to be denied twice in a row. He comes down two minutes later and sets another course record, beating me by two hundredths of a second. He, too, has won a classic downhill, his first major victory. Steve, eighth on Friday, is third today.

Although we had won difficult downhills before, with the double victories on the classic courses we are finally given the attention and respect our results merit. The Crazy Canuck appellation continues to stick because it is convenient, but with Kitzbühel and Wengen under my belt, the European racers and journalists now begin to view the Canadians as true equals.

We are no longer referred to, snidely, as "world training champions." In Vienna's prestigious daily, *Die Presse*, Charlie Kahr is quoted as saying, "Those boys have pluck. They've really helped improve the sport." The headline above the article reads, "The series of crashes at the Canadian Corner was the birthplace of a new World Cup machine." Another Viennese paper, the tabloid *Der Kurier*, says, "The Canadian ski star Ken Read from Calgary is now entrenched as the Olympic favourite, having won the most difficult tests, the race of kings on Kitzbühel's Streif and the fiftieth Lauberhorn race within the same week." In the opinion of the *Tribune de Lausanne*, there has been a "battle royal" involving downhill racing's three powers, Austria, Switzerland, and Canada.

A measure of our new stature is that I am invited to appear with Müller on a Swiss television show commemorating the Lauberhorn's golden anniversary. The host, Karl Erb, tells the audience that as far as he is concerned, the past two days have been the greatest in the history of ski racing. Later, I am asked to address a banquet for Swiss ski officials, volunteers, and former Lauberhorn winners. It is not much of a speech; just a brief "thank you," in English, French, and German, for the fine show they have put on for us on the mountain.

(But the weekend in Switzerland seems to have really struck a chord with the Swiss. To this day, people still come up to me in Switzerland to talk about the races in 1980, the television program, and the speech.)

Ironically, because I've been trooping around town to attend these functions, I miss the special Canadian team dinner that has been laid on to celebrate eight days of intense downhill racing. I end up wolfing down some food late at night in the Club Mediterranée with our slalom team, which has just arrived for the Lauberhorn slalom tomorrow.

The Wengen race represents a watershed of another sort. CBC producer, Jim Thompson, has been trying to interest his hard-nosed superiors in ski racing for the new *Sportsweekend* program. For the first time, at Wengen, he has finally won the battle. The Canadian Broadcasting Corporation provides same-day coverage of both downhills. With ABC broadcasting the Kitzbühel race, and the CBC at Wengen, Canadians have the opportunity to witness a pair of victories, and a second and third place finish, by two of their own. In a way, it is a little late for me and my teammates, but I think it may provide the extra motivation for the men and women from Canada who follow us to Europe.

FROM
CHAMONIX TO
LAKE PLACID *CHAPTER FIFTEEN*

January 21-27, 1980

WE ARE ON THE ROAD again on Monday morning, wending our way southwest along the margins of Lac Leman by way of Geneva to Chamonix, France, for the last race before the Lake Placid Olympics.

It was at Chamonix in 1978, after a disastrous World Championships, and after two years without a victory, that the Canadian downhill team was reborn. David Murray was just back from a knee injury, and two inspiring Europa Cup downhill victories at Artesina, Italy. He posted the fastest training times from the third seed in the final two days of training. I was second.

Les Housches at Chamonix is not a difficult course, but it has a few generous bumps and lots of rough, washboard-like terrain. Back in 1978, David and I figured out that the line was critical. We had to jump on it quickly, and then have the confidence and precise timing to ride out the bumps, which were capable of throwing us twenty or thirty metres down the course.

Race day in 1978 was foggy and sullen. In the flat light, locating the bumps was difficult. Nonetheless, from start number six, I posted the fastest time in the first seed: 2:08.11. Immediately I was set upon by a swarm of journalists eager to grab some quotes and quit the hill. "No, no," I told them. "Let's wait for the guy who's been fastest all week." David, whose previous best World Cup result was a seventh in 1975, had number 36, so the wait was a gut-wrenching half hour. It was an eerie feeling, stomping my boots together in the finish area, hoping he'd do well, but naturally anxious that if he did as well as he'd done in training, I would be pushed out of first place.

Through the first and second interval timers, David was still the top gun. From mid-course, I heard the coaches report by radio that he was hitting the bumps right and maintaining speed. Watching him hurtle into the finish, I was sure he'd bested me by a fraction of a second, but the scoreboard said otherwise. I had won by sixteen hundredths of a second. Canada had its first one-two finish in twelve years of World Cup racing!

"We did it! We did it! We've finally got them!" I said as I ran up to David. After two winters of frustration and disappointment, finally, in 1978, we had displaced the Europeans with a one-two finish.

So Chamonix holds pleasant memories for me. Now, in 1980, I look forward to seeing it again. After my last three results I am almost invincible. This is easy to state, but difficult to explain. I have achieved a certain mesh of mental, physical, technical, and strategic elements necessary to win. In my present state I can read a course, and calculate exactly what kind of action is needed to squeeze a few hundredths of a second out of it. If I make an error, it seems to me to be trivial. I have the self-confidence to recover immediately.

In a fifteen- or sixteen-week season, the idea is to try to peak for the four or five most important races. For the first time in my life and with Lake Placid just three weeks away, I feel I am in the middle of such a streak.

As we discovered in 1978, the trick at Chamonix is to hit those knee- and thigh-jarring jumps perfectly and then, with hands outstretched, fight our way down through the rough spots. Unfortunately, not every racer has the proper trajectory figured. The 1978 Hahnenkamm champion, Sepp Ferstl of West Germany, ended his career on Wednesday in the first training run. He went off a blind roller near the top of the mountain and impaled himself on a fence.

The World Cup downhill title hinges on the result at Chamonix. I am lying second to Peter Müller, but if I win and he finishes third or worse I can pull it out. Peter Müller was fourteenth in 1978 in Chamonix, and in training has been foundering on the bumps. I have won several of the timed trials.

On the day before the race, a warm front moves into the

Haute-Savoie from the Mediterranean, and training is cancelled because of rain and fog. On race day, we wake up to
more of the same, murky weather. A band of fog shrouds the
bottom half of the mountain. Above the cloud, the rest of the
course is bathed in glorious sunshine.

We go through our usual pre-race drill in the morning,
climbing the mountain at 8:30 to limber up. But I have an
ominous feeling that nothing is going to be possible. The track
is soft from the rain, and the bank of fog still imprisons much
of the piste.

US President Jimmy Carter announced this week that
American athletes will not be going to the Moscow Summer
Olympics because Soviet troops have invaded Afghanistan.
What all this portends for the upcoming Lake Placid Games
is anybody's guess. As we hang around the lodge near the start,
and await word on the weather, I read an *International Herald
Tribune* article which speculates upon the tension that would
attend a chance encounter between American and Soviet athletes at, for example, Heathrow Airport.

Across the way the Soviet racer, Vladimir Makeev, who with
his coaches keeps most of the World Cup supplied with fur
hats and caviar, is kidding good-naturedly with the American,
Karl Anderson, about superpower rivalry. It makes me think
how wrong men such as President Carter are. In sport, it sometimes appears as if nations are pitted against nations, but at
the end of the day it is an individual or a group of individuals
against another individual or group. Athletes study each other's
strengths and weaknesses and compete to win, but when the
contest is over, they are usually better friends than before.
Vladimir and Karl are proof of this.

I have a lot of time for serious contemplation and reflection
this morning. An hour after the scheduled start time the fog,
like Mr. Carter, hasn't moved an inch. The Chamonix race is
abandoned.

THERE IS ALWAYS A SENSE of frustration when a race is cancelled.
These feelings are naturally most acute when a racer is on a
roll. When you fancy your chances, but are denied the opportunity to race, it feels as if you have competed and lost. A
week is gone from your life and there is nothing to show for
it, but some more dirty laundry and another stamp in the
passport. That's how I feel as we pack our belongings and drive

north to Zurich for our flight home to Canada.

January 25-February 7, 1980

THERE HAVE BEEN a few occasions when we have been welcomed home with news conferences at airports, but our reception in Toronto and Calgary the day after the cancellation of the Chamonix race is like nothing I've experienced before or since. Why one fellow actually has a "Ken Read for Prime Minister" banner!

Airport arrivals in Canada, after months of traipsing around Europe, are always somewhat awkward. We're generally pooped after eight or nine hours in the back of a smoke-infested aircraft. Then, suddenly, we're set free, but we still have to wrestle several tons of gear and apparel on to a squadron of trolleys, go through customs and walk upstairs. Today, in addition to all that, we have to make our way past a crush of well-wishers, into a room full of journalists, there to discuss quietly and patiently our most recent and pending activities.

Canada seems to have been transported by our successes of the past few weeks. Lake Placid is virtually a Canadian Olympics, because it is so handy to our greatest population centres in Ontario and Quebec. Our races have been broadcast across Canada; now the journalists are keen to tell Canada about us. There seem to be hundreds of them, jockeying for position and attention. Of course, they want what we jokingly refer to as "world exclusives." Michel Farber of the *Montreal Gazette*, even flies to Calgary to sidestep the competition.

At the news conference, the president of the Calgary Olympics bid committee, Frank King, flits about, putting in telephone calls to federal and provincial government officials. Calgary has just won the Canadian rights to bid for the 1988 Winter Games. Now, in an attempt to establish immediate world-wide credibility, King tries frantically to bring the cancelled Chamonix downhill to Alberta, and my home course, Lake Louise.

Incredible as it will seem in later years, when Canadian races become a regular feature of the World Cup calendar, the Crazy Canucks have never been able to race at home. The one downhill race that was scheduled at Whistler twelve months ago, was cancelled at the last moment because the FIS race jury and World Cup president Serge Lang decided that the course lacked sufficient security measures. This was balder-dash, but it underlined again that ski racing is a European sport.

As the news conference in Calgary winds down, King comes in to report that Molson Breweries and several other parties are interested in backing a Canadian bid for the race to demonstrate Calgary's commitment to the Games. Everyone is delighted by the initiative, but skeptical about King's ability to pull it off. We're sure the World Cup Committee will never agree on such short notice to send fifty or sixty racers to an untested course in western Canada, especially with a Swiss skier leading the downhill table, and a Canadian in second place behind him. Peter Andrews, our World Cup Committee member, now has to horse-trade with the Europeans against their choice of Bad Kleinkircheim in Austria.

(But we are wrong. After several days of haggling the Europeans accede to Canada's request. The federal and provincial governments, and Molson, agree to put up $125,000 to stage the event. The Lake Louise Ski Club and the Canadian Ski Association agree to do the rest. I am to have another chance at the World Cup title, and under the most favourable terms imaginable.)

Coming back from Europe, and the high that comes from being the toast of the Alps, I take a few days off at Lake Louise to relax and shake free of jet lag. I have to re-build my conditioning because, in the competitive cycle of Europe, it has slipped a little.

To regain optimal conditioning, I set myself a rigorous free skiing program that includes lots of work on technique, so I can maintain the faultless flow I have gotten into over the past few weeks. I am not yet back in peak condition when I fly to Montreal and Mont Ste. Anne, where the coaches have arranged a brief, pre-Olympic camp, but I don't want to be. I am close, and that is good enough.

The folks at Mont Ste. Anne do a marvelous job, making us feel welcome and preparing the slopes for our work. It is a good test, because the terrain and artificial snow are similar to Lake Placid's. This should give us a bit of a leg up on the Europeans, who are continuing to train on real snow back in their home countries.

We are the object of intense media scrutiny. A seemingly interminable series of news conferences and public functions follow one after another. Much as we would like to appease everyone, and meet all the demands that are made of us, we also need to prepare in an orderly way for our ultimate goal, the Olympics. But the CSA is apparently incapable of saying no to the media or to our corporate sponsors. No rules are established to restrict access to us, and we are sucked steadily into an abyss. During the period prior to the opening of the Lake Placid Games we endure no less than seven public appearances.

It would be amazing if, on the eve of the seventh game of the Stanley Cup finals or the World Series, a journalist called up Wayne Gretzky or Dwight Gooden and demanded an hour-long interview about their parents, their youth, and their dreams. When dealing with professional athletes, the journalists know better than to ask. And if they don't know better, the teams' flaks either fend them off, or limit the time given to interviews, to protect the athletes. But amateur athletes are not so protected. It seems to me that after ignoring our achievements for years, journalists have declared an open season on us.

After three days at Mont Ste. Anne, we troop into town for a news conference sponsored by Shell Canada, which is contributing $150,000 towards the Canadian Championship. Fair enough. They have always stood by us. But tonight we are informed that the next day's training is limited to only two runs. We know we have a major press reception laid on in Montreal for the *première* of Lauron Productions' newest film, *Those Crazy Canucks*, which was filmed in the fall and winter. A fund-raiser is to follow with a lot of high rollers in attendance. This, too, is a necessary evil, because the team needs public contributions, but it is a long way from the playing fields for a team that is preparing for the Olympics.

Only on the drive to Montreal do we discover why our training is being aborted after only two runs. His Worship, Mayor Jean Drapeau, has expressed an interest in meeting with us. It turns out that this get-together is the idea of a woman who is responsible for yet another CSA fund-raiser. We are going to meet the mayor as a favour to her. My reaction is, "Nice favour." It's fine to hob-nob with the mighty, but I'd rather we come away from the Olympic Games with medals around our necks. After the Games is the time for fund-raisers. We lose about five hours of training time.

As receptions go, the mayor's gathering is a nice one. Later the same day, at the ski team fund-raiser, the local media takes a keen interest in my tenuous connections with "la belle province." (My father was born and raised in Joliette. My mother is from Westmount. My maternal grandmother, Mary Burden, has lived her entire life in Quebec. She becomes the peg for a story by French Canada's most enthusiastic and knowledgeable ski reporter, Mario Brisebois.) Monsieur Drapeau is very kind. He wishes us luck.

The next morning we leave by road for Lake Placid.

LAKE
PLACID

CHAPTER SIXTEEN

February 8-14, 1980

A T THE UNITED STATES border crossing, a few kilometres north of Champlain, New York, there is a minor hold-up while, for the first time, US officials explain to me what "dual nationality" is.

Although I was born in Ann Arbor, Michigan, both my parents were Canadian citizens and my arrival was registered with Canadian authorities within hours of my birth. I have lived almost all my life in Canada. I knew that until I was twenty-one, I had a choice as to whether I wished to be Canadian or American. After that, there is a three-year grace period during which I could apparently still opt for US citizenship. As I am now twenty-four, this possibility is about to expire. According to the fellows from US immigration, there is a small catch.

"Have I gone before a judge to renounce my US citizenship?" they ask me.

No, I haven't.

That, they say, means I still have a shot at US citizenship if I want it. There is a long pause.

"Well, given the fact you're on the way down here to represent Canada, we'd better let you in as a Canadian without further delay," they say. "But you never know when US citizenship might come in handy. You might want to work down here one day. Think about it, huh?"

I figure I'm a prime candidate for the military draft, if President Carter decides to re-institute it. (Later, of course, the US military wouldn't want me. My knees will be so scrambled by skiing that they'd consider me a cripple.) Anyway, after twenty-one years in Canada, and seven years on the national ski team, I am going to my second Olympic Games. My choice was made long ago. I'm Canadian.

My slender link with the United States always seems to crop up, especially when I am doing well. ABC commentators, Bob Beattie and Frank Gifford, are forever saying, "And here comes Ken Read, the American-born Canadian downhill racer . . . ." US magazines and newspapers also regularly tout this fact.

Later, at the Games, I actually meet a reporter from Ann Arbor who seeks me out to do a feature story on the local boy who made good. I explain to him, patiently, the circumstances surrounding my birth and subsequent patriation to Canada. He says it doesn't matter. I spent almost three years in Michigan, and that is good enough for him.

When we arrive at Lake Placid, the first order of business is to take the small sideroad past Whiteface Mountain in order to catch a glimpse of the distant course. What strikes me is that, except on the hill itself, there is no snow anywhere. The mountain is brown and looks forlorn. There may be a problem: where are we going to free ski until training begins in three days?

As I survey the hill I get my first real taste of the Olympics. Rosi Mittermaier, the West German "golden girl" from the Innsbruck Games, shows up with a ZDF (southern German network) television crew. Suddenly, four photographers pop out of the woodwork and begin taking pictures of us with Rosi.

I actually stood at the top of this course five months before. To get a sense of the hills that lie below and what they are made of, I have often hiked on downhill courses during the off-season. I did the same the previous autumn at Kitzbühel and it helped me a lot.

On Whiteface, I only got as far as the second bump above the finish before a watchman told me to leave: there was blasting in progress to re-arrange the face of the course for the Olympics. I had just flown from Calgary to Montreal, and then driven to Lake Placid, so I was a little peeved, but the hardhat was only doing his job. To avoid him, I took my rental car up the back of the hill to a weather observatory. About 200 yards down from the tower was a sign warning of the blasting. I deked under it and walked down to the start area, and then followed the course until the second corner, where I heard earth-moving equipment. I went no further, but I had a pretty good sense that major modifications were being undertaken. What I had learned about the course in the pre-Olympic test the previous winter was not going to be of great value.

As we enter Lake Placid we see that the Thunderbird Motel, smack in the middle of town, has a vacancy sign up. We chuckle to ourselves because, for days, all we have heard is that Lake Placid has extremely limited accommodation. Because of the shortage — it turns out to be true — extortionate prices are being asked for hotel rooms, houses, and even bedrooms.

But back to the real world. These Olympics are to be unlike anything I have experienced before. On the Olympic village site security heavies, big and self-important, with sunglasses, nightsticks, and walkie-talkies are everywhere. A sacred, laminated piece of paper identifies us as athletes; without it we would be non-persons. We have to carry our accreditation with us everywhere, except on the downhill run.

From the accreditation office we drive inside the outer perimeter of the Olympic village. When we get out of our cars we are instantly inundated by a mass of journalists who have been following us for some time. As one of the first groups of Canadian athletes to arrive, we become prime fodder for their interview-starved microphones and cameras.

Next on our Olympic tour are the airport-style X-ray machines through which we, our paraphernalia, and our companions, the journalists, all have to pass to reach our residences.

The needs of a downhill racer and his coaches are many and varied. To serve them we have enough gear to sink a frigate. Much of our kit, including our ski boots, is made partly from bits of steel and aluminium that set electronic eyes squawking. Thank heavens most of our skis, which also have metal in them, have been off-loaded at Whiteface Mountain.

From the second security perimeter and the X-ray conveyor belts, we are trundled off to our accommodation. This consists of ATCO trailers of a very ordinary, bush-camp design. I can tell you, they are not looked on with any delight by their tenants.

The nonsense with the media continues. They want to get pictures of me opening the door to my temporary home. I am beginning to to feel that there is nothing the media won't do to remain with us. But, then, miraculously, their invasion of our privacy ends when I close the door. When I see the room I am to be lodged in, my jaw drops. Each room is, say, two metres by three. With the cupboard open, the room is completely filled by its door and the bed. Four of these cubbyholes, two bathrooms with showers, and a very small sitting room make up the Crazy Canuck suite. Gear is stowed anywhere and everywhere we can find a place for it. Much of it ends up piled in heaps that reach the ceiling.

So, as they'd warned us before we got here, and the Thunderbird's openings notwithstanding, space is certainly at a premium. We are living in a virtual prison (in fact, that is what it becomes after the Games). The Austrians, meanwhile, are moving into houses their federation has rented for the month.

The first thing I always do in any new locale is case it for likely places for exercise. My needs are not unreasonable. A hill for sprints, and a more level area for gymnastics and circuit work, are sufficient. I find early-morning and late-afternoon workouts best — they fit around prime skiing hours — but occasionally, if I am bored or antsy, I go for a third leg-stretcher in the evening.

The Olympic compound looks great for what I have in mind. It is surrounded by a fence that is about a mile and a half around. On the other side is a strip of cleared land. The whole area is well lighted. I can easily see and avoid any dips or holes. Ideal!

I decide to dress up in my new Olympic togs. There has been a lot of energy expended in the hoopla associated with our arrival. Now is my chance to escape the media and get back into my usual pre-race drill.

I go through the security cordon, turn to my left, and start to run. Within three strides I am confronted by a man in uniform, his hand on his holster. I stop.

"What the hell do you think y'er doin'?" he snarls.

"Going for a run."

"No y'er not."

"Why not?"

"This is a secured area. No movement is allowed outside the perimeter of the fence. You want to run? Do it inside."

So I wheel around and return to the compound.

Welcome to the Olympic Games! How is that for a "hello"?

Of course, there are very good reasons for the extensive security at the Olympic Games. The Munich Summer Games, where terrorists seized and slaughtered athletes, is the sad example of what can happen if appropriate counter-measures are not taken. However, the Winter Games attract nothing like the same degree of world attention as the Summer Games. I'd like to think this para-military atmosphere is unnecessary.

It is ironic that here, in the isolated and postcard-perfect wilderness of the Adirondacks, some twelve kilometres from Lake Placid, we are surrounded by cops sitting in big cars twenty-four hours a day, their engines spewing noxious fumes. Within the fence, other security forces occupy prime space, too. It means my daily constitutionals have to be squeezed within a small, winding circuit. After five laps I start to go a trifle dizzy.

ON OUR SECOND DAY in the village, we head out of the trailer at the hour appointed for dinner. As we near the dining area, the coaches catch up and tell us that the meal has to be delayed. A press conference has been arranged. We know nothing about it, but dutifully comply. It is mostly senior sports writers from newspapers across Canada. For ninety minutes, they contrive in a variety of ways to make us say that we are going to win the downhill gold medal. We stick, with equal determination, to our standard line: "We've got a reasonable chance. It's a competitive field. In ski racing there are many variables to be taken into account . . . weather, equipment, start number, mood, ease or difficulty of the course. We'll sure give it our best. If that means a medal, great. If it doesn't, well, that's life."

They aren't very satisfied by our bland answers, but we refuse to be pinned down. To say that we have it in the bag only gives ammunition to our rivals, and sets us up for a fall.

At Mont Ste. Anne we were on snow and then, as suddenly, we were off it. This pattern has continued through the transit stage, in Montreal, and at Lake Placid itself. At one point, with Whiteface closed down because of insufficient snow, we have to drive two hours east to Pico Peaks for free skiing.

I am having difficulty adapting to man-made snow. My years at Camp Fortune, near Ottawa, taught me a lot about it, but the lessons I learned there were forgotten in western Canada, where snow conditions are softer and more forgiving. In Europe, where I spent most of my time racing and training, artificial snow is seldom encountered.

Real snow that has been turned to ice by Nature, is easy enough to ski on. It is only a question of deciding how hard to plant the edge before carving a turn. However, the pasty effluent that is shot from a snow-making gun is nothing like that which falls from the sky. For one thing, it is significantly denser than real snow. Carving turns is very difficult. To be fast, you hit a corner and you get off your edges as quickly as possible. It feels like skiing on ballbearings.

My problems with man's version of snow have reached the stage where, to avoid mayhem, I am trying to tiptoe down the course. What with this, and the increasingly unreasonable demands on our time, I am slowly unravelling. Two nights before the Games, I've had enough.

Would the Canadian ski team please attend a function tonight being hosted by Pepi Fischer? The Opening Ceremonies are thirty-six hours off. We've endured media gatherings and public receptions at Montreal and Lake Placid. As has always been Alpine skiing's custom, the ski journalists are still getting us for half an hour every day at the hill after training. Enough is enough. I tell the coaches I'm not bundling myself through security checks any more to attend parties. I'm staying home to think about the race.

From this time on, it is as if a door has been slammed shut. All access to us is tightly restricted. Journalists are instructed not to approach us in the village. We will be available in the finish area; otherwise our privacy is to be respected at all times. It has taken a long time, but the CSA and the Canadian Olympic Association finally understand the need to protect our privacy.

It's a reporter's job to get whatever story he thinks is out there. Like a racehorse, if he's given full rein he'll take it. If he's not, he'll try to seize it, anyway.

I think we feed the problem, too. As a group, we seem to be regarded as well-spoken and thoughtful. Except when asked to provide answers to questions of the "How are you going to do?" variety, we provide long, reasoned, full paragraph responses to most questions.

Journalists perform an important function at competitions such as the Olympics. They interpret and disseminate information to a public that is eager to know. They need to have access. But there is so much at stake for the competitors that some form of control simply has to be implemented.

THE DAY BEFORE the Fischer invitation, we attended the Canadian Olympic Association reception for athletes and the media. It was here that the name of the Canadian flag bearer for the Opening Ceremonies was to be announced. After milling around for a while, meeting with the other athletes, the Sport minister, Steve Paproski, announced that I would be the thirteenth Canadian to carry our standard at the Olympic Games. I said a few words and left the dais a very happy, thankful man.

Carrying the flag at Lake Placid is perhaps the proudest moment of my life. Twenty-three thousand people are crammed into a village of 2,700 to watch 1,300 athletes from thirty-seven countries file by. U.S. Vice-President Walter Mondale takes the salute and utters about thirty words declaring the Games open. The great American speedskater, Erik Heiden (who will win five gold medals in the next ten days), recites the athletes' oath. As a result of the Afghanistan-Moscow Olympics boycott, President Carter declines to attend the ceremony.

I am a strong Canadian nationalist. I have been fortunate to be able to represent my country internationally. I know it sounds maudlin, but I regard the distinction conferred upon me here, at Lake Placid, as a chance to pay Canada back in a small way for all my country has done for me, as a racer, and as an individual. I can demonstrate what the Maple Leaf symbolizes to me. It is an occasion I will never forget.

However, being the flag bearer puts an additional strain on my Olympic schedule. The race is tomorrow. We've just come down from our final timed trial, and have barely enough time to slip into the huge, red, team parkas and white ski pants before the festivities begin. The Opening Ceremony leaves me with a bit of a sore back, but I would never have traded this cool day in the Adirondacks for anything.

In an odd way, the Opening Ceremony brings me relief from the anguish my training results are giving me. With so many distractions in the village and on the hill, I have been losing my concentration. I am increasingly worried that I may be losing the momentum that made me unbeatable at Kitzbühel and Wengen.

The first few days of timed trials at Lake Placid have not gone well. I've been struggling with results between tenth and twelfth. But after closing the door on outside distractions we are once again a cohesive little group. Instead of feeling on the defensive all the time, we begin to enjoy the Games. Not coincidently, my skiing begins to improve, too.

On the second-last day of training, I creep into the bottom end of the first ten. On the eve of the race, I am fourth and fifth although, if the last run had been a race I would be placed one notch higher because Herbert Plank, of Italy, who finishes ahead of me, misses a gate.

I begin to feel that if I ski as well tomorrow, and everything breaks properly for me, I may have a shot at a medal. If I improve again I may have a chance at the top spot. It isn't going to be easy. It's never easy.

After the final training run, we stand around answering questions. ABC's *Good Morning America* does a low-key, live-to-videotape interview with me for the next day's show. Over visuals of my training runs they pump me, treating me as the pre-race favourite. At the end, I am asked to stay on a little longer to say, "Good Morning America. I'm Ken Read and I'll be competing later today in the men's downhill." But I am numb from the cold and can't say the words properly! I beg their pardon and ski to the base lodge a few hundred metres away to get warm.

I am flattered and surprised at the way the American media is going out of its way to make a big deal of all the Canadian racers. For Americans and for ABC Sports, this is unbelievable. They love nothing better than to wrap themselves in Old Glory and celebrate their own.

I conclude that our American cousins focus on us because we are proven winners who speak unaccented English. It is one of the joys of being a Canadian that one is accepted and acceptable all over the world.

Meanwhile, back in the Olympic Village, life is becoming slightly more bearable. On the first day we were almost alone, but now the village is filled with hundreds of great athletes. It is a shock to me, as one used to the narrow World Cup routine of "train, race, travel, train, race" to be thrust into a much larger milieu with other sportsmen.

The populating of the village helps to make the Games less unfriendly, but it remains an armed camp located a long way from the competition venues. Having an Olympic village is a sensible, efficient way to administer a large group of athletes and coaches, but it should not mean that it is impossible to have a friendly place where people can get to know each other.

The Games should provide a chance to step out of our usual competitive roles and learn new things. Instead, the Lake Placid setup is fraught with problems for us. For example, our masseur and servicemen, and several of our assistant coaches, live about half an hour from us. It is one more aggravation to contend with.

WHEN WE WAKE UP on race day, there is mixed cloud with occasional snow squalls blustering in from Canada. The course is in superb condition. Man-made snow from top to bottom and as hard as rock. There is not a big crowd — 10,000 people — but that is about all that can fit into the spectator space available on the margins of the 3,028 metre Olympic course. Millions more are watching on television, including many people north of the border, who are watching Canada's first-ever live telecast of a downhill race.

The Swiss and Canadians have several serious contenders, but the Austrians have the strongest team. We are all fascinated by what has been going on within their camp. The Austrian coaches are under extreme pressure to win. They elected to leave their great Olympic champion and the darling of the nation, Franz Klammer, at home. In his place they selected the defending world champion, Sepp Walcher; eager young Peter Wirnsberger, who won at Val d'Isère and at the pre-Olympic trial last year; bad boy Werner Grissman, who has a string of top three results, and a World Championship silver medal; their newest boy, Harti Weirather, who was second to me at Kitzbühel; and Klammer's drinking buddy, the amiable, Pinocchio-nosed giant, Leonhard Stock.

It is a reasonable decision. Klammer has not performed well all year, and these other skiers have. But it still hasn't gone down very well with the commentators or the public who thought their beloved Kaiser deserved another Olympic chance.

It must be understood that special rules apply to the Olympics. At World Cups, each country is allowed to include ten racers in its team. At the quadrennial Games, five skiers are allowed to train for the downhill race, and entry on race day is limited to four.

For countries with only a few good racers, such as Canada, the choices are relatively easy to make. For some of the European nations, it is like walking through a minefield. Does a fourth at Kitzbühel and third at Val Gardena equal a second at Val d'Isère and a sixth at Villars? Who's to say?

The scuttle-butt at Lake Placid is that Stock, a master technician with good giant slalom results, is to be the Austrian alternate. There is no way he will run the Olympic downhill unless one of the other four is injured.

Hallelujah! That is fine by us. We figure that Stock would be hard to beat on this course. The top third of the mountain consists of a series of difficult, high-speed turns and is followed by a mind-numbing high-speed glide to the finish. If Stock, the giant slalom turner, works his usual magic above and carries sufficient momentum on to the flats, he could win.

Stock, realizing the impossibility of his position, seizes the initiative and creams the field in the first two practice runs. The Austrian head coach, Charlie Kahr, ever the pragmatist, promptly reverses himself and announces that Stock is in the downhill team. It is up to the other four racers to fight for the other three places. The uproar this causes among the Austrian racers and their fans at home is unimaginable. Kahr's reversal puts the rest of us on our mettle, too. Stock will be *very* hard to beat.

When we get to the top of the hill on race day, Stock is already warming up. The man left out of the Austrian line-up is the world champ, Walcher.

The incident demonstrates Kahr's rare nerve. Austria wants nothing less from the Games than a gold medal in the downhill to go with the ones that Klammer, Toni Sailer, and Egon Zimmermann have won.

If Kahr's gamble does not pay off with a first place finish, it is altogether possible that the people of Austria will go *en masse* to his hotel and restaurant in Schladming, and set the place alight. After all, Sepp Walcher is a Schladming boy, too.

Given that the snow still handles like ballbearings, I feel good on my skis as I warm up with Steve Podborski. There is lots of space in which to let loose, so I give myself a couple of good, high-speed runs. Then I take the lift up to the holding area beside the women's start where I climb into my new Descente downhill suit. The suit is made of a new fabric of ultra-fast design. Canada's suits, in keeping with our race colours this season, are silver. We have taken to calling them the "silver sausages." The black maple leaf shoulder patches that come with them have been imprinted upside-down. Last night I took a felt pen to fix mine up.

I have drawn number fourteen and am pleased to have it. Steve has number fifteen.

I begin my final, pre-race warmup routine, which takes ten minutes, as Harti Weirather, starting first, makes his descent. A good, muscle extending, sweat-producing warmup is particularly important this morning. It is chilly, and a fair gale is rattling through the firs that guard the course on both sides.

I collect my race skis and receive a few words of quiet encouragement from Hans Rammelmueller. From Hans I proceed to another Austrian, Joe Bachler, my Salomon rep, to make sure the ski bindings are mounted and adjusted properly. He goes through the usual routine.

Then I slide past Steve into the starting gate. We know how lucky we are to be blessed with such late start numbers. Those down the hill before us have blown the new snow away. The snow underneath is so hard, it is not likely to deteriorate at all before we start.

This may be the most important race of my life, but I am trying my hardest to treat it like any other, as far as pre-race preparations are concerned. But when I push out of the hut the plan begins to fall apart.

The first fifty metres are flat, encouraging aggression. In my exuberance to get underway, I make four poling movements instead of my usual two or three. The fourth one is a waste of time. Still, it seems to have done me no harm as I swing through the first turn, a mean left-hander, and enter a flat that course officials have dubbed "Hurricane Alley" because of the wind. Dropping into the second turn, a fall-away which begins a series of four quick bends, I begin to accelerate.

Then, near the point I stopped at when I looked over the course months before, my upper ski hits a ripple created by the forerunners and first thirteen racers. Suddenly I find myself sliding on my side. I immediately relax and try to absorb the shock of my low-speed collapse. I come to a quick and gentle stop, and regain my feet without even thinking.

The stomach-sinking realization of disaster hits just before I stop. The routine which I meticulously rehearsed this morning in bed is not unfolding as it should. I am supposed to be skipping across the snowfield. Instead, I am standing on the hill minus one ski. My Olympic Games have lasted exactly twelve seconds. My ski has fallen off.

Whether in a race or in training, whenever a ski becomes unhinged or something else causes me to go down early in a race, I am flooded with feelings of frustration and impotence. It's like being swindled out of a fortune. There is no appeal. I will have no second chance.

Within a few minutes the magnitude of what has happened dawns on me. The thousands of hours of travelling, training, and racing that have led to this moment on the side of the Olympic mountain flash through my mind.

Real anger is welling up inside of me, but I don't act on it. Instead, I stand in abject silence, poking my poles in the snow. Later many people will say that I didn't react normally, that I should have been thwacking my good ski or screaming to the heavens. That I do nothing of the sort may be due to a lesson I learned from Canada's *première* Alpine racer, Nancy Greene.

In 1977 — a terrible year for us — I had finally put together a reasonable run in the final race of the season, and was second at the last interval timer. But between there and the finish I made a silly mistake, and bought it in an easy turn. In anger I swung my pole violently across my skis and broke it.

Thinking nothing of it then, I picked up the pieces and proceeded to the finish area. Nancy was there, waiting. Without even saying "hello" she went up one side of me and down the other. The essence of what she said was that I wasn't just Ken Read, I was a representative of Canada. Others had invested a great deal of time and money so I could ski race. In return I had to do more than savage a ski pole to celebrate my own bungling. Frustration on the hill had to be dealt with internally. If I needed to express it, why didn't I do it with some good results? Young people looked to me as a role model. Such behaviour proved I was not a "champion." With hard work we could win again, but only if we showed maturity. . . .

At the time I was furious with her, but I eventually came around to her point of view.

I have never felt greater frustration in my life than I feel today on Whiteface Mountain. A ski marshal thoughtfully returns my errant ski. There is nothing wrong with it.

All that happened is that a ripple in the snow knocked my

inside ski away. It's not unusual to lose a ski in such circumstances. I probably had a little too much weight on the outside ski to grip the artificial snow. My full weight was pushing down upon it when it might better have been balanced on both skis.

There is no injury and no one to blame. Zilch. My equipment has functioned as it should. My chance for the gold medal is gone. Heeding Nancy's advice, I plant my poles in the snow and stare straight ahead, resisting a public display of the fury that rages inside of me.

I am brushing myself off when Steve comes careering towards me. He almost mows down a gate in the snowfield, but he reels himself in at the last moment and makes it. In a second he is gone, blasting blissfully down the mountain.

At the next corner, as I slowly ease myself down the course, I run into Toni Buergler. The young Swiss racer is in a foul mood. He didn't make the gate that Steve flirted with, and ended up on his head. Blood oozes from a dozen small cuts on his face. It's never fun to smack into a gate, but it could have been much worse. It can always be worse.

A few metres later, as I continue to thread my way down, I run in to my aunt and uncle at the top of Victoria pitch, where I was supposed to have rocketed by at 140 kilometres per hour. They say they came to watch me race and didn't really plan on having a chat.

I am still clad only in a downhill suit and am beginning to feel the bitter winter air creeping into my joints. I am not looking forward to what lies ahead. I steel myself for the inevitable questions from racers, coaches, servicemen, and journalists. What happened to the favourite? Why?

Reaching the racer's corral, I see Stock and Wirnsberger hoisted aloft by the Austrian delegation. Steve Podborski is being mobbed by the North American media. At a glance it is evident how the race has ended.

Stock's gold medal makes Kahr a prophet. Wirnsberger's silver makes Kahr a saint. And Steve aced the top turns and rode a subtle flat ski most of the rest of the way to a well-deserved bronze.

Then, whammo.

"Why Ken?"

"Was it a conspiracy?"

"Did you lose your balance?"

"What's the name of the guy who did your bindings?"

"Can you sue him?"

"Can you sue Salomon?"

"No! Then was it your fault?"

For an hour or more the inquisitors come at me from every direction, by turns mean and skeptical, gentle and sympathetic. There is no facile or adroit answer. There is no way to sidestep their questions. I try as patiently and politely as possible to explain what I think has happened. No matter what I say, my answers have a hollow ring. What true answer is there but the trite one? I tried my best, and lost. That happens sometimes in life and in sport.

Near the end of this ordeal, someone gives me a track top to wear. It helps a little, but not enough. I am frozen stiff. George Duffield, a radio reporter from Toronto, takes me into his heated booth to warm up. It is there that I give my last interview on the events of my twelve-second day.

When I return to the finish area, about ninety minutes after the race began, there is not a soul in sight. I mention this because an elderly Ottawa columnist writes very nastily, later, about how un-cooperative Kathy Kreiner and I have been with the media. He said she refused to do interviews, which is untrue, and that I shirked the press after my ski fell off, which I didn't. It is the only complaint of this kind I will receive in nine years of high-level competition.

With no one around, I sling my skis over my shoulder, and begin walking the final 400 metres to the base of the mountain. I can see a huge crowd gathered at the bottom to honour the new Olympic and world champion, Leonhard Stock, and the silver and bronze medallists.

It is a very lonely, bleak moment for me. I stand and watch from a distance as Stock, Wirnsberger, and Podborski wave ecstatically to the throng from a makeshift podium. In the crowd, many Canadians are flourishing our flag.

SALOMON TOOK MY SKI BINDING back to the factory at Annecy, France, and tested it repeatedly. In every way, it was found to meet the company's very exacting standards.

Studies have shown that in an average downhill race each ski bounces against the track about 5,000 times. The force and torsion created by these repeated impacts is so great that, to prevent a ski from coming off inadvertently, downhill racers must always have their safety bindings screwed down much more tightly than recreational skiers. But the fear of losing a ski as a result of such pressures must be balanced against the fact that if a racer falls, the binding must let go, or he risks a severe leg injury. It defeats the purpose of the bindings to be clamped down so snugly that the skis won't release when they should.

What happened to me in 1980 at Lake Placid had happened to me occasionally before in training on rough glaciers and washboard-like tracks. Usually, I didn't give such occurrences a second thought. Having it happen at the Olympics should not have made a great difference, but with half of the Western world tuned in, and being one of the favourites, it did.

If anyone felt worse than me about what had happened, it was Joe Bachler. In the aftermath of my humiliation, sales of Salomon's bindings slumped precipitously, and there were (ultimately unsuccessful) moves afoot to sack Joe. I liked and trusted him. I still do. That's why, at the very next race, at Lake Louise, I made a point of ensuring that Joe Bachler checked my bindings.

There was no point in blaming Joe or Salomon. They had loyally provided me with support for many years. They had done their job competently. It was time to forget this unpleasant episode.

Could I have won the gold medal? That's a $64,000 question that people still pose. In retrospect, when I reflect on all that was swirling around me and within me at Lake Placid, and after appraising what I had achieved in training, I believe I would have had no better than an outside chance at first place. Videotapes show that Stock, Wirnsberger, and Podborski had excellent runs with only one or two errors. On that day, the way I had been skiing, I do not believe I could have matched Stock for the gold. The silver? Or the bronze? We'll never know.

There are two factors that set the Olympic downhill apart from other races of equal or superior competitive quality. The obvious one is that it is only held every four years. Clearly, it is much harder to capture the top prize than at World Cups, which are raced ten or eleven times annually.

Secondly, the limelight cast by television, and the unabashed jingoism of the media, create national expectations that often can't be met. Men and women who have never thought to watch or read about sport, are suddenly booking off work to watch the Olympics on television or in person. Competitors know it. It is another burden they take to bed with them every night. My own experience at Lake Placid was indicative of the extraordinary public attention which envelops athletes at the Olympic Games. It can consume those who are unprepared for it.

If the officiating is fair, a figure skater such as Katerina Witt, a sprinter such as Ben Johnson, a gymnast such as Nadia Comaneci and a swimmer such as Alex Baumann, only have to perform at their best to have an excellent chance to win. Oh, that is was so easy for us! In Alpine racing, there are many variables that affect performance. Dozens of other people — coaches, servicemen, scientists — are involved in getting a racer and his equipment into the starting hut. Skis, wax, bindings, suits, weather, and start number can assist a racer or hurt him.

It is little understood in North America that downhill racing is unlike other individual Olympic sports such as figure skating, track and field, gymnastics, and swimming. Why? Because it is frequently performed on a platform that is not especially well-suited to the best downhill racers' skills.

The downhill is the most difficult of the events to be staged because the course must have a vertical drop of at least 800 metres. This minimum posed significant difficulties for organizers at Lake Placid and Sarajevo.

In the case of Sarajevo the tallest mountain, Bjelasnica, was found slightly wanting so the enterprising Yugoslavs built the lift terminal and a restaurant at the very crest of the mountain, put a long ski ramp through the middle of the roof and met the requirement with one metre to spare. Unfortunately, the course was not very challenging, and it threw up a less than exceptional winner, Billy D. Johnson, a skier of modest talent, if not of modest demeanour.

At Lake Placid there was more mountain to play with. With a smidgen of that famous American ingenuity and know-how, it could have been made longer at both ends. Instead, from the very beginning, it was obvious that the organizers had a fixation: downhill as a death-defying spectacle. To enhance this perception they constructed mini-launch pads all over the place. The further we flew off their man-made creations the happier they were. By constructing the course like this, they missed a chance to use their fancy earth-changing hardware to make a more challenging, technically-interesting downhill. If they had, their Olympic race might have been truly riveting in the way that Innsbruck was in 1976. To win at Innsbruck, Klammer had to pull off a truly Olympian feat.

Leonhard Stock maintains his reputation as a technician capable of carving the loveliest turns and handling the most generous bumps. Proof of this is his high standing in the super-G. But in four years of racing before Lake Placid, and eight years of racing since, he has not won another downhill. But no one else has his Lake Placid Olympic memories.

March 4, 1980

FROM LAKE PLACID we move on to Lake Louise for Canada's first men's World Cup downhill. In four weeks, my many friends there have pulled together a world-class event. The showdown for the World Cup title is set. It is a two-man race for the championship between me and Switzerland's Peter Müller. My loss to him by two hundredths of a second in the second downhill at Wengen, in January, looms large. Five more World Cup points for me, and five less points for him, would have made the contest even tighter. As it is, I've got to win.

March 4, 1980, dawns crystal-clear and cold. The Rockies look magnificent. Although it's a Tuesday, over 12,000 Calgarians have made their way to Louise. The White Circus has truly arrived in the Great White North! The circumstances could not have been better for my triumph.

But the showdown never materializes. Whether I'm too anxious, or lack sharpness after the Olympic shock, I don't know. I finish ninth after a poor race. There is no satisfaction in it, but Müller does even worse, placing fourteenth. The title is his. I am second. If I had won in the second race at Wengen, our standings would have been reversed. My only consolation is that I have won North America's first World Cup downhill medal.

VI

THE LAST OF THE CRAZY CANUCKS

THE
PODBORSKI
STORY

I DID NOT REALIZE IT at the time, and I'm sure Steve Podborski didn't either, but when he clattered by me as I stood helpless in the snow at the second bend at Lake Placid, the Crazy Canucks entered their final chapter, the Podborski years.

Since the mid-1970s I had shared centre stage with Jim Hunter, David Murray, and Dave Irwin. I had held Steve at bay, but just barely, in 1980, by winning the coveted classic double. Now it was his turn to show the way. I was not to win another race, while he was on his way to seven World Cup victories and a World Cup downhill title. For the next two seasons he was only to finish worse than fourth in one race.

The timing of Steve's ascension may have been a rude shock for me, but it was really — honestly! — no surprise. Already, ten years earlier, in camps in western Canada, South America, and Europe, I had seen evidence of his sweet touch on skis, his lightning-quick intelligence, and his vigorous competitive spirit. By the spring of 1979, when I was in Furano, Japan for the World Cup final, I said in interviews that the days when I could keep up with Steve were numbered. Every index showed that he was creeping up on me.

Perceptive Europeans had also figured it out. Three weeks before the Olympics, for example, Beat Kaspar, a World Cup regular from *Basler Zeitung*, wrote that irrespective of where anyone else stood in the standings, Podborski was the best racer in the world. This educated judgment was based upon Steve's relative youth, and a careful reading of interval times from all the races that winter. He won at Schladming in December, 1980, by more than a second, but the result was annulled because of fog and snow. At Kitzbühel, a few weeks earlier, where I won, Steve recorded the fastest interval time at the top before going head-first into some safety netting. It was the third time that happened to him in two months. At Wengen, in the second race, he finished only an eyeblink behind me. That result and his bronze medal at Lake Placid were the first of more than twenty consecutive world class results which would prove Kaspar right.

There is no one in the world that I have spent as much of my adult life with as Steve Podborski (I've only been married since 1984!). It was, for the most part, a mutually-rewarding partnership.

Steve and I joined the team on the same day in British Columbia in the fall of 1973. Nine months later, after traipsing around North America together on the Can-Am tour, Scott Henderson chose us on the same day in Chile for his World Cup squad. In the public mind, we have been linked together forever since.

Whether intentionally or through inadvertence, from our first moments on the Can-Am team, coaches and racers tended to lump us together, to think of us as a couple. It was a marriage of convenience, not of two people with mutual interests or similar personalities. No one knew quite what to do with the tykes once they left the hill, so they left us with each other.

My prattle was full of earnest references to miles logged, interval timers, and FIS points. Steve's was sarcastic, loose, flippant, smart-alecky and, in the beginning, a little too off-the-wall for his more staid teammates. He wore a diamond stud in his left earlobe — a gift from his girlfriend in Toronto — and was always laughing and having a good time.

On the hills, our personalities became a little mixed up. I was an intense charger, an impatient overachiever with a bizarre, windmilling style. I often seemed to be on the verge of catastrophe. Paradoxically, I was also a good glider, although always a little short of technique.

Steve skied with exuberance, but he also possessed as solid a technical base as any skier Canada has ever produced. He could carve magical, geometrically precise turns, slicing snow as easily as a hot knife slides through warm butter. He made it look so simple. On skis he was most self-assured.

Physically, there was almost nothing to choose between us. I was a little taller, with a slightly longer trunk. He may have been a few kilos heavier and stronger than me in the thighs and calves.

In 1973, I was the serious, worldly-wise eighteen year-old but Steve, who was sixteen, was the more accomplished skier. A check of almost any training chart from this period shows him beating me by small margins almost every time we skied.

Steve would probably have stayed ahead of me forever, because of the depth of his talent, if I had not already had a year in Europe under by belt when we landed there in 1974. That first winter, he was zapped by the light, and space, and excitement that surrounded ski racing on the fabled White Circus. So much was new to him: the languages, the travel, the food, and the adulation. There was no question that it amazed and excited him, but it also intimidated him.

At the season opener at Val d'Isère, in 1975, for example, the jaded, fading Austrian superstar, David Zwilling, who had been world champion in downhill in 1974, was to start immediately behind Steve in the second group. At the last instant, Zwilling tried to push his way in front of Steve and start before him. If he had succeeded, Steve would have been disqualified. Steve held his ground and won the battle, but it was illustrative of the little tricks that could upset a young racer. The older boys, like older boys everywhere, weren't averse to throwing their weight around, or bullying those coming up. Steve, with his brash good nature and his earring, was a prime target. I didn't have this problem. I was in the first group!

It was quite a while before Steve adjusted to his new circumstances. While he was making peace with Europe, I drew on the experience I had gained in Switzerland two years earlier. I scooted past Steve, and set my sights on Dave Irwin, David Murray, and Jim Hunter.

That winter, Irwin and I spoiled the European skiing party by becoming the first *aussenseiters*, or "outsiders," to win World Cup downhills. My quick progress was extremely unusual. In skiing, the race is not always won by the hare. The traditional path to World Cup success is a rough-and-tumble, five-year apprenticeship, with results in FIS points, which determine start numbers, improving in increments of five or ten every year. This was Steve's way. He was the tortoise, methodically lumbering to his goal.

By the fall of 1975, Steve was showing much greater maturity. He began to handle the whirlwind we operated in with the assurance and poise which typified his later years as a racer. Then, at Kitzbühel, in the final training run for the Hahnenkamm, exactly a week before the Innsbruck Olympics, he blew his knee out in a wild crash. His parents were *en route* to Europe to see him race for the first time. He was flown home to an uncertain future. His dream was on hold.

In those days, we were all desperately trying to establish ourselves on the team. There were only a few places available in the cash-starved Canadian operation. Naturally, some jostling for position and favour was going on. But most of the time, our life on the road was relaxed and friendly. We were good with each other because we had to be. What was the point of fighting when we had to spend eight months of the year practically on top of one another in European-style double beds?

So great were the talents, and so few the places, that the big European teams were usually involved in unfathomable, internecine battles. There were reliable reports of a fist fight in a hotel room between two first-seed racers in the Swiss camp. It was flattering to have the Europeans write: "These handsome young men from Canada get along so well."

Despite spending a lot of time together during our first three seasons, I would not say that Steve and I were any more dependent on each other than we were on our older teammates. We were as dissimilar temperamentally as two people can be, so it was trying for both of us to spend long periods of time in each other's company. We were also from very different parts of Canada. He was from the suburbs of industrialized Toronto, while I grew up in Peter Lougheed's oil-rich province, in the shadow of the Rocky Mountains. Despite our differences, we competed and got along well.

As David Murray would say, when confronted with questions about the apparently contradictory relationship among teammates: "Us? Rivals? Yeah, sure. For two minutes every week we're enemies."

And that's as close to the truth as I can come in explaining how Steve and I had come to feel about each other. What sets ski racing apart from many other individual sports, such as tennis, boxing, or car racing, and what makes it possible to have a close relationship with those who may be one-hundredth of a second better or worse than you, is that your Nemesis is not your opponent — it is the environment. You don't conquer the field; you tame the mountain.

Typical of the moments Steve and I shared off the hill were our occasional visits to the local *konditorei*, or pastry shop, for an espresso and *apfelstrudel* or *Wiener Torte*, or to the hotel bar for a quiet pint after dinner. On a rare day off, we'd deke out to Zurich to see some bright lights and a movie, or to the Rammelmueller home at Grieskirchen, in the Bohemian forest, to enjoy some calorie-laden Austrian food and a few beers with some of Hans' pals. Once in a blue moon we'd go girl-chasing together, although this was never a priority with either of us. During this period Steve had a regular girl in Toronto. I had a few, not-so-terribly serious or successful romances on the circuit and in Canada. Ski racing was our real passion.

This relatively subdued winter lifestyle was necessary. To race at the highest level demands a dedicated work ethic, and a very disciplined routine. It seems melodramatic to say it, but it was a life-and-death situation every day on the hill. With rocks and trees zinging past us at up to 140 kilometres per hour, neither of us wanted to be in anything less than our best condition.

Until the Lake Placid Olympics, I got most of the press ink because I was winning, but we were equals. Steve was clearly establishing himself as a contender for every race. Then, when he won Canada's first men's Alpine medal, he began to receive as much or more publicity than I did. The reality, in North American terms, was that the public considered an Olympic bronze medal to be of equal or greater value than my victories at Kitzbühel and Wengen. It was a clear demonstration of the power of the Olympic Games.

In the spring of 1980, Steve and Hans Rammelmueller and I made a pact that we would continue to work together, whether with Fischer or another ski firm. No one in the secret triad would sign anything unless we were all satisfied with the deal that was being offered.

We visited with Hans several times that spring at Grieskirchen to explore the possibility of switching to another Austrian ski manufacturer. Ultimately, we decided to stay with Fischer, because they offered us the best financial terms, and what we felt were the most reliable skis.

In May, a few days after all this had been resolved, Steve blew apart the repair job that had been done on his right knee in 1976, while testing skis in very heavy, wet snow at Hintertux. It was a freakish accident. Although he fell, he never actually crashed. It was more as if he had keeled over. Watching from the bottom of the run with Hans as he picked himself up slowly, I said, "Oh-oh."

After it happened, he skied down gingerly on one leg and announced to us matter-of-factly: "I've just destroyed my knee again. At least I think so. I'll have to get it checked when we get home."

He flew home and had another operation. It was a messy one, that re-routed muscle tissue from his thigh through his knee, to replace ligaments which had been torn.

As soon as Fischer found out what had happened, all hell broke loose. They accused Steve of negotiating in bad faith. The company said he must have known that his knee was close to becoming unhinged. He should have told them of this. As his worth was now greatly diminished, they demanded the contract be voided.

To bring them around to a more reasonable position I went to them and said: "If you really are going to try and void Steve's contract, you can void mine, as well. If you drop Steve, you lose your whole Canadian program."

That was the last we heard of the matter.

For the second summer in a row the team — minus Steve — flew to New Zealand's South Island to train in wintry conditions at Mount Hutt. Without Steve to cruise with I had a little extra time on my hands. I spent it with my old British sidekick, Konrad Bartelski.

While in the Antipodes, I received a little warning signal that all was not well with my skiing, although I didn't really pick up on it at the time. In the first of two downhills fellow Calgarian, Chris Kent, who was a member of our C team, upset me. In the other, Bartelski beat me by one-hundredth of a second. For someone who was supposed to be one of the top three or four racers in the world, it was unsettling. I put it down to insufficient concentration and increased my workload.

When we returned to Europe in October, 1980, I knew it was going to be a little tougher for me because, with Steve still in the process of recovering from the knee operation, I would not have the best barometer available to compare myself to.

Training went badly. Most of our camp, which was at Hintertux, was snowed out. I felt that I had not had nearly enough training, and Steve also thought he would benefit from more work. We went to John Ritchie to ask that we be allowed to return to Europe a week before the rest of the team in November. To our surprise, Ritchie tried to squelch the idea. He told us he thought it unnecessary. We were already spending too much time in Europe. What we had proposed undermined the team concept and his authority. Fortunately, we carried enough weight within the association to have him overruled, and he knew it. When push came to shove, he acquiesced.

Hans met us at Geneva Airport and we went off to train at Tignes, France, with the always obliging Currie Chapman and the Canadian women. For five days we skied from dawn to dusk. Every mile we logged counted for a lot. Steve answered every uncertainty about his knee by posting progressively better training times. Incredibly, by the end of our mini-camp, he and his battered knee were only a tiny bit behind me.

The weather for the season opener at nearby Val d'Isère was miserable. First there was thin snow cover, then it snowed like crazy for forty-eight hours. The race was delayed for two days.

On the third day, after our morning jog, we saw the Austrians outside their hotel, ready to leave. They were always eager to leave a country where German wasn't the principal language. We radioed our coaches on the hill. They advised us to stay put as nothing had been decided. After breakfast the word came down from on high: "It's blustery, but it's a go. It's definitely on."

Sure enough, across the street, the Austrians were frantically unpacking. For us, this scene was delightful.

Steve had won the final training run, completing the cycle of ever-improving times which he had assembled the preceding week at Tignes. He didn't win the race, but he was third to our good Austrian friend, Uli Spiess. I placed second; Chris Kent, a World Cup newcomer from Calgary and a member of our C team, was fourth; Irwin was fifth; and Murray was seventh. Pete Patterson, of the US was sixth. It was North America's greatest day ever in downhill!

Only two Austrians were in the first fifteen; only one Swiss in the first ten. Even the Russians, Vladimir Makeev and Valeri Tysganov, had done better.

"A Canadian Tidal Wave," the *Tribune de Geneve* called it. Zurich's *Tages Anzeiger*'s headline read, "The Wild Canadians Have Learned to Calculate the Risks." The Swiss weekly, *La Semaine Sportive* said: "Les Crazy Canucks, maybe are not so crazy," while Vienna's *Der Kurier* quoted Austrian head coach Charlie Kahr: "By all means, I'm pleased that Spiess won, but the aggravation of what the Canadians did gives me more to think about. We have to find out what happened."

What had happened in Steve's case was that he had thrown every ounce of himself into recovering his old form. Daily five- and six-hour sessions with weights and hydraulics had rebuilt him. He was a self-made, bionic man.

At the next stop, Val Gardena, Pod was third again and starting to doubt, just a little, that he would ever make it to the top spot. I was out of it, eleventh, and furious with myself for having hooked an edge and almost bought it in a twisty meadow. Poor Chris Kent had gone down in the notorious Camel Bumps, a series of three prodigious jumps, where he pulled knee ligaments. Most regrettably, Chris never regained anything like the form he had displayed at Val d'Isère.

The last race before Christmas, 1980, was on the Corviglia course, above St. Moritz. It was to be Steve's present to himself. Seven months after tearing his ligaments he became a winner in a time of 1:54.31, one-tenth of a second ahead of Austria's Peter Wirnsberger. Unlike his victory at Morzine, in 1979, which came from my disqualification for wearing the infamous, "wind-proof," illegal downhill suit, or his win at Schladming, eleven months later, which was annulled because of deteriorating weather, this one was untainted and fully-deserved.

Spiess, the dominant racer until that week, was one of several high-flyers who crashed. The Tyrolean ski-school operator's son had flown sixty metres off a bump, banged his head, and torn all four ligaments in one knee. He was flown to Innsbruck by helicopter for repairs, but his downhill career was over. He returned for one more year of competition, but was never again a contender.

It was a mad week, like an excerpt from a Vietnam war documentary. The helicopters arrived every few minutes to ferry out the wounded. Among the fallen: Italy's Alberto Ghidoni and Herbert Plank, and France's Pierre Pacini.

On the second-last training run, after posting the second-best interval time, I, too, crashed a few metres from the finish, cracking my head. It was my second fall of the week, and by far the more serious. For the longest time I could not remember where I was, or what I was doing. I walked up to long-time friends in the finish area and introduced myself to them as if I was a stranger.

The tumbles really shook my psyche. John Ritchie said it was an axiom on the World Cup: Ken Read almost never fell and if he did he never, never hurt himself. For the first time in my life I had learned what it was like to be intimidated by a mountain. I dreaded the thought of racing and my result showed it. I was ninth, more than one second behind Steve.

The course was above the tree line, a few kilometres from St. Moritz and its millionaires and jetport. It had not been raced on for six years. Since then, equipment had become better and so had the racers, but nothing to do with the course, or course safety, had been changed. Most of us were unable to handle the higher speed. Five racers were lost for the season.

While all those about him were losing their heads Steve sailed, undaunted, down the Corviglia track with the style that is so much his own. He was quiet on his skis, compact of body and smooth through the corners and off the bumps. He could have had a videotape made of his run, and sold it to the rest of us as a training film.

Our roles were now reversed. Pod was the pre-eminent Canadian skier. For the first time since 1974, I was playing catch-up.

At home I followed my usual Christmas procedure, taking a couple of days off, then hitting the boards hard for a few days at Lake Louise. I was determined to shake the frightening effects of St. Moritz, and regain my composure in time for the coming battle.

The White Circus reassembled at Garmisch-Partenkirchen, in the first week of January, 1981. Steve and I were rooming together as we had in December. There was no question that we had a tremendous competition going. We were not only trying to outdo each other in training, we were also trying to be the fastest past all the most difficult section timers. It was a strange time — as a writer for *Sports Illustrated* wrote in an article which appeared the following week, Steve and I roomed together, chummed together, coached each other and then, for two minutes a week were tigers, each doing all in our power to beat the other guy.

When I came down the mountain at Garmisch on race day, my section times indicated that I would have finished third or second or first — if I had been able to make it past the last curve and across the finish line.

Twenty metres shy of the mark I provided the audience with a macabre thrill. In an attempt to shave a little more time from my result, I cut close to a gate on my left. As I did this, I caught my left ski on some loose snow and fell on my face. Splat! I jacknifed in the snow. Within two or three seconds my speed declined from 120 kilometres per hour to zero.

Ligaments in my left knee were shredded like spaghetti. My nose was broken, and a gash above my right eye required five stitches. My season had come to an abrupt end. Forty-eight hours later I would be under a surgeon's knife for the first time in my life, in a hospital nine times zones away, in Vancouver.

Steve then came down the Kreuzeck-Kandahar course and established a new course record. It was a marvelous achievement, because the Garmisch downhill was so completely unlike the course at St. Moritz — it had smooth, high-speed turns, and several languid flats. It was hard to believe the same skier could master both.

I'm sure it was a bitter-sweet victory for Steve. His win, by more than a third of a second over Switzerland's Peter Müller, was a stunner. But a guy he'd spent thousands of hours working with had been wrecked before his eyes. In looking at videotapes later, I saw him watching course workers load me into the ambulance. He actually looked sadder than I did.

That night, he was super. Instead of celebrating his victory with champagne, the man who was now the toast of Europe spent hours with me in the hotel room. He brought me food. He answered the telephone, which was ringing constantly, and he packed all my gear for the trip home. It was really a pathetic scene. On one side of the room was his huge winner's trophy; on the other side were my crutches.

In retrospect, I realize that I got carried away at Garmisch. In my haste to climb back to the top, I started to gun too much. With Steve skiing exceptionally well, I was taking unacceptable risks to keep up. In the last day of training, I was fastest in both training runs for the first time ever. I should have cooled it a little, and waited to best him in the next few races. After all, the towns of my two greatest successes, Kitzbühel and Wengen, were the next stops.

Steve had a tremendous season, winning his third consecutive race at Kitzbühel. He was only narrowly edged out for the title by Austria's Harti Weirather, in the last two races of the season at Aspen, Colorado.

That summer, for the first time, I was the one with a knee injury to recover from, not Steve. He could not have been more helpful. His most useful piece of advice was that my knee was like a person, and I must listen to it. "If it hurts, don't do it. If it's tired, stop. If it's swelling up, you're doing something wrong. If you listen to what it has to say, you'll do fine. The knee is a beautiful joint, but when it blows up it must be treated very carefully."

Many athletes feel that they have to rush to get back into action after they're injured. I didn't. Because my knee had popped in January, there was no way I could compete in the last eight weeks of the season. I had the luxury of an eleven-month recovery period.

When I rejoined the team late in the summer of 1981, in New Zealand, Steve was not there. After working so hard in the previous summer, and after his three victories during the winter, he needed a rest. To keep sharp, he cycled.

None of the other senior members of the team wanted to go south that summer, so I was in with the junior members. They were to be my new training competitors.

On the long, winding road up to the Mount Hutt ski station, I was very anxious to find out how my knee would perform. After taking in the breathtaking panorama of the southern Alps, and the table-flat Canterbury Plain below, I went over to the beginner's hill, put a knee brace on and slapped my skis down. A service rep adjusted my bindings, making them as loose and easy to wear as possible, and I was off.

The first turn was to the left, on my good left knee. No problem, of course. The next was to the right. And it felt the same as always. Within a few hours I was on the advanced hill, my confidence growing by the minute. In the next few weeks I experienced no problems on the soft, natural snow. In fact, my progress was so rapid that I foreran the New Zealand downhill championship, although not exactly in Crazy Canuck fashion.

In the fall, when Steve rejoined the team, our roles were reversed from the previous year. Steve was setting the standard, while I continued my recovery.

I sensed a rather interesting alteration in the way people dealt with us during that period. I had been the leader in the late 1970s. Now Steve was top-dog . . . an Olympic medallist, a three-time World Cup winner, and like me, a conqueror of Kitzbühel's treacherous Hahnenkamm.

Before, the Canadian team had always been just that, a team. After Steve began winning, the results of the rest of the Canadian team collapsed. When I returned, I had naïvely expected the situation to be as it was before, but it wasn't. With me gone for half a season, Steve had gone about business by himself. He didn't need me any more, but I needed him. I was struggling back from an injury. I was trying to get into the thick of things as quickly as possible; but not wanting to overdo it and suffer a relapse. I wanted his counsel, and I didn't get it. The rapport, the camaraderie, the sharing of ideas and problems, were no longer there. Our relationship had changed. He was polite, but cool and distant.

I was greatly troubled and sought the advice of our downhill coach, Heinz Kappeler. He and Hans Rammelmueller were my closest allies on the team.

"Look," Heinz said, in his almost-Canadian English. "Until your accident, he always felt he needed the help of others. He's spent half a year doing it on his own now, and he now knows he can do it without you or anyone else. He's simply carrying on with the pattern that brought him success."

It was hard for me to accept what I was hearing, but I knew it to be true. Steve had matured enough to carry on alone. I felt very strongly that the team concept was what had made us special. Somehow I was adrift. I was hurt.

"Well, this is only a training period," Kappeler said. "Try not to worry about this. When we get to Val d'Isère, be at the top of the mountain early. Do your warmup and when inspection starts, be there, ready to do it as you've always done it . . . together. If he comes up to you and says, "Let's go," inspect the course together. I don't know, for sure, but I think that's what he'll do. But if he skis past you, there is nothing you can do about it. You'll know things have changed forever."

On the morning of the first training run for the Test of the First Snow, at Val d'Isère, I stood leaning on my ski poles beside the start hut waiting for the course inspection. I was also waiting to resume the relationship which had been so successful for the preceding seven years. It wasn't too long before Steve poled up beside me. And continued down the course alone.

There was no fight. No sharp exchange of words. There couldn't be. It was not a matter of who was right or wrong. I had resolved to do things as I always had done them, with him. He had obviously resolved to do things the way he had learned to do them the previous winter — by himself. The things that had brought us together in the past no longer mattered. We were to go our separate ways on the World Cup. It was as if he'd spread his wings and left the nest.

GOVERNMENT AND SPORT

CHAPTER EIGHTEEN

S EBASTIAN COE, the celebrated English middle distance run-
ner, set me thinking about government and sport when
he described to me a thorough study the British Ministry of
Sport had made of our system. As a performing athlete and
I guess, as a Canadian, I used to scoff at government and
politicians. In my active years, I paid scant attention to their
activities.

Sebastian sits on the British Athletic Commission. He is
quick, shrewd and commonsensical. It struck me that, if he
and the British sports leaders thought we had made something
worthwhile, perhaps something worth imitating, maybe I had
better reassess my own experience and reactions. What is it
we have which is unique and worthwhile? How did it come
about? How has it affected our ski teams? What does it presage
for the future?

It's not corny or being Goody Two-shoes to want your country to have a workable, sound system for administering sport.
If I had one penchant above others which helped my skiing,
it was a penchant for a system. I am a systematic type. I have
to plan and organize and schedule my days and hours. Perhaps
it is something of an obsession with me. Being loosey-goosey
and just doing one's thing may be fun, but not forever; in fact,
not for very long. There's nothing profound in this. Athletes
and teams simply must have intelligent plans and goals.

Government organizational support and funding are not
merely the necessary underpinnings of a national sports program; they are also an expression of pride and faith in the
talents of our young people. I depended on them. Pod did. So
did everyone on our teams.

One of the oldest themes in high-performance sports is "the

natural," the athlete who just has it, who can't miss. I guess the obvious example in our generation is Wayne Gretzky. But those who think he just happened, don't know of the literally thousands of hours he trained, and practised, and drilled. His family, his neighbourhood, and ultimately his government provided and supported the facilities and the coaching and so on. All meshed together with Wayne's talent and will-power, so we have an athlete who is both a common denominator for Canadians, and a real symbol of our national identity in this quarter of a century.

Wayne Gretzky shows us what Canada can produce. And out of ourselves we have also produced a system for supporting and advancing amateur sport. It's not like the British, or the American, or the gold medal-rich East German system. It's unique.

I have tended — and still do — to take "government" to mean the federal government, that is, Ottawa. For many of us, government is personified by the Minister of Sport; say, the graceful Iona Campagnolo, or Otto Jelinek, the gold medal pairs skater who turned to politics. By adopting this national emphasis, I know I am overlooking the complex realities of government in Canada. I do it as a Calgarian, knowing full well the essential parts which the Alberta government and the city of Calgary are playing in the grandest festival in our winter sports history — the Calgary Olympics.

I find it interesting, occasionally flattering, and sometimes presumptuous that people will suggest, either in the media, or in tentative chats, that I may be considering a political career. Not so; at least not yet. But I have boned up on our sports system since I left competitive racing.

Have I any particular insights into government and sport? No! At least, not beyond a rational appreciation that politicians meet in sport exactly the simple, durable dilemmas of democracy in general.

How does one square the need to foster excellence with the principle of broad participation? Ken Reads and Alex Baumanns are all very well, but is their level of achievement what government should be concerned about?

Rather than lavishing funds, expertise, and special facilities on these few, shouldn't government be supporting the vast mass of kids, seeing that they get access to good, handy facilities and competition?

Someone once told me that the late Lloyd Percival, the "radio coach" of thirty years ago, and the father of the present Canadian sports system, believed there is a plain link between gold medals at world-class level, and mass activity at the recreational level, in all competitive sports.

Percival talked of "the pyramid" at the peak of which were the leaders in skill, heart, and fire, who were drawn from among the thousands who made up the base. Not only was there no gap in his conception between the stars and the "fun" athletes, but great success at the summit could only come, in a genuinely democratic country, through a welter of popular activity. Percival's theory wasn't of a "trickle down" effect, but of a pushing up.

It's a simple idea — the pyramid — but I like it. I'm part of the pyramid, myself. Over the years, tens of thousands of kids have skied in junior racing programs such as the one I skied in at Camp Fortune. Of all those kids, seven or eight made it to the national team. If the pool had been smaller, the number of racers who would have made the national team would probably have been smaller, too. Maybe Ken Read wouldn't have been one of them. Who knows?

You can see the pyramid at work best in Canada in the organization of ice hockey. So many boys have played the game that, when they become men, they form a natural audience for the sport. In the United States basketball is so popular now — perhaps even more popular than football or baseball — because so many Americans played the game in their youth. But look at the sorry state of Canadian football. It is withering away, and the main reason is that so few Canadian high schools are still playing the game. Why, twenty years ago, football was a big deal in Calgary or Ottawa! Now far fewer follow it, because the base is gone. We musn't let that happen to skiing or other sports.

My aim in the years ahead, as a vice-president of the Canadian Olympic Association, and as one who believes there's value both in playing games and in striving for excellence, is to help where I can, perhaps by making government more intelligible to both athletes and citizens.

Government in Canada came late to sports activity, in a formal way. The official history seems to begin with the Diefenbaker government's creation of the National Fitness and

Amateur Sport Act of 1961, but the big federal push came as we headed into the 1970s. In 1969, a task force on sport headed by an oil industry executive, Harold Rea, made a lot of recommendations to Pierre Trudeau and his government. Our finest, pound-for-pound skier, Nancy Greene, was one of the three task-force members.

Before 1968 and Trudeau, Ottawa had never spent more than $3 million a year on fitness and amateur sport, although the 1961 act permitted a ceiling of up to $5 million. This year (1987) the federal spending figure will be over $70 million. The biggest jump came in the mid-1970s while Ms. Campagnolo was minister. But federal spending figures only tell a small part of the story.

In 1969, none of the provinces really had a cadre of sports officials. It has been estimated that in sport itself, aside from those serving golf and tennis clubs, there weren't a hundred people in Canada who could be classed as full-time amateur sports administrators. Less than two decades later, there are 15,000 at the federal, provincial, and municipal level, or working for sports associations or clubs. All provinces but one now have their own sports bureaucracy. Most of the bigger provinces sponsor or partly fund a variety of provincial amateur sports associations. All have emulated the federal model.

More than anyone else, it was John Munro, who in 1969 was Trudeau's minister of health and welfare, who picked up the ball created by the task force report and ran with it, hard. Munro created Sport Canada, a distinct segment within the huge federal bureaucracy, to direct federal activity, especially funding, to *élite* amateur sport. Sport Canada, to put it succinctly, was shooting for the best. The plan was to lift amateur sports organizations off the kitchen tables. The National Sport and Recreation Centre sprang up in Ottawa. It housed half a hundred or more sports associations, and aided them in providing technical and administrative support to their members. One of the best, computer-based information centres for technique in sport was established; so was a national association for coaches.

But the idea that has attracted the most interest from other countries was Sport Canada's "Game Plan." This is simply a financial-assistance program for athletes. It's first great purpose was to strengthen our chances in the Montreal Olympics of 1976. It continues to provide basic financial support to athletes who qualify by reaching, or nearly reaching, world-class levels.

Game Plan was much like the programs developed federally on the arts front in the 1950s and directed by the Canada Council. Perhaps in sport it is simpler, because there are fewer arguments about what constitutes excellence. There are winners and losers.

In essence Ottawa, acting for the nation, recognized in the 1960s that athletes were representing Canada at the Olympics and the various world championships, and that Canadians wanted them to do well. To do well requires good coaching, the best competition, and a modicum of financial support. For most sports, serious training demands six to eight months a year, or more, of concentration and effort. Alpine skiing, as an example, requires so much training it effectively denies an athlete the chance to find or hold a regular job, or take a full course load at high school or university.

Another sensible and welcome inducement to athletes was provided by Sport Canada. Athletes who spent the years normally devoted to attaining a higher education, in competitive sports, could later have their university tuition and some other expenses taken care of.

On the whole I think the best thing I can say about our system, centred on Sport Canada, is that it kept a sense of proportion while remaining unobtrusive.

We do not have the chauvinistic Eastern-bloc system, with truly massive spending, rigid controls, rigorous streaming, scientific experimentation, and the intense expectation of medals for the Motherland or the Fatherland that goes with it. Nor do we suffer from the delusion that sports superiority is indicative of a superior political system.

We didn't take the American way, either, with its enormous dependence on volunteerism, free enterprise, and jingoism on one side, and the huge role played by the educational system, from grade school to university, on the other. Athletes in the United States, once they are outside of the educational system, are often unable to remain involved in their sport. A lot of talent falls through the cracks as a result. Our system of "carded athletes," and our support for teams, also helps to keep as many as possible of our budding athletes in Canada, rather than allowing them to be lured away by the athletic scholarships and grants-in-aid which American universities offer.

What has been working for us is the typical, perhaps notorious, Canadian gift for compromise: government involvement without government domination.

From meagre success in the 1950s and 1960s, we've been coming on strong. In many sports we're now ranked second or third in the Western world, despite our relatively sparse numbers. Perhaps what I like best is that we've had no major fusses over government involvement. Although Ottawa underwrites some forty per cent of the Alpine skiing expenses, and as much as ninety-nine per cent for some other sports, its interventions have been few.

We, on the ski team, had a high enough profile to be drawn into direct contact with the politicians. From time to time, we had the chance to see the ministers responsible for sport at close hand. I wasn't old enough to meet John Munro and his successor, Marc Lalonde. I gather that each one, although a remarkable contrast in style and personality, was a mover and a shaker. Each had clout in the political drama. Neither was himself a keen participant or fan of high level sport, but they both recognized its significance to national spirit and pride. Both seized the point that regular events, like the Canada Games and the Olympics or World Championships, could provide the occasions to build across Canada an array of top-flight facilities: pools, courts, and tracks. And so we got structures and programs. And the provinces followed the federal lead, Quebec and Ontario with a vengeance.

It was against the background of this burgeoning governmental activity that my skiing career was played. I first came face-to-face with government, most pleasantly, in the person of Iona Campagnolo. For all her great looks, I saw and see her as a straightforward MP from Skeena, a small-town person from the northern BC wilderness. To me she exuded both enthusiasm for sport and a sense of frugality. Her message was that we all had to do our best with limited dollars. I was happy, not critical, when she seemed to parlay the profile she gained with the sport portfolio to her later role as president of her political party.

The next minister I knew, Steve Paproski, had a run of less than a year, before electoral defeat in early 1980 sent him back into opposition. Steve, a broad-beamed and beaming ex-lineman with the Edmonton Oilers, followed a proposal put forward by Joe Clark, and took Ottawa out of direct sponsorship of lotteries for fund-raising purposes.

A deal was struck with the provinces for the sake of better relations. In effect, the federal lottery franchise was "farmed out" for an annual, indexed rental, which last year came to over $30 million. This sounds like a lot, but it's a smidgen beside the much larger profits the provinces retain.

What has this to do with sport? Two things. First, it was sports people who campaigned for the legalization of lotteries, and the profits from the original ones were dedicated to sports. (Remember the Montreal Olympics?) Second, the proliferation of lotteries has diverted a lot of discretionary spending away from sports groups. Raffles, draws, and special sales were once the staples of amateur sport financing. Now the money goes to Lotto 6/49, Western Express, and the rest.

My hunch is that Steve Paproski never understood what he was supposed to do as minister for sport. He had a few hundred of us to a $50,000 "dinner for champions" under the magnificent chandeliers in the National Ballroom on Parliament Hill. We met Prime Minister Clark and he praised us. I had the honour of presenting a track suit to Maureen McTeer. Six weeks later, the Clark government ordered many of the athletes at the dinner out of the Moscow Olympics, because Soviet troops had invaded Afghanistan.

A few days into the Lake Placid Olympics, our minister was part of a defeated government. Trudeau was back in power, and the new minister for sport was the very experienced ex-premier of Nova Scotia, Gerry Regan. Although Regan was given other duties (first labour, then international trade) he gave those of us in sport the feeling that he had time and thought for us. Of course, he played to the hilt the "godfather" part, handing out cheques, dedicating stadiums and introducing athletes to the House of Commons. He had influence in cabinet and gave me the feeling that the politics of sport were in good hands. He was also the first politician to recognize the potential role our leading amateur athletes could play as ambassadors for Canada. The best-known Canadian athletes overseas are not Wayne Gretzky or Guy Lafleur. They are people such as Gaetan Boucher and Alex Baumann. Regan had the Department of External Affairs arrange for such high-profile athletes to appear at meetings like the Davos World Economic Symposium, and the Winter Sports Trade Show in Munich, to spread the good word about Canada. We were also called on to actively support Calgary's Olympic bid.

After Regan, Senator Ray Perrault assumed the sport portfolio. He lasted nine months from the time he was appointed in the fall of 1982. It was clear that as a Vancouverite, he had a priority — to bring major league baseball to the coast to play in Canada's first completed domed stadium. He was also the minister during much of the wrap-up of inter-governmental negotiations on the Calgary Olympics.

Then, in 1983, the ministerial door began to swing. After Ray Perrault we got Céline Hervieux-Payette, Jacques Olivier, and then "the Kid," twenty-eight year-old Jean Lapierre.

Hervieux-Payette was a bad sport minister because her attention was on other matters. Olivier seemed a most uncomfortable bird of brief passage. Lapierre never had a real shot, regrettably. At least, those in Sport Canada who would know, tell me he was an eager, sensible doer.

Lapierre's term was a mere flick of an eyelid. His successor, a Tory MP from Toronto, Otto Jelinek, has been in charge since September, 1984, the first ex-athlete of renown in the post. He's sensitive to athletic issues. I would guess he's been the most single-minded and intense of all the ministers of sport.

As part of a cabinet dedicated to reducing the federal deficit, Jelinek has had to be a trimmer, not a spender. And so he's fixed, sensibly, on raising more "outside money" for sport. If we're to reach the top rungs of the world sport ladder and stay there, more backing is required. Jelinek took the lead with a plan to draw corporate sector money to amateur sport. This entails a lot of horn-blowing, for example, by athletes like me. We all know that corporate financing for sport is almost certain to tumble after the 1988 Olympics, unless we do something about it. And so we have to brag and strut a bit to draw and retain backing.

I am much less taken with Jelinek's reluctance to tackle the sponsorship of sport by tobacco companies. He's never been less in tune with the chimes of change. No matter how sharp the cries from tobacco growers and cigarette-makers, tobacco and sport are incompatible.

An issue very much to the fore these days is that of politics and international sport. Of course, everyone with some common sense knows that governments will sometimes use sport, or bend it for the purpose of political advantage. There has been steady agitation, for example, to boycott the athletes of South Africa.

Competitors at international sporting events can usually get along well, perhaps better than their various countries, politically-speaking. Although the Olympic ideal of amity and understanding through sport may still not be proof against any number of international crises and pressures, I see it as an ideal worth pursuing. Certainly, most of our skiing races were held far beyond our borders, and done in company with rivals of many nationalities. You know by now that I thought it worthwhile.

PAST,
PRESENT,
AND FUTURE___ *CHAPTER NINETEEN*

T HE CRAZY CANUCKS remain exceptions in the history of
Canadian ski racing. The enduring story remains our female
ski racers — our "Golden Girls."

True, the men have won downhill races eighteen times in
World Cup competitions. In doing so, they have enjoyed much
public attention, but they have won only two World Championships and one Olympic medal. It's the women who have
brought Canada most of its skiing successes. It makes for a
long paragraph.

Lucille Wheeler was the first Canadian to make the international grade, winning a bronze medal in the 1956 Olympics
at Cortina, and two gold medals in the 1958 World Championships at Badgastein. Next came Ann Heggtveit. She won
the slalom gold in the Squaw Valley Olympics by the largest
margin ever. Nancy Greene won a slew of races, and the first
overall World Cup title in 1967, repeating in 1968. She is
perhaps better known for a gold and a silver in giant slalom
and slalom in the Grenoble Olympics in 1968. Betsy Clifford
won the giant slalom gold medal as a sixteen year-old at the
Val Gardena World Championships in 1970, and a downhill
silver medal in the 1974 World Championships at St. Moritz,
after recovering from a pair of broken heels. Kathy Kreiner
stopped the Rosi Mittermaier sweep in the Innsbruck Olympics by winning the giant slalom gold medal in 1976. The gold
rush rolled on in 1982 in the World Championships at Haus,
when Gerry Sorensen won the downhill. Today we have Laurie
Graham and a small cadre of women planning medals for
themselves in the Calgary Olympics.

The question is obvious: Why have Canadian women done
better than the men at ski racing?

I believe it has to do with the available talent pool. Many of the most athletically promising boys in Canada choose ice hockey as their winter sport. It's in the ice game that they and their parents see a future career and glory. Other boys turn to other team games such as football, baseball, or basketball, or to any one of the more than fifty other sports which the federal and provincial governments subsidize.

Ours is a small population and, as I see it, men's skiing does not draw much of the cream in athletic talent; not as much as in Austria or Switzerland, for example. But women's skiing is another matter. Hockey rarely entices our girls away from skiing, and so the coaches in skiing begin with better female athletes. You see it in Alpine skiing, and as clearly in figure skating and diving. Another, much less obvious factor, I believe, is that downhill skiing demands a very assertive personality, and North American women tend to be much more assertive than European women. They have much more confidence, because most of them have been treated to greater equality at home and in school.

Certainly, Alpine Europe remains a very chauvinistic, male-dominated society. In the mountains women are still in the kitchen. In our country, particularly since the 1960s, girls and women have come to expect a chance to pursue what they want. They're willing to push for it. Their determination is reflected in their skiing successes. Canadian women have tended to do better in the past decade in the most assertive and demanding event, the downhill.

After the retirement of Clifford, Judy Crawford, and Kathy Kreiner's older sister, Laurie, there was a falling off in the results of Canadian women. Only Kathy was in the first seed. While the men took over the limelight, the women were slowly regaining confidence under a new coach, Currie Chapman. He was a member of the Canadian team of the late 1960s. He was one of those athletes who never reached the heights himself, but became a very successful coach.

Why did Currie make the top grade as a coach? I believe because he's such an analytical thinker. He thought long and hard about why he, himself, didn't make it as a racer, and what might have been done to make him succeed.

Chapman injected enthusiasm into the women's program. He gathered a competent staff, led by his downhill specialist, Don Lyon, and Max Gartner, an Austrian technical specialist who moved into the Alberta program last year. In profession-alizing the women's team, they also identified and remedied the one great weakness: the women weren't in excellent phys-ical condition. Peter Kopp and Bill Gvoitch were brought in to work on dryland conditioning.

In his first coaching years, Currie had his team train closely with the men's squad. In the interaction that resulted, the women picked up the men's knack for aggressive skiing. Tough downhill training made the races themselves that much easier for the women. Success came quickly to Gerry Sorensen. On a demanding course, she was unquestionably the fastest, strongest, and bravest woman in the world. At times she resembled a loose cannonball. No one could touch her. A few years later, Laurie Graham stormed into view with much the same daring. If conditions were appalling, she could be counted upon to do well.

There were costs and casualties, however, as a result of this "total downhill" philosophy. Short-term success for the few athletes who could handle the rough going may have been at the expense of longer range success for several others.

Someone who might have become a winner was Dee Dee Haight. She grew up in the same valley as Nancy Greene in the British Columbia interior. In 1981, she became the first Canadian to win the Europa Cup, or B circuit, narrowly edging out Brigitte Oertli, of Switzerland.

Haight was a fine technical skier who might have done well in slalom or giant slalom. For short-term advantage, she was pushed into downhill, where she scored several top fifteen results. But she also suffered three severe leg injuries which led her to miss almost three complete seasons. To fulfil her promise as a technical skier would have taken longer, but it is likely that she would have been hurt less. She retired last winter, her confidence shot. Her Europa Cup challenger, Oer-tli, finished third overall in the 1987 World Cup.

The same might be said of Liisa Savijarvi. She had a crisis of confidence and then a horrible, career-threatening injury at Vail last March, after fine results a year earlier. She felt the intense pressure to succeed. Liisa was a more difficult riddle to solve than Dee Dee Haight. She probably needed slower nurturing to re-establish her progress.

If I have seemed to denigrate Chapman's record, by citing examples of women who did not thrive within his program,

I still acknowledge and admire his achievements. He made the Canadian women's team stronger and deeper than it had ever been before. His methods were particularly well-suited to Laurie Graham. She has been the third-ranked woman downhiller in the world for two years now, and is Canada's leading prospect for an Alpine medal in the 1988 Olympics.

Although Haight and Savijarvi were stronger, technically-speaking, neither one had Laurie's psychological make-up. Laurie could block outside influences, and narrow her focus, so that only the hill was on her mind. In Currie's words, "Laurie is a racehorse."

A list of other Canadian women racers with medal chances at Calgary must include Alberta's all-rounder, twenty-one year-old Karen Percy. Although she has not won yet, she has finished in the top fifteen several times in the past few seasons, including a bronze medal result in the Husky World downhill at Banff in 1986. Karen's youth, her growing confidence and grace under pressure, and her great physical strength mark her as a future champion with a good medal chance in the Alpine combination as well as downhill. Another possible medallist is technical specialist, Josée Lacasse, of Brossard, Quebec, who began to gain prominence two seasons ago with top-ten finishes in giant slalom. Last season she became the first French Canadian to stand on the podium in a World Cup race, finishing third at Waterville Valley, New Hampshire.

It is not easy to coach women racers. As Currie's assistant, Don Lyon, has said: "They cry when they win and they cry when they lose." It takes a unique person to ride the emotional roller coasters with them. Currie has done a better job than any women's coach I know. It's true he's closer to some team members than others. It's a difficult thing to accept, but a coach can't be everything to everybody. A good coach, like Chapman, counts on his assistants to step in and fill the gaps.

Chapman has also tried to expand his program beyond the usual flight to Europe for a glacier training camp, and three intense months of racing. He has introduced some genteel, low-key aspects to the European experience, by moving his team to cities like Rome and Venice, and for short holidays in the south of France. These breaks, which have even included dryland training at Club Meds, have helped his team members hold a higher interest level. It's a canny strategy.

MY ONE GREAT SADNESS about the Calgary Olympics is that my good friend and former running mate, Todd Brooker, will not be there. He was the bridge between the Crazy Canucks, and the new generation of racers. As the link between the past and the future, Todd was in a difficult position. During the most crucial years of his career, after the Sarajevo Olympics, he was the only Canadian in the first seed. But it is difficult, if not impossible, to win consistently on the World Cup without some teammates to push you. A series of nasty knee injuries obliged him to retire last winter.

One of the reasons Todd was alone after the last of the Crazy Canucks retired in 1984 was that Scott Henderson's replacement as head coach, John Ritchie, did little to develop a group of racers to replace the Crazy Canucks.

It is, of course, a coach's job to win, but it is equally, if not more, important to develop new talent. In fact, the measure of a coach's success is not the talent he inherits, but the talent he builds. During Ritchie's six-year tenure, only one world-class talent emerged — Todd Brooker. From the beginning, in November 1977, Ritchie focused all his attention on the best racers, ignoring those who were coming up. This approach was disastrous for promising young racers like Tim Gilhooly, Mike Irwin, Robin McLeish, and Chris Kent. These skiers were not given the quantity or quality of training which Scott Henderson insisted upon in the mid-1970s. Whereas Scott required that we all train and race in slalom and giant slalom events, as well as downhill, in order to build a strong technical base, John directed a program focused on downhill almost exclusively.

My problems with John Ritchie began soon after he joined the team, a few months after Heinz Kappeler was hired as a downhill specialist. It is not surprising when the personalities of certain racers mesh better with different coaches. I developed a close relationship with Kappeler. We communicated well and effectively about what line to pursue and how to handle course conditions. He was a technical expert. I turned his instructions into results. We were a winning combination.

John was never a strong technical influence on the program. We simply could not trust his judgement on technical matters. For example, in 1982, at Aspen, I skied the course well on the first day of training, but I was having trouble in a section we called the "Spring Pitch." John had been stationed in that area. His only comment was that both my runs had been excellent. On the second day, following a review of section times and video film, I decided to try two different lines. On the first run I followed the one I felt was fastest. On the second, I followed a line that looked best on video. On inspection following the two runs, John's analysis was that I was right on line with excellent runs. I was floored! In each run my line had been purposely different. I needed accurate feedback and just wasn't getting it. I told Steve Podborski about it. He just shrugged and said, "John is sometimes too proud to wear his glasses. He can't see what we're doing." From that day on, until I retired, I listened to John with scepticism.

John never seemed able to accept my close ties to Heinz. Moreover, he became terribly defensive about the frequent description of Heinz in the European media as the "real coach" of the Canadian team. European journalists viewed Ritchie as excess baggage. I defended John against these slurs many times. My line of argument was that it was not his job to be the downhill coach or the technical expert. He nonetheless played a strong, effective managerial role for the team. He co-ordinated our schedules, made travel arrangements and hotel bookings, and acted as another pair of eyes on the hill.

But I lost my desire to stick up for John when I noticed how he began to undermine Heinz's position. John complained about Heinz to the CSA. He started to represent himself as the mastermind of Canada's downhill success, neglecting to mention the other coaches and support staff, or those who had gone before him. By 1982, the situation had become intolerable: Heinz had no choice but to quit. The team concept that had been established years before was in ruins.

In a show of loyalty and respect, ten of the twelve racers on the team sent a petition to the CSA, demanding that Heinz be recalled and named head coach. In retrospect, it is not surprising that the CSA stood behind John. Steve Podborski had just won the World Cup. To replace John with a Swiss coach would have been politically difficult.

During the uproar in 1982 John insisted he would remain with the team through the Sarajevo Olympics. Less than twelve months after Heinz quit, John did, too. He announced his departure before the end of the season, creating additional pressure and uncertainty for the athletes.

Fortunately, the errors of the early 1980s have been acted on. Even as early as 1984, the ski team identified lack of depth in the downhill program as a significant problem and initiated remedial work with the emphasis on basic technique. In the last three years under the new regime, young talent has begun to blossom.

It was a wonderful surprise to me last winter when the Canadian men's team became winners again with a first by Rob Boyd at Val Gardena. A few weeks later, the fair-haired British Columbian confirmed his status as a world-ranking racer by placing fifth in the World Championships at Crans Montana. This was the best Canadian result ever.

Others pressing Boyd for a place on the podium include Brian Stemmle and Felix Belcyzk. Under the quiet tutelage of their Austrian downhill coach, Heinz Stohl, they have begun to develop something of the momentum and internal dynamics that characterized the Crazy Canucks.

Of the Canadian men, I would rate Boyd, whose enthusiasm and maturity have impressed me very much, as having the best chance for Olympic success, but it may be too early in their development for these young fellows to win medals at Calgary. They lack experience. They will, of course, have the advantage of racing at home on a course they are familiar with. This counts for a lot.

Our men's technical team will face a far more competitive field in the Olympic slalom and giant slalom races. Canada has never had serious challengers in these events. We lack a sufficient base, and those who show promise have not been given enough opportunity to compete against the best on the World Cup. My brother Jim, and Alain Villiard represent our only chances for good technical results. Regrettably, their medal prospects are remote.

WHAT IT ALL MEANT

I CHOSE TO RETIRE just before the 1984 season, and the Olympics in Sarajevo. All that winter, I was asked why I had quit before the most important event in the Alpine quadrennial. I am still asked about it occasionally today.

Some have speculated that I decided to retire in 1983, even before my final season began. This is not so. I went into that season with my head up, ready to assess my feelings about ski racing. My health, and the level of my desire, were the key questions facing me. I began the 1983 season healthy and hungry for a World Cup title. I looked forward to the trial run on the Olympic downhill course as a significant test. My results there would have a lot to do with my future plans.

Well, Sarajevo was a disappointment. Although the Yugoslavs had tried their best, and had used the tallest mountain in Bosnia, there just wasn't enough mountain. It was not a great challenge. To invest another twelve months of my life to work towards a race on a marginal course did not make sense to me. I had finished fifth at the pre-Olympic trial. In the finish area that day I decided to retire.

The decision was the culmination of a winter of serious thought about my future. Many factors played a part in my decision to quit.

A delightful young woman had entered my life, bringing with her a joy in skiing and a fresh perspective on training. She made skiing fun, always with a laugh to carry us through the sweat and grind of pre-season preparations. Lynda Robbins was an outstanding ski racer in her own right. This fact immediately limited the amount of time we could spend together. Growing frustration with the ski team's regimented lifestyle meant we were ready for a change.

I had already enjoyed the positive aspects of two Olympic Games. I had been a player in the drama of the greatest downhill race ever, at Innsbruck, in 1976. Lake Placid had been a disaster for me, but I had good memories of the Opening Ceremony, in which I carried the Canadian flag.

Another factor pushing me towards retirement was that I felt increasingly alone on the White Circus. Over the previous five seasons, I had established a deep personal friendship with our downhill coach, Heinz Kappeler. When he quit the team, much of my zest for the sport disappeared. Through the 1982-1983 season I formed a good relationship with Heinz's successor, Joey Lavigne. I had known him for years and appreciated his congenial, relaxed manner, but I missed the intimate understanding of the sport I felt I had when I discussed skiing with Heinz. Any athlete who has had a personal mentor will know what I mean.

Yet another factor in my decision to leave the team was that I was making slow progress towards my degree in economics. Although ski racing had provided me with valuable communication skills, and a chance to learn languages painlessly, I was ready for new challenges.

Ski racing was a succession of goals. Certainly, at the outset, I had no visions of World Cup victories. Canadian men had a history of mediocre results. I did have a burning ambition to turn these results around. I've never subscribed to the so-called Canadian inferiority complex. It has always been my firm belief that if we give ourselves the tools for success and put our minds to it, we are as capable and competitive as the best.

One might call my career one of missed opportunities, taking into account the Lake Placid disaster, Morzine, and my knee injury. I look at it differently. When I began, no Canadian male had ever won a World Cup race. I broke the barrier and created a whole new mind-set for Canadian skiers. From that point on, everything was possible.

Every ski racer wants to win the World Cup. I was no different. But for my disqualification at Morzine in 1979, and the loss by two-hundredths of a second in the second downhill at Wengen in 1980, the title might have been mine. But, by 1983, I realized that this goal was slipping further from my grasp.

I had one other goal in my final year as a ski racer: to complete my recovery from the 1981 knee injury. The 1982-1983 season had thrown every possible curve at me: relocated races, snow storms, early start numbers. Nevertheless, although I didn't win in 1983, I had my most consistent and rewarding season in nine years. Above all, I wanted to retire on my own terms, not as a fading champion, but as a formidable competitor: I think I achieved that. I announced my retirement two days prior to the last race of the 1982-1983 season. Appropriately, it was on my home course, Lake Louise.

A crowd of more than 10,000 people came out to see the race — the largest crowd in North America up to that time. But they didn't get to see me ski. Twenty seconds into the race I hooked an edge and went down. It was only 250 metres from the spot where I had fallen in my first downhill race, fourteen years before.

RETIREMENT BROUGHT GREAT CHANGES in my life. I was twenty-seven, a ski analyst on CBC's *Sportsweekend*, a full-time student at the University of Western Ontario and a devoted husband.

So I finally joined the real world. There were bills to be paid, papers to be written, garbage to be put out.

To fill the void I felt after leaving the comfortable, if disciplined, life of a ski team member, I attempted to remain as busy as possible. In my spare time I devoted myself to achieving something for those still involved in sport.

My association with the movement for a racers' union had stimulated my interest in the politics of sport. I became Alpine skiing's representative on the Canadian Olympic Association athlete's committee which considered whether Canada should join the Western boycott of the Moscow Olympics. As a result of that meeting, the COA decided to form an Athletes Advisory Council, to represent the interests of Canadian athletes. I was once again chosen as the CSA's representative. With a friendly nudge from Canada's bobsled Olympic gold medalist, Victor Emery, I sought the chairmanship of the council, and won it. Suddenly I was plunged into a different sports world, attending COA executive and board meetings.

A whirlwind of committee work began that continues to this day. I am now a vice-president of the Canadian Olympic Association, assistant inspector for Alpine skiing competition runs at the Calgary Olympics, and a candidate to become a technical delegate for the FIS. I also serve on the IOC's Athletes Commission with sportsmen such as hockey's Vladislav

Tretiak, track and field's Sebastian Coe and Edwin Moses, and gymnastics' Nadia Comaneci.

Sports has been good to me. It has opened doors of opportunity and experience. To give something back, committing time and support to our future athletes, is a small way of saying thank you to those who did the same for me.

A FEW MONTHS AFTER my last race, when I was in Aspen, shooting a print advertisement for Salomon bindings, I stayed with Jean-Claude Killy's close friend, ski and tennis photographer, John Russell. On several hot Colorado afternoons, we talked together about the World Cup, retirement, and future goals. It surprised me when he described the identity crisis Jean-Claude went through when he left ski racing after the Grenoble Olympics in 1968. Even the greatest ski racer of his time, and the greatest ski businessman of subsequent years, had endured withdrawal pains.

While I was staying with John Russell, I came across a couple of lines in a magazine which were then a sort of inspiration to me. The lines, by Rudyard Kipling, are inscribed on the wall of the players' holding area at Wimbledon:

> If you can meet with Triumph and Disaster
> And treat those two imposters just the same

It made me think of the winter of 1980, when I won the double at Kitzbühel and Wengen, and then lost my ski a few seconds into the Olympic downhill at Lake Placid.

Kipling knew nothing of *élite* sport as we know it today, but in those few words he captured my dreams and disappointments. The poem gave me a renewed sense of purpose: to accept the past, and use it to build my future.

As Pierre de Coubertin stated in the Olympic motto: "The most important thing in the Olympic Games is not to win but to take part, just as the most important thing in life is not the triumph but the struggle. The essential thing is not to have conquered but to have fought well."

The Crazy Canucks fought well.

APPENDIX

CANADIAN WORLD CUP VICTORIES

Since the Crazy Canucks showed the way in 1975, to the end of the 1986–1987 season, Canadian men have placed first in World Cup competition eighteen times.

December 7, 1975	Val d'Isère, France	Ken Read
December 21, 1975	Schladming, Austria	Dave Irwin
February 11, 1978	Chamonix, France	Ken Read
December 10, 1978	Schladming, Austria	Ken Read
January 6, 1979	Morzine, France	Steve Podborski*
January 12, 1980	Kitzbühel, Austria	Ken Read
January 18, 1980	Wengen, Switzerland	Ken Read
December 21, 1980	St. Moritz, Switzerland	Steve Podborski
January 10, 1981	Garmisch, West Germany	Steve Podborski
January 17, 1981	Kitzbühel, Austria	Steve Podborski
December 21, 1981	Crans Montana, Switzerland	Steve Podborski
January 16, 1982	Kitzbühel, Austria	Steve Podborski
February 13, 1982	Garmisch, West Germany	Steve Podborski
January 22, 1983	Kitzbühel, Austria	Todd Brooker
March 6, 1983	Aspen, USA	Todd Brooker
January 7, 1984	Garmisch, West Germany	Steve Podborski
March 2, 1985	Furano, Japan	Todd Brooker
December 13, 1986	Val Gardena, Italy	Rob Boyd

* Ken Read finished first, but was subsequently disqualified